Anthem for Millie

Roberta M. Sahr

ISBN: 1505349311
ISBN 13: 9781505349313
Library of Congress Control Number: 2015906491
CreateSpace Independent Publishing Platform
North Charleston, South Carolina

For
Mother

Thanks

To all the people who encouraged me to write Millie's story, especially: John and the kids; Tom, Erin, RoseMarie, Muff, Marlys,
Nayda, Val, Lisa, Pat, Jan, Linda, Peg, Mary Ann, Gwen, Joy, Dick,
Diane, and all the writers in my SCC writing class, their interest
and their patience. Most of all, I thank my editor Dean Wright who
gave me the courage to forge ahead when I faltered because he
knew I needed to tell Millie's story to my children.

They Came Before

In 1652 John and Tomasin Milby arrived in the New World on the shores of what later became the Commonwealth of Virginia. About the same time from Europe came Nicolas "the Swede" Albertson, and later the Peterson, Fis(c)her and other hardy families. Their descendants became plantation owners, ship captains, businessmen, and farmers, and many of those descendants defended their freedom and livelihood in every battle from the French and Indian Wars through the Civil War to the present while their wives struggled at home to keep their families safe and sustained. Inevitably, they moved westward with the frontier, building roads, schools, libraries, places of worship, towns and had personal experiences that shaped their family lore. They practiced and spread their faith, be it Quaker, Protestant, or Catholic.

They often died young of typhus, consumption (TB), war, accident (being run over by a horse), infection, or childhood maladies. More than a few women died in childbirth or shortly thereafter, and many of these families were large, often nearing or exceeding a dozen children. Martha Albertson Fisher, my great grandmother, gave birth to her 11th child Scott shortly after moving from Ray County, Missouri, to Los Animas County, Colorado by wagon when she was forty-five. At that time her oldest son was twenty-seven and the father of two.

It was in 1898 in Trinidad, Colorado that Martha Albertson and David Fisher's daughter Effie met Arthur Milby at a church picnic. Courtship and marriage followed, and a few years later the couple and their two children moved to Moriarty, Territory of New Mexico, where Arthur became the manager of a trading post near the old Santa Fe Trail. And so it was that two hundred and fifty-six years after her seventh-great grand parents came to the New World, an ordinary child nicknamed "Millie" was born. This is her story.

Roberta Sahr

Wedding photo of Effie and Arthur Milby @ 1899, Trinidad, Colorado

1

A Bitter Winter Day

New Mexico Territory, 1908
The storm; Banishment to a chicken house; A baby is born

IN THE EARLY MORNING HOURS of January 11, 1908, a weather system calved off the southern Rocky Mountains and pushed its way over the 6,220-foot high desert mesa between Santa Fe and Albuquerque. The system then spread over north central New Mexico Territory carrying a pack load of frigid temperatures and howling winds, was met by a mild but stubborn Texan front, and stalled. Initially the two systems sparred with one another, locked in a kind of sandlot pushing and shoving contest during which they dissipated just enough moisture to wring out a modest few inches of powdery snow. In the subsequent three weeks bitter temperatures and gusty winds made conditions so miserable on the high rolling mesa where the homesteads, settlements and towns of Moriarty, Edgewood, Estancia, and Cline's Corners huddled, that daily life shuddered to a halt while their inhabitants tried to cope with the storm's fury. One by one, businesses pulled down their shades, schools closed, and for miles around, ranchers cut their chores to a bare minimum. Just for a few days, they said, until the storm eases up. Then the phone lines went down.

This was not a time of easy fixes, rescues or emergency services. In 1908 people living in rural areas all over the West were virtually on their own and expected to be prepared for winter. Few homes had electricity. The oil lantern was the light in the window. In New Mexico Territory phone service was so new that both in winter and summer it was common for lines to be down somewhere. This was especially true in the vast triangular expanse between Moriarty, Santa Fe and Albuquerque.

In remote towns like Moriarty, horse and mule were still the primary mode of both transportation and work force. Henry Ford wouldn't produce his first Model T until later that year. Families stuffed newspapers and strips of cloth in leaky window or door frames and huddled around their oil heaters, wood stoves, and fireplaces waiting for each winter storm to end. Running water inside a home was rare. Pipes usually froze in the winter. While indoor toilets, electricity and party-line telephones were slowly beginning to replace the hand pump, the privy, the lantern, and isolation in rural America, it would be many more years until these new conveniences would outnumber their predecessors. Life in the developing areas of the West did hold promise, but progress took time.

In New Mexico Territory the old Santa Fe Trail linking Mexico to Missouri along the ancient trade routes of Native Americans and Mexicans was still viable for traders of all kinds by horse, mule and wagon. Small settlements grew up shack by house by trading post by railroad siding. Range lands began to disappear, fences were built, streams were diverted and wells were dug. Large groups of settlers, miners, farmers, ranchers and other entrepreneurs moved into the vast expanse of the West soon after the outlaws Jesse James, Billy the Kid, the Younger brothers, Black Jack Ketchum, and their imitators had disappeared, been shot or hung. Law and order morphed into regional protocols that were not always standard or just, but were enforced by the status quo or the powerful, often a former gunslinger who now had your back.

By 1908 railroads had all but replaced the Oregon Trail, making it easier for "suitcase farmers" to move west, prove up an acreage, find a job, send crops to markets, receive supplies, and keep in closer contact with far-away families. In 1903 Moriarty had sprung to life in the high desert plains near the Santa Fe Trail when the Santa Fe Central Railroad built a branch line through the area in the hope that it would become an important supply center in the expanding southwest. In 1908 the Santa Fe Railroad became The New Mexico Central Railroad and linked Moriarty to Santa Fe and El Paso, Texas, with connections to Chicago. It would not be long until mail to Moriarty, which still came once or twice a week in a saddle bag, would ride the rails, weather permitting.

On the second of February 1908, the storm had been unrepentant for three weeks. At 6,225 feet above sea level and with no nearby hills to protect the open and arid grassland, the wind, freezing temperatures and snow were unforgiving. Most people living in this remote section of New Mexico Territory were accustomed to dealing with periods of snow and cold on and off throughout the winters, but they could usually count on shorter stormy periods and more temperate winter interludes when they could check to see what stock had gone missing or if the cows had begun to calve or the ewes had held on to their lambs for a little longer. They depended on supplies in the trading posts.

Besides neighbor being cut off from neighbor, the potential of getting lost in the drifting snow was frustrating especially because there was so little of it. Erratically swirling snow in the biting wind made it difficult to determine where the edge of the road was. Once again, supplies from Santa Fe had not come in for several days. It was just plain miserable to try to go anywhere, and many businesses including the Moriarty Trading Company General Mercantile, the largest trading post building west of the Mississippi, had been forced to close for a few days, much to its manager Arthur Milby's dismay.

A few miles from town the clapboard Milby farmhouse rattled and shuddered in the ashy gray light of early morning. Wisps of chimney smoke were caught and flung away as if by a petulant child. Cattle leaned into the lee of the barn, eyes shut. Their faces and eyelashes were crusted over with frozen crystals. Chickens hunkered down in their nests or on the rails of their coops sensing danger if they ventured out into the chicken yard. Dogs burrowed under porches, and cats curled themselves into tight balls in the hay for hours on end. Even the mice disappeared.

The rutted, uneven frozen ground made walking difficult between the house and its outbuildings. Needing to go out for even the barest of requirements such as chores or using the outhouse, was to risk a bad fall, or being blown into a fence post or a piece of farm machinery. Surrounding the house, skiffs of crystalized snow lay in rippled rows ready to be flung about like angry swarms of wasps stinging faces and hands. None of the people residing in the little house wanted to be the one whose turn it was to bundle up and trudge to the barn to milk, feed, and water the cow, feed and break the ice in the trough for the horses, or dash to the chicken coop hoping to find eggs. Most of the hens had elected to quit laying for the time being anyway.

The two Milby children, Harold and Florence, ages six and nearly four, were excused from these chores. For more than two weeks playing outside had been nearly impossible for them. They quickly became afraid of falling after they had first discovered the thrill of running and sliding on the lumpy frozen ground or patch of ice while standing upright. The problem was that when they fell down, it hurt awfully. Then, if they paused to nurse their bumps and bruises, their tears froze on their faces and their fingers and toes tingled angrily. Soon they were too chilled to enjoy sliding any more again and went banging into the house to demand something more fun to occupy their time while they shed their frozen coats, boots, and mittens near the warmth of the stove. They were bored.

Effie, the children's mother, listless and swollen from a difficult pregnancy, lay in bed. She had not ventured outside since the stormy weather had begun. The family's seventeen-year-old hired girl, Ellen Foster, was in charge of cooking and tending to the children as well as the needs of her pregnant employer. Thus, the outside chores were left to Arthur and his brother Fred, whose jobs at the mercantile were temporarily on hold. To complicate matters, Effie had not felt well for several days and was restless and irritated by the howling wind. During the previous night when she became certain her discomfort was the beginning of labor, she had moved to Ellen's downstairs bedroom that she and Ellen readied for the birth of her third child.

That morning Arthur had come in from the barn shaking and stomping and swearing about how the weather had wrought such an indignity on the entire world. He was frustrated by the inconvenience the storm had wrought upon him. Ellen, small in stature but whose tongue she could snap like a bullwhip, retorted to Arthur that his was not the hardest job being done at the moment, "thankyouverymuch!" She knew how heavy her own responsibilities would be in the next several hours. Few people were willing to cross Ellen, except Effie who depended upon her.

As Ellen finished up the breakfast dishes between tending to Effie's needs, her attention to her morning chores was periodically disrupted by the two boisterous children. Both men sat by the stove and smoked their pipes ignoring the children's noisy chatter except to offer a "Quiet down there!" or "Shush!" or "Do you need a whatfor?" now and then. Ellen was not one to coddle children, and they usually obeyed her, but even when she gave them explicit directions about their behavior, their attention spans were short.

As the morning progressed, so did Effie's labor, but all was not well with her. By mid-day Ellen was concerned that Effie should get help while it was still daylight. Effie finally agreed that she would like the doctor to come, and that Arthur should go retrieve him, despite the road conditions. Ellen put it to Arthur bluntly: Despite the weather, he needed to drive the horse and buggy to fetch the doctor in Moriarty.

The major question at the moment, however, was, "Where exactly *was* the doctor?" for they had heard in passing only a few days before the roads closed that the country physician had been called somewhere south of Moriarty to attend a family in which the mother was seriously ill with pneumonia. Everyone in the area who had a phone, including the Milbys and the doctor, had had no phone service for several days so they couldn't reach him that way. Suppose Arthur did get all the way into town only to find that the doctor had not returned?

Their second choice was to fetch a birthing nurse who was living temporarily east of Moriarty toward Cline's Corners. She had no phone there (the line was down anyway), so someone would have to try to find her. Her no-nonsense reputation was the focus of many a tall tale in the region, so she was not the Milbys' first choice, but she was apparently good at her job. Even though Ellen had previously assisted her stepmother during the birth of two or three of her younger half-siblings, she believed Effie's labor was not going well. Effie agreed that this labor was different from her first two experiences of giving birth. Hard labor had come on swiftly, but the baby was not in a hurry to be born.

And so the debate of what to do created its own storm inside the little house. Effie's moans and the wailing of the storm outside set the tone for the discussion. The children became alarmed while they listened to their mother, then became petulant about why no one was helping her. Then they complained about being bored and neglected, and wouldn't someone please play with them?

Frustrated and concerned for Effie, Ellen finally took command. Hand on hip, she shook her finger at the children and ordered them to put on their coats, hats, mittens, and boots and go play in the chicken incubation house. This was a small shack behind the house and near the outhouse, hardly larger than a corn crib, which was warmed by a small kerosene heater. They were instructed to go there and not come back until they were given permission to do so. None of their pleadings moved Ellen, who was becoming alarmed by the situation. She got no assistance from the men: neither wanted anything to do with the birthing process, and they would not deal with the children, yet agreed something should be done about them. So when

Ellen gave the children their unusual marching orders, she dared the men with a glare to countermand her.

Finally, with the children dispatched to the outbuilding where they could, at least, keep warm, Arthur reluctantly agreed to harness up the gelding and leave immediately for Moriarty in hope of finding the doctor at home. At the same time Fred would saddle the mare and ride east to try to find the family where the nurse was staying. There was great concern that either man could get blown off course on their respective routes. Ellen was adamant that they had to go, while they had light. "Both of you, go. Now!"

Reluctantly, but resolved, they did. Ellen was left alone, completely in charge of Effie whose distress was increasing. Ellen still felt she could be a help to Effie at least for a few more hours, but Effie was clearly beginning to struggle in her attempt to deliver the child. An hour passed. Then two, then three.

Arthur returned first. He was alone. He'd found the doctor's home, but it was as feared. The physician was still away caring for the other sick family, but his wife said she would tell him to come quickly if he returned *"...in the next day or so!"* Clearly Effie could not endure that long. An hour or so later as daylight began to wane Fred returned. He, too, was alone and very, very cold. Like Arthur, Fred had not found the nurse he had sought, but he happened to locate the nurse's cousin who said he was willing to ride a little further up the road where his cousin was at a friend's to get the message to her to come as quickly as she could. Soon it would be dark. Ellen lit the lamps, and in the last dim light of the winter afternoon the nurse, cold, crabby and imperious, pounded on the door.

Within minutes the atmosphere inside the farmhouse changed. Tension because of Effie's condition had already set the adults on edge. Then a brief confrontation between Ellen and the nurse brewed over who was in charge. Ellen had truly taken command until then and was not the least bit willing to cede any territory to the bristling, demanding, much older nurse. Eventually the two caregivers worked together in spite of each other, and within two hours were able to help the exhausted woman give birth to a tiny, squalling infant whom Effie named Mildred Lorraine Milby. Thankful that the ordeal was over, that both Effie and the baby appeared to be fine, and after the older children had been released from their confinement in the incubation house and met their little sister, relief poured into the household even as the storm howled outside. Despite the odds, the day had ended successfully.

Who could have foretold on that bitter winter day that the new-born child would be motherless soon after her ninth birthday; or that she and her siblings would contract the Spanish flu in the pandemic of 1918; or that Mildred would be exiled by her father from her home at fourteen; or that in the Great Depression she would go against her aunt and uncle's vehement objections by leaving their Oregon home to put herself through college so she could become a teacher; or that her older brother and sister would later sue her over the guardianship of their Aunt Ellen. (Were they still angry for having been banished to the incubation house all those years earlier?) Who could have guessed then that the tiny, squalling child born on that difficult day would become not only the glue, but the peacemaker in her family?

Moriarty, Territory of New Mexico @ 1909
L-R: Back: Effie Milby & neighbor child.; Sitting: Ellen Milby
holding neighbor child, Mildred, Florence, Harold.

2

The Train to Brownsville:

A wedding; The baby wanders off; David's last gathering

IN THE TWO YEARS FOLLOWING Mildred's birth a series of events began to have a profound effect on the Milby family. By autumn of 1908 when Harold began the first grade it had become increasingly clear to Effie that her two older children, Harold and Florence, needed to have more substance and discipline in a more formal school setting than was available in Moriarty. At home Effie's attention was too divided between her new baby, the big garden she grew, her egg business, her frequent boarders who, although they brought in a little income, were also a distraction, and the sewing that she did to pay for art lessons. Even with Ellen's help, the household was often frenetic and Effie did not have the time or the energy to hover over the children and their lessons in the afternoons or evenings.

In the meantime Ellen continued to enjoy the attention of her handsome young beau who invited her to go to local dances with him. He appeared to be seriously courting her, which was not only flattering, but it gave her an occasional break from her household duties. Above all, she discovered that she loved to dance. At the same time, Fred began to feel the stirrings of attraction himself. He became enamored of Ellen's forthright demeanor, her pert attitude, and her skill in accomplishing whatever the family required of her, including helping at the Mercantile. Ellen was a counterpart to Fred's quieter, gentler disposition.

Moriarty Trading Co @ 1906; Arthur, center in hat; Ellen Foster to his left.

Ellen had had her eye on Fred ever since he began working for Arthur in 1907. Years later as an adult, Mildred often tried to get Ellen to admit that she purposefully led on her young suitor to ignite Fred's interest in her. Eventually, Fred decided he'd better take action and began showing up at the local dances where he watched Ellen and her beau dance their evenings away. He finally became bold enough to ask her to dance, and from that first dance, Ellen knew she could catch him. Her young suitor vanished into the countryside when Ellen began to turn down his offers to go dancing with him, but for the remainder of her life, Ellen kept the three leather post-cards he sent her from his self exile and wondered if she had, indeed, broken his heart. Fred and Ellen were married in August 1909 when the baby Mildred was about eighteen months old. Ellen was nineteen and Fred was twenty-three.

As a gift to the newly married couple Effie created a pastel chalk likeness of the head of a St. Bernard, but Ellen never hung it. Ever blunt, she blurted out, "Who would give a picture of a dog as a wedding gift?" Ironically, because it was in Ellen's possession, it would be Effie's only surviving artwork of her many paintings and sketches, and would be greatly cherished by her descendants.

In the fall of 1909 Fred was offered his own general store to manage further up in the mountains. Arthur was surprised that Fred would consider the job, but Fred, new husband and competent businessman in his own right, was eager to try. Besides, he was tired of being his brother's lackey, for Arthur never let Fred out from under his thumb. Fred was flattered to get the chance to demonstrate his capabilities, but it meant leaving the Milby family in Moriarty. He and Ellen would have to move to a much more remote area.

Ellen put her foot down. She made two demands on Fred that she thought would never get fulfilled. First, she wasn't going anywhere without her piano, which Fred had given her as a wedding gift. Secondly, she would go only if she could take 'baby 'Mil' too, for she had been Mildred's second mother for a year and a half and truly adored the child. Effie was horrified that Ellen would dare to ask for such a thing and told Ellen that there was no way she would let her take Mildred with her. The final blow came when, to Ellen's surprise, Fred managed to arrange for a wagon freighter to take both the piano and a milk cow into the remote area where his job was waiting for him. Ellen was despondent, and tearful when they left Moriarty.

Effie deeply missed Ellen and Fred after they left. Without Ellen's assistance, Effie grew more and more concerned about the need for a stronger school setting for her two strong-willed older children. In addition, both Arthur and Effie were worried about their future in

Moriarty. The great influx of people that Arthur's boss in Denver, Mr. Dunlavy, had predicted would come to the Moriarty area by way of the established trade route along the Santa Fe Trail and support the growth of his trading post had not materialized. A number of their patrons, artists and musicians who had been coming from the East to enjoy the moderate summer and pleasant autumn weather of Moriarty, and with whom Effie had made numerous friendships, left in the fall and were not planning to return. Several of them found other pleasant sites such as Taos and Santa Fe, larger communities that offered more diverse social and artistic opportunties to offer. It was because of Effie's interaction with these artists and musicians that she had begun to blossom as a singer and painter—and she missed the stimulation they brought to her life. Thus, Effie and Arthur decided they had to seek new employment opportunities for him, better schools for the children, and more artistic stimulation for her.

As these events were taking place in New Mexico, Effie's parents in Trinidad, CO were experiencing changes, too. David Fisher was nearing eighty, and Martha, in her seventies, was also slowing down. David was no longer able to do the hard work of his and William's dairy farm in Trinidad. Their youngest son Scott, now in his mid-twenties, had preferred carpentry to milking cows and was about to leave Trinidad with his new wife Florence Putnam. Their daughter Ida Fisher Jones had moved to Milton, Oregon, and extolled its virtues. George Washington Fisher, their fourth oldest son, who had become very involved in the Seventh Day Adventist Church, as were several of his siblings, answered a missionary call to Brownsville, Oregon. George bought a leather glove factory on the bank of the Calapooya River, and became active in a Seventh Day Adventist church there. David, Martha, and Effie had not been won over to the new faith, but many of the other children, now adults, had become active evangelists. As David's health became a serious issue, Martha and David decided to move to Milton, but they stayed only a few months there before moving to Brownsville where George gave his father a job in the glove factory.

Even with gentler work, David's health continued to decline. It wasn't long until Effie heard from her older sister Mattie (Martha) that the family was concerned that David would not last the winter of 1909-1910. Effie was determined to see her father one more time. Her dilemma was what to do with the children since Ellen, having moved out of Moriarty with Fred, was not there to take over in her absence. In the interval since Mildred's birth, Effie had not completely regained her strength and was nagged by a feeling that something was wrong with her own health. Then, she was dismayed to discover she was pregnant again, and attributed her malaise to that condition. Arthur and Effie's plans to leave the Moriarty area also had to be put on hold while Mr. Dunlavy found a new manager for the Mercantile.

All fall Effie and Arthur gathered what cash they could spare, and in February, bought Effie a ticket to Brownsville by way of Portland, Oregon, and packed up the three children to go with her. Harold had celebrated his eighth birthday and was the only child who was old enough to require a ticket. However, since money was tight and he was small for his age, Effie believed she could pass him off as a younger child. On the way to Portland, though, Harold let slip to the conductor that he had had his eighth birthday the previous September. The conductor confronted Effie who admitted how old her son was, so when she and the children changed trains in Portland, the conductor told her she would have to purchase a ticket for Harold for the remainder of the trip.

Effie pleaded she did not have enough money to buy the ticket, but the conductor was adamant. He would be on that leg of the journey, too, so she had no choice. After she and the children disembarked in Portland, Effie hurried to the ticket window, took Florence, age six, with her and left Harold in charge of the baby and their luggage, which she had piled on the platform near the next train they would take. The ticket man demanded the full amount for Harold and would not yield to Effie's pleas to give her some consideration because she was traveling by herself with three children to see her ailing father. In desperation, she removed her wedding ring and asked how much he would give her for it. He said he would exchange it for a ticket, and would keep the ring until she returned in a few weeks with the money to redeem it.

Effie grabbed the ticket and ran back to where she had left Harold, the baby and their luggage, pulling a tired Florence along behind her. But when she got there, Harold was nowhere near their luggage. He was standing further down the platform watching the conductor put up the steps as the train prepared to leave. There was no baby in sight.

Effie panicked and ran to Harold demanding to know where the baby was. He had no idea, and seemed unconcerned to boot. Effie grabbed him by the ear and hauled him back to the luggage, also dragging the now-sobbing Florence. Effie told Harold if he moved from that spot she would leave him at the station, and then she ran up the platform desperately trying to spot baby Mildred, fearing as she ran that the child had fallen under a train. Suddenly, she caught sight of a man holding a wailing baby and she rushed up to him and swept the child out of the man's arms. He loudly berated her for her lack of responsibility for the child as she ran back down the platform to the train, which was gathering steam to leave. Pleading for assistance from the conductor who was just stepping onto the train, and with the howling infant under one arm, she hauled unhappy Harold, crying Florence, and their luggage on board and leaped onto the steps just as the train began to move.

For the rest of his life Harold thought the story of how they just made the train to Brownsville was amusing. His mother told a different version. She scolded him for the entire two hours it took to get to Brownsville He later maintained that his mother was wrong to have placed such a burden of responsibility on such a little boy. Effie never forgot the near tragedy.

When Arthur found out that Effie had pawned her ring to get money for the ticket, he was acutely embarrassed, and wired her enough money to redeem it on her return to Moriarty as well as to have enough for their stay with her family.

While Effie was visiting her parents, several of her brothers and sisters and some of their children gathered at the Fisher's home for a meal together. It would prove to be the last time that most of these brothers and sisters would ever be together. Effie's premonition that she would never see her father again if she did not make this trip proved to be accurate. David Fisher died May 10, 1910. He was buried in the Brownsville Cemetery.

Mildred, age 2

Fisher family: Brownsville, Oregon, 1909

Center: Martha and David Fisher

Center right from David: George W. Fisher, Effie Fisher Milby; Martha "Mattie" Fisher, Mary C. Fisher (George Fisher's wife); Melvin Jones (son of Ida Fisher Jones); Harold A. Milby,

Adults from Martha's right (moving left): Carrie May Lucas Wyant (daughter of Mary Ellen), Ida Fisher Jones, Alex Lucas(?), Mary Ellen Fisher Lucas, D. Scott Fisher (?)

Girl children sitting in the picture (L-R): Florence Milby, Bernice Wyant; Nina and Effie Jones,

3

Milton: The First Hard Years

On death and dying

"I often think about how something in life will
trigger one of those hard memories..... I hope that
my sadness hasn't gone on to my children."

— MILDRED'S JOURNAL, AGE 98, SPOKANE, WASHINGTON, 2006

IN THE EARLY SUMMER OF 1910 as Effie began the final preparations to move
their household from Moriarty to Milton, Oregon, the death of her father continued to weigh heavily upon her. Effie had long realized that
she was indebted to her father for her love of music. Although David
had not had much formal education as a boy, he had taught himself to
play an old pump organ left behind in the Colorado farm house he had
purchased when they had arrived in Trinidad in 1882. David moved the
organ to a small parlor off the dining room and there Effie and some
of her siblings would gather in the occasional evening to sing along with
their father as he played. Of all the eleven Fisher children, Effie was
perhaps the most talented. She learned how to play the organ and was
able to take a few music lessons on the piano at the Methodist church.
Her sweet voice had matured into a lovely contralto by the time she and
Arthur were married.

Effie could picture her father at the organ surrounded by the flowery-papered walls of the parlor and she was grateful for having had the opportunity to forge this special bond with her father through their mutual love of music. For Effie, to have lost her father and then most of her artist and musician friends when they left Moriarty was emotionally difficult.

Physically, the move to Oregon was difficult for Effie. From the time she returned to Moriarty from Brownsville, Effie had not felt well. She was frequently tired, had headaches and was depressed. She thought her malaise might be caused by her pregnancy and because she was so far away from family. Fortunately for Effie and Arthur, Fred's new job at the outlying trading store southeast of Santa Fe had not gone well. Once the coldest part of winter was over, the newlyweds decided to move back to Moriarty, with piano and milk cow in tow. When Ellen arrived she found Effie thrilled to have her friend and sister in-law back, and Ellen gladly took over the responsibility of caring for baby Mildred, now two years old.

Arthur and Effie's decision to move to a larger community in Oregon would also enable them to be close to Effie's sister Ida Fisher Jones. Upon inquiry, Arthur found a job in a grocery business in Milton. Mr. Dunlavy expressed his sorrow that Arthur was leaving for he had done an outstanding job with the Trading Company. Now that the household was again under Ellen's efficient directions, the two women packed both families up for the move to Milton while Arthur and Fred prepared Dunlavy's Mercantile & Trading Company for new management. They boarded the New Mexico Central Railroad at the new depot in Moriarty and transferred in Santa Fe to a northbound train. This time Ellen's piano and the milk cow went together with the family's household goods in a boxcar!

Initially, the two Milby families could not find houses to buy or rent either in College Place or in Milton. For a few weeks they stayed in a hotel in Walla Walla, which was over the Washington State line north of Milton by about ten miles. Arthur and Fred used the electrically powered interurban street car to come and go from work at the Economy Grocery Store which Arthur later purchased from the owner, Mr. McIntyre. Soon the family was able to board with a Mrs. Smedley in Milton for several months. On October 12, 1910, Cranston David Milby was born in Milton. While the birth was relatively easy, Effie remained exhausted and bedfast for over a month.

Effie was heartened to be near family once again. Her sister Ida Jones lived in College Place and Ida's husband Tom operated the Milton Bakery. Ida, too, was pleased to have her sister near. However, Ida and her husband were experiencing marital problems. She was distracted by that and was not much help to either of the Milby families. Ida had three small children of her own: a son, Melvin, and two daughters: Nina and Effie (named after her sister). Then her husband Tom suddenly left town. His whereabouts was not known for many months.

That fall Florence and Harold were enrolled in school, Arthur and Fred were busy with the new store, and the family began to settle down in their new town. When Mildred was three and Crans one, the family moved into a farm house on 7th Avenue on the edge of town. Fred and Ellen found a house to rent a few blocks away.

The move to Milton could have been a good change for the family, had Effie's health not remained questionable. For a full year it appeared that she had never fully recovered from the move from New Mexico or the birth of her youngest son. No matter how hard she tried, her headaches, fatigue, and aching persisted. She even developed a rash that stretched from one cheek across her nose to the other and would not go away. This was distressing to this fastidious woman who was very particular about her appearance.

By early summer of 1911, Effie went to see a doctor about her symptoms, but nothing resulted from his examination. When the hot summer months bore down on them, Effie was miserable. She could not bear being in the sunlight and her fatigue persisted. Arthur rented a small cabin in the cool mountains near Joseph, Oregon, where she and the children went to stay for a few weeks. One day Effie received an urgent message from Arthur that Ellen was in great distress. Nine months pregnant, Ellen had been in hard labor for three days and was in danger of dying. Effie quickly packed up herself and the children and hurried back to Milton where she found that Ellen had, indeed, nearly died.

When Ellen and Fred had announced they would be parents a few months after moving to Milton, the whole family had been overjoyed. Ellen set about making a christening gown for her baby using pieces of two handkerchiefs trimmed in hand-tatted lace for the bodice and cap which had been made by Ellen's mother before her death in the 1890s when Ellen was very young. These handkerchiefs were the only things Ellen possessed of her mother's. Ellen who had always been in robust health had gained weight rapidly during her pregnancy. Neither she nor her doctor were concerned about her weight gain even considering her small stature and bone structure. By the time she neared the end of her term she had gained over sixty pounds. When she went into labor the doctor realized that her baby was very large and was having difficulty progressing through the birth canal.

After three days of hard labor Ellen lay exhausted and unable to aid in her baby's birth. To save her life and with Fred's permission the doctor was forced to compress the baby's shoulders together to deliver it. In doing so, the baby's lungs were crushed and the robust boy died within minutes of his birth. There was little anyone could do to comfort Ellen who was later told by the doctor that she was not built to be a mother and would not survive another difficult pregnancy. There could be no more children for her. By the time Effie had returned to Milton from her mountain retreat she found that the child had not survived. While Ellen remained at home the family buried the infant the next day. The little boy was never named. Effie was bereft that she had not been by her sister in-law's side especially since it was Ellen who had made so many important decisions when Effie was having a difficult time giving birth to Mildred three years earlier. It was a hard blow to the whole family, but Ellen, as resolute as ever, regained her health gradually and resumed her everyday routine, keeping her heartache suppressed

A month or so after the death of her child, Ellen packed the christening dress away and tried to put the tragedy aside in her mind. She remained saddened by her loss for the remainder of her life. Over the years she unwrapped the gown several times and retold the story to Mildred who eventually took the carefully wrapped box and kept it among her own things. Eighty-four years later, Mildred's great granddaughter Paige Elizabeth Calcagni was the first baby to be christened in the dress made by her great great grand aunt.

Milton, OR: the house at 14 SW 7th Avenue where the Milby family lived from 1911-1922. It was located near the Little Walla Walla River and was surrounded by trees. In back there was a barn where they kept their milk cow. A peach tree was in the front yard on the left. Picture was taken @ 2003.

4

Battles at Home and Abroad

1914-1917
World War I Begins; Another Train trip; Effie Fights for Her Life

IN THE FOUR YEARS BETWEEN the birth of her brother Crans and her sixth birthday Mildred experienced the most normal years of her entire childhood. Florence and Harold were very happy in Milton. They liked having new friends and new activities. At home one of their favorite activities was to make up plays in which their little sister Mildred was frequently drafted to play a minor role: a dog whining or barking, a cat meowing, a cow mooing, a lamb, a baby. As a four year-old, she was usually thrilled to be included in her older sister's and brother's activities. On one occasion, the plot required a baby to cry, so Mildred was instructed to cry on a certain cue. But when they practiced it, her little "wahs-wahs" did not meet the criteria of director Harold's instructions.

"Do it again and louder!" Florence instructed Mildred. So they practiced the scene again, but Mildred still did not deliver her crying role effectively. Harold was getting angry, but Florence said, "Never mind, she'll do it right next time." They began the scene again. This time when it came time for Mildred to cry, Florence rapped her little sister a good one on the head with her knuckles. Mildred howled in earnest. Florence and Harold were elated. This was exactly the sound effect they wanted.

Their mother called up the stairs, "What's wrong with Mildred?" Florence shushed Mildred and answered,

"Nothing. We're doing a play and she's in it."

They all held their breaths including Mildred who had learned that if she got her sister or brother in trouble for being mean to her, they would ambush her later when their mother was not around.

Looking back on that period of her life Mildred was amused that she would one day audition to be in plays and operettas, and that in her professional life she would direct them.

When not being drafted as a minor character in her siblings' plays, Mildred enjoyed playing near her mother who was frequently hard at work at her sewing machine. The few memories Mildred had of this happy time when her mother's illness was not the dominant factor in the household involved occasions when her curiosity got her into trouble:

"I liked to pick up her scissors and she would tell me not to touch them, but I kept doing it. So she said, "Now Mil if you touch my scissors again, I'll spank you." But I couldn't keep my hands off them and picked them up again. So she took me into the bathroom to spank me, and when she was pulling my panties down to give me a swat, I looked up at her and said, "Momma, you might bust me," and that was the end of the spanking."

Mildred was fascinated when her mother got all dressed up in fine clothes and fancy hats. She loved to shuffle around in her mother's shoes, and wear her necklaces and hats with feathers. While watching her mother nurse her baby brother, Mildred mimicked her with her own doll. Then one day as Effie prepared herself to nurse a howling Crans, Mildred was surprised to see her mother bend over the kitchen sink and express some milk out of her breasts.

"Momma," I said, "What are you doing?" and my mother replied, "I have too much milk for the baby and I don't want to drown him."

One day while the children were playing games in the house, Mildred ran away from Harold who had begun to chase her. Effie had always warned the children that they must not run in the house. But Harold loved to scare Mildred to make her scream and run away, then he would chase her while he made growling noises and laughed wickedly.

"...This happened when I was about three and Harold was nine. When Harold didn't have anything to do he would chase me. I was afraid of him when he did this, but he thought it was fun to make me scream and run away from him. There was a little room off the living room they called the parlor and there was a rocking chair in it. The lights were always off in there. So this time when I ran in there to hide, I tripped on the rug and hit the sharp end of one of the rockers with my forehead. The chair was facing me. It had no arms. It was a sewing rocker. The point end just missed my temple and my eye and I was bleeding. It was late in the afternoon. They got ahold of the doctor by phone (an old crank phone) and he came right away. He said it had to be sewed up. They put me on the dining room table which wasn't set [for dinner] yet. They gave me chloroform so I was out. Harold and Florence were still running around in the room. It turned out that they put me right where I usually sat at the table. And while he was sewing me up I wet my pants. Harold thought that was the funniest thing. Later on he didn't mind telling the story in front of company to embarrass me. He didn't ever get into trouble. My mother spoiled him I think because he nearly died [of pneumonia] when he was little and we lived in Trinidad..."

In January 1914, when Mildred was nearing her sixth birthday, Arthur decided to make a trip to Missouri to see his parents in Breckenridge. They were in their seventies and their health was declining. With Florence and Harold enrolled in school, Arthur and Effie decided that Arthur would take Mildred with him on the train. Since Effie had not been feeling well again, all she would have to do during the day while he and Mildred were gone was care for Crans who was three years old. Effie sewed a traveling outfit for Mildred. Every piece of her clothing was black, even her bloomers so that the soot from the train would not show. Arthur arranged to stop over in Denver to have dinner with his former boss, Mr. Dunlavy.

Mildred remembered how thrilled she was to be her father's traveling companion. Mr. Dunlavy and his family made a big to-do over the little girl at dinner in their lovely home and seemed pleased to have the opportunity to visit with Arthur. In Breckenridge, Mildred met her grandmother Florence for the first and only time. Florence, after whom Mildred's sister was named, was a petite woman, not quite five feet tall who wore black clothing every day, winter and summer. Like her Fisher counterpart, she was a feisty, sharp-tongued woman who ruled the roost. Even if her husband William was out of sorts, she would wink behind his back so that Mildred would not be afraid of him. Florence insisted that Mildred take a nap every day, which Mildred felt she too big to do. Florence would shoo the little girl into her own bedroom where both of them would cuddle on the large black leather chaise near the window. There Florence would read to Mildred and then tickle her. It was a special time for Mildred to be the focus of that kind of attention. She had her sixth birthday in Breckenridge shortly before they left for home. Arthur never saw his parents again for they both died a few years later.

In 1914 the United States became embroiled in the Great War in Europe. Nearly fifty years after the end of the Civil War in which Arthur's father William had fought and had been wounded at Shiloh, Tennessee (The Battle of Pittsburg Landing), Arthur and his wife Effie found themselves under a siege of their own in Milton.

In the four years since the birth of Cranston in 1910, Effie had continued to suffer from extreme fatigue and headaches, which caused her to spend many hours and days in her darkened bedroom with cold compresses on her forehead. She became depressed. When she tried to will herself to be strong and involved with her children and couldn't, her depression increased. Finally, shortly after Arthur and Mildred's return from Missouri, Effie went to another doctor in Walla Walla who recognized Effie's symptoms. It was to be her death sentence.

All the symptoms which Effie had been experiencing for several years in increasing intensity: extreme fatigue, headaches, skin lesions, anemia, reaction to sunlight, dizziness, abdominal pain, arthritis, and the tell tale "butterfly" rash (the malar rash) across her nose and cheeks led the doctor to make a positive diagnosis: Systemic Lupus Erythematosis, or SLE, a chronic auto-immune disease.

Most people in the early 1900s lived only a few years after being diagnosed. Effie's last two pregnancies, which were accompanied by soaring hormone production, probably caused her body's defenses to surge into a more advanced fighting mode against itself as her immune system continued to be compromised. In some cases, a pregnant woman with SLE can pass the disease on to the child in utero, but none of Effie's children came down with neonatal SLE or developed it later in life.

When Effie was finally diagnosed, her SLE was full-blown and she was given few options, none of which could save her life, only postpone her death. Opiates such as laudanum were still available over the counter at pharmacies, but new guidelines in the 1914 Harrison Narcotics Tax Act restricted the manufacture and open distribution of opiates, which included laudanum. A "tincture" of laudanum had been commonly prescribed to aid sleep, to help calm those who were anxious, had meningitis, heart problems, and to alleviate pain. At that time it was even given to babies and young children who were fretful or coughing. In 1897 the drug and dye firm Bayer began perfecting salicylate medicines which, while effective in reducing inflammation and other aches and pains, caused several undesirable side effects such as stomach ulcers. By 1899 Bayer had patented Aspirin, which rapidly became distributed throughout the world. Thus, to lessen the effects of her debilitating symptoms, Effie used quinine, the principal medicine for the aches and fevers of malaria; laudanum prescribed by her doctor to help her sleep; and aspirin to help reduce inflammation and pain in her arthritic joints, but the lupus had already begun to ravage her body.

The doctor in Walla Walla encouraged Effie to travel to Portland, Oregon, to a medical center there to see if there were any other available options to treat her lupus. He told her that in some cases, surgery to remove the organs most involved in the active part of her disease could lengthen her life. These organs included her reproductive organs and her spleen. Weak and miserable, Effie travelled to Portland twice for surgeries: the first a complete hysterectomy, and the second, the removal of her spleen. After the first surgery, Effie made a valiant effort to recover, but to little avail. She was now in constant discomfort, which caused her to become less and less involved in the life of her family.

As Effie's health continued its spiraling decline, the family struggled to function normally. Florence and Harold were thriving in the Milton school system, which was well staffed and provided its students with a solid education. Even though Harold had been required to repeat the third grade, he was able to fill in all the skills he had missed in Moriarty. Mildred started school in the fall of 1914 and loved it. Many additional enrichment opportunities were available at the newly established Columbia College in Milton which had built

an attractive class building in the center of town. Arthur, his grocery store business flourishing, paid for piano, voice, and elocution
lessons for his daughters. The children soon acquired many new
friends. For the three older ones life had improved immeasurably.
But Crans, who started school in 1916 and who had enjoyed his lack
of supervision, mourned the loss of his freedom to do as he wished all
day long. Early on he resisted the regimen he was required to follow
for the whole day. He loved lunch time and recesses, but he found it
hard to concentrate or sit still on a hard seat for hours on end.

Harold and Florence entered their teenage years and went
through all the throes of adolescence just as their mother's illness
began to impact everyone in the household. Out of necessity the two
older children became increasingly independent and self-sufficient.
They were not pleased when they were told to be quiet because their
mother was ill, nor did they want to be responsible for additional
household duties. Mildred, the shyest of the children, began to feel
invisible. She had only Crans to play with at home. She was afraid
of Harold who was loud and boisterous and she felt she was a bother
to Florence.

Like Mildred, Crans missed his mother's attention and became
more and more a part of the woodwork. He was prone to not getting to the toilet in time. The teens were spending more time in the
household's only bathroom and refused to yield it to the smaller children. Florence was furious at her younger brother when he had an
accident. Her anger at having to help clean him up caused him to be
less and less willing to ask her for help. By the time he was six years
old he had began spending much of his free time at the neighbor's
where he could always find a cookie, a friend and a toilet.

In late December 1916, now seriously ill and desperate for some
kind of hope, Effie made a second trip to the medical center in
Portland, but this proved to be futile. When the surgeon opened her
up he saw that her internal organs were fully involved with the disease
and there was no hope of respite, much less recovery. Furthermore,

as her immune system gradually broke down, her skin lesions became more numerous, deepened, became infected and very painful. The surgeon did remove Effie's spleen, which was no longer functioning, but it served little purpose to do so.

Effie was in such a weakened condition during the two months following her latest surgery that there was some doubt if she would survive long enough to make the trip home by car to Milton. However, still fairly alert even with the drugs she was given, she remembered she had been absent from her husband and children at Christmas, so she insisted that she make the trip home to Milton to be with her family. With a heavy heart Arthur took the train to Portland to bring his wife home to die.

The four Milby children in 1911

5

Motherless

Two sad birthdays and a funeral

APRIL 7, 1917. SPRING HAD officially arrived just two weeks earlier. Buttercups peeked out from the cover of the tall grassy riverbank near the house. Meandering crowds of dandelions had begun to open in the unkempt front yard. Buds on the branches of two tall Lilac bushes in back of the house were beginning to swell, and somewhere doves were cooing their love songs. But the sky was overcast and a chill still hung in the air. The neighborhood was unusually quiet for a Saturday afternoon. No one in the Milby household heard the sounds or saw the promise of that springtime day. For them the message was hope defeated, prayers forsaken and fear of what lay ahead. Melancholy filled little house on Seventh Avenue when Arthur brought Effie home.

The family had made a bedroom for Effie in the small parlor off the dining room because they knew it would be too difficult to carry this frail, pain-shrouded woman up the stairs without jostling her. A single chair near the bed was for the person who would be visiting or sitting with Effie around the clock. The woman Arthur had hired to stay with the children while he went to Portland to bring Effie home stayed in the room with his wife when Arthur was resting or at the store. She could sleep on a small cot near her patient while Effie was dozing.

Effie's brother D. Scott Fisher and his wife Florence drove from Athena, Oregon, to spend some precious time with her the next afternoon, a Sunday. Effie's friend Mrs. Munselle, whose husband owned a furniture store as well as the mortuary in Milton, her sister Ida Jones, and her sister in-law Ellen Milby visited her for brief periods throughout the day.

The children could scarcely bear to visit their mother for more than a few minutes at a time. Any movement, no matter how slight, increased Effie's pain considerably. She could not embrace them nor hold their hands. She could not lift her head to give them a kiss, or offer words of comfort. Her breath smelled sour. She could barely lift two or three fingers to pat their hands. Even the effort of trying to communicate just a few gasping words to them caused her to weep in frustration, pain and grief, and the children could only stand there silently and weep beside her. What do you say to your mother when she is dying in front of you? Her last desperate prayer for a miracle gone, Effie had now accepted fully that she was not going to see her children grow up. Once her visitors had returned to their homes, and the children had left her room, she made no attempt to be brave and lay there weeping and gasping and waiting for the inevitable. Everyone else waited in their own way both inside the house and out.

Mildred had had her ninth birthday six weeks before her mother was brought home. But there had been no celebration. Christmas and her February birthday had come and gone with little acknowledgement that year. Harold and Florence were old enough to be able to pretend to function normally, but Mildred and seven-year-old Crans did not comprehend the full extent of their mother's condition. The two younger children concentrated on staying out of the way and not calling attention to themselves because Arthur, Harold and Florence were focused on their own emotions and stratagems for getting through this difficult time. They often displayed their grief and frustration by being short-tempered and brusque. The older children had grasped how dire their mother's situation was and that nothing could be done to save her life. No one had completely explained to Mildred and Crans what was happening, or if they had, the fact that Effie would die still did not fully register in their young minds. Yet they feared it. They feared the unknown.

It seemed heartless to Mildred that after their mother returned home from the hospital for the last time, Harold and Florence dealt with their mother's imminent demise by spending most of their daylight hours for the next few days either at school or with their friends. They were not equipped to be of any use in these circumstances, they had no experience in giving comfort to someone as ill as their mother was, or even knew to ask what they might do for her. Their friends and their friends' families comforted them and gave them solace, so it was to them that they turned for comfort. As long as Arthur could go to work at his store, he found comfort in that routine. There, life was normal. The store became his refuge. Effie's only solace was the blessed release from pain by sliding in and out of consciousness with the aid of her medications. The two youngest children remained in the shadows of the house where they were anonymous.

In those last few days of her life Effie could not bear to have anything heavy touch her skin, which was covered with angry and often festering lesions. Her immune system had completely shut down. Her body was at war with itself. Her abdominal pain was severe as her organs began to shut down. Her headaches were monumental, and her joints were painfully swollen and inflamed. Day and night her moans could be heard throughout the house along with the murmurs of whoever was sitting with her trying to ease her pain with cold compresses on her forehead and giving her small doses of laudanum.

Mildred was so affected by these sights and sounds that they became a part of her dreams for many years. A melange of scenes flitted through her mind wherein the dreamer wanted to shout out a warning or go get help, but no sound emerged from her lips no matter how hard she tried. In one of the darkest of them she imagined herself being reluctantly reeled in like a fish into her mother's dim room by unknown hands, and as she was forced closer to where her mother lay, she heard Effie plead hoarsely that she needed water. Suddenly Mildred's legs turned into tree stumps and she had no feet. "No!" she shouted in the dream as she tried to turn around and go back out the door, "I have to help her; I have to get her something! She needs water." Turning, she faced the doorway and willed her wooden feet to carry her away, but they were so heavy she could barely move them. The scene repeated itself over and over: she was back in the doorway being pulled into the room again, but she had not had time to go to the kitchen for a glass of water. The fingers that gripped her dug in deep and bruised her flesh. Low, echoing voices seemed to overlap one another as they moaned, "Come in here," and "Yes, you must'" and "She needs you." The scene would repeat itself several times in slow motion until she woke up crying, her heart beating wildly.

She never got that glass of water for her mother nor did she completely reach the bed where Effie lay. She was powerless to help her dying mother in reality as well as in her dreams. Years later Mildred could never distinguish between what she had actually seen and heard in that room and what she had dreamed, or what others described about what had happened. By the time she had turned eighty, she had finally been able to wake herself up and not dream the whole dream.

"I had that bad dream for a long time," she wrote. "But I have forgotten most of it now. ...It still makes me feel sad and I can't even remember it."
(Mildred's journal entry)

About 7 am, on Wednesday, April 11th, 1917, Effie's heart could no longer endure the tremendous battle her body was waging against itself. She made one last shallow, hiccupping gasp and slipped away. The woman sitting with her watched Effie closely and waited for a minute or two, lay her hand on the patient's chest to see if she was breathing, and when it was clear that she was not, went quietly up the stairs to awaken Arthur who had fallen into an exhausted sleep in his room. A quick phone call to Munselle's Mortuary alerted the men who arrived shortly to remove Effie's body, but not before her children had come downstairs for breakfast before going to school. They witnessed their mother, covered from head to toe with a sheet, being carried out the front door on a stretcher. There would be no school for the children that day or the next. Ellen had come quickly and selected Effie's dark church dress for the men to take with them to the mortuary.

Later that afternoon the mortuary returned Effie lying in a casket, dressed and prepared for the viewing. The open casket was placed on the dining room table, which Arthur had moved into the small parlor after removing Effie's bed. Mildred had to kneel on a chair to be able to view her mother's body. At first, she did not recognize her mother. She was initially relieved that the body in the casket wearing her mother's dress was some other woman. Hopeful for a fleeting moment, she felt that her mother had not died after all and that her father would tell them it was a big mistake. "It's not her," the voice in her head said. In actual fact, Effie had lost so much weight that in death Mildred could not easily recognize her mother's gaunt features. But as she peered longer at the corpse's face she saw how much the woman's aquiline nose and her high brow resembled Effie's. When her gaze fell on the woman's thin hands gracefully clasped under her bosom she recognized the long slender fingers of her mother for whom music and art had been a life-long passion. Her sister Florence had placed a few sprigs of dried lavender blossoms in her mother's hands. They were, without question, the mother's hands that had helped the little girl find chords on the piano, had combed and petted her curly hair, and had laced her fingers through Mildred's while the little girl sat in her mother's lap listening to her read from her story books.

People came to call that evening, but Mildred's memories of their presence remained dreamlike, as if she were a ghost among other shadowy forms swirling soundlessly around the parlor, the voices murmuring sounds, but not words. Just before bedtime, when no one else was in the room, Mildred was drawn back to the parlor archway to take one final look at her mother, but couldn't bring herself to approach the casket. From the doorway she could see some of her mother's hair and her facial profile and knew without a doubt that the woman lying there had to be her mother. She did not remember how her older siblings behaved that evening, but she had watched as six year-old Crans took one look, fled from the room, and disappeared.

Effie's funeral was held the next afternoon in the Methodist Church. It was Mildred's first funeral. While she knew they were praying for her mother, the impact of the service still did not register fully in her mind. She was cold, like her mother. She shivered. After the service Effie's casket was placed in the hearse and driven to the Milton Cemetery. The family and a small knot of friends followed in their cars, parked, then walked from their cars up a hilly slope to the Milby family plot. Florence took her little sister's hand and they walked silently with the group of mourners who trailed after the men carrying Effie's casket to her grave. Ellen and Fred's baby was buried nearby. Nobody said a word until the minister cleared his throat and began to speak. Mildred's strongest memory about her mother's illness and death was how hard she shivered in her thin coat on that chilly, blustery day.

"I couldn't stop shaking," she said. *"I just couldn't. Florence even told me to stop it, but I couldn't. I was freezing. I shook all the way home"*

It was the 12th of April, 1917, Effie's thirty-eighth birthday.

6

Lost and Alone

Fall and winter 1917-1918:
Christmas; a missing horse; tonsillitis

"I think my father did the best he could. I didn't
blame him then or now for not being more
attentive to his children's needs at the time..."

— MILDRED, AGE 97, SPOKANE, 2006.

SADNESS PERMEATED THE HOUSEHOLD FOLLOWING Effie's funeral. Like a "crazy" quilt, the Milby family had no established pattern for day-to-day activity. What fell into place was like the way a crazy quilt-maker puts random pieces together. There is no specific arrangement other than to join odd shapes, colors, and sizes of scrap fabrics into blocks and rows. The Milby quilt was like a daily amalgam of what was on hand: bits and pieces of an old wool coat, a dress or a shirt; worn out clothing; parts of other blankets. The inside of a crazy quilt, if the maker was fortunate to have it, was usually wool or cotton batting, and the underside was often another patched, thin blanket, sheet, tablecloth or curtains. Stitches holding the pieces together were large and not intended to be beautiful, but sometimes a decorative "blanket stitch" added interest. Pioneer women were famous for their crazy quilts because they let nothing go to waste and these heavy quilts kept their families warm during long bitter winters before coal, oil, gas, electric heaters or wood stoves replaced open, drafty fireplaces. Mildred always thought these stitches looked like caterpillar legs. The Milby quilt barely hung together.

Mildred and Crans would have been the gray border of the family quilt. Florence would have been both passionate red and elegant plum in the design and Harold, always seeking stardom, would have been an effervescent yellow or greens and blues, colors of exuberant life. Arthur would have been a deep midnight blue, undecipherable and displaying his hue differently depending upon how the light shone on it. Here and there would have been reminders of Effie: her lavender wedding dress; the sleeve of her dark brown traveling suit; small faded forest green squares of her church dress; and perhaps there would have been a bit of lace or embroidery from one of her handkerchiefs. Small traces of Ellen and Fred would surface here and there as contrast in somber burgundy or rust, and were bold and steady.

Weighted down by these heavy layers of family fabric each of the Milby children began to return to the daily business of life in Milton. They were left to their own devices while Arthur poured himself into the concerns of his store. His primary focus was to pay off the large medical bills that his wife's illness had amassed in the last seven years as well as making enough to support his children.

In this family where feelings were not expressed openly, there was little attempt to ease anyone's grief or facilitate their emotional healing, but their superficial emotions ran high. Arthur felt Harold and Florence were old enough at sixteen and fourteen to be responsible for their younger brother and sister while he was at his store, but like typical teenagers they had their own agendas: Harold had discovered girls, and Florence had discovered boys and parties. Contrary to their father's expectations, they felt Mildred, nine, and Crans, seven did not need close attention and could easily fend for themselves. Both

Harold and Florence had well-developed social skills and without a mother's intervention or words of caution, they had the freedom to put those skills to frequent use.

Harold looked forward to graduating from high school in two years and was determined to go on to college. This would be his way of moving beyond the hard years leading up to his mother's death and leaving behind the trivia of small town life. He dreamt of a glorious and lucrative career in a big city. He was determined to attend the University of Washington in Seattle. Florence, while just as academically capable, was not thus inclined. She enjoyed her elocution lessons and walked around the house dramatically emoting long passages that she later presented in recitals. She had no desire to go on to college after high school.

Mildred poured herself into her 4-H Club activities. Her piano and voice lessons transported her happily into sunny places in her mind's eye far from her home where gloom enveloped her. Crans, largely ignored by everyone, began to disappear for hours on end as the days of spring and summer lengthened. When he returned home he was often dirty, silent, and usually late for dinner. This behavior angered Arthur. He began to whip the young boy with his leather barber strop when he could catch him. However, fear of being beaten kept the young and unrepentant Crans away from home even more, and one of Mildred's saddest childhood memories was listening to Crans wail while his father took out his frustrations on him. She also learned the hard way that if she did not want to get a 'licking' herself, she should not defend her little brother. She often stood at the bathroom door crying along with Crans while she tried to gather up enough courage to plead with their father to stop. But after the first time when she, too, got a thrashing for telling her father, "Crans is just a little boy. He doesn't know he's being bad!" she no longer stood up for him. She carried that guilt for the rest of her life.

April dragged into May. The sweet, cool air of spring morphed into a hot, humid summer Mildred was swept gratefully along into the new "now" of her life, tucking away her emotional pain, ever wary, until she arrived at a place in her life where she began, like Crans, to perfect her own individual survival skills: how to get from day to day without being noticed.

By late summer what little had remained of the former household "quilt" began to come apart at the seams. Florence and Harold, ever territorial, began to bait each other and have raging fights. Their father worked long hours and was not emotionally involved with any of his children. He himself had not experienced nurturing in his youth except when his mother stood up against the tyranny of his own father. The four Milby children had no mother's firm guiding hand to keep order, nor a soft lap to cuddle on. The older children began take their frustrations out on each other as well as on their younger brother and sister.

On one occasion when Mildred did something to make her sister angry, Florence cuffed her a good one. Unfortunately this happened at the top of the staircase and Mildred fell down the stairs to the bottom where she lay stunned and began to cry. Florence did not want to get into trouble with her father so she stomped down the stairs and picked Mildred up roughly, grabbed her by the arm and told her not to tell their father or she'd get it even worse next time. The little girl wore a sweater for a week to hide her bruises. Mildred had already learned to stay out of Harold's way after the rocking chair incident. She had also seen Harold roughly throw Crans across the room a couple of times. From then on, both Crans and Mildred stayed out of everyone's way as best as they could. Mildred silently began to wish that when this Christmas arrived surely they would have some happiness.

As with the previous Christmas when their mother was in Portland awaiting surgery, Mildred was hoping for a new doll. As Christmas 1917 approached Mildred did not know what to expect. Arthur's attention in 1916 and 1917 had been on his ailing wife, certainly not on buying Christmas gifts for his children. Mildred remembered that Christmas morning while her mother lay ill in a Portland hospital....

"...Harold and Florence had been after Dad to get them a horse. They told him since they already had a barn where they could keep it, they would take care of it. I was only nine, but I knew they wouldn't. They said they had to have one because many of their friends had horses and could gallop out into the countryside for picnics or ride to the Natatorium in Walla Walla [to go swimming]. Because the Milbys had no horse, Florence and Harold were left out of these adventures. Well, Dad told them "No!" every time they asked. They wouldn't let up on it. They must have asked him again just before Christmas because when we all came down stairs on Christmas morning, (I remember this because my mother wasn't there and I wondered if there would be anything in my stocking) we all rushed over and took down our stockings which we could see had been stuffed. I think Florence even looked out the window to see if a horse was tied up there in the yard. Well Harold and Florence dumped out their stockings onto their laps and they started shouting, "What is this? What is this?" Crans and I looked over at them and saw that on their laps with the paper-wrapped candy and oranges and nuts were several brown lumps that looked like horse poop. Oh, were they mad! Then I looked at Dad who said with a little smile, "Well, I bought you a horse but he got away." Crans and I didn't have any horse poop in our stockings so we thought it was a wonderful joke, but we had to laugh behind our hands because Florence and Harold were so mad. They were sure mad at dad anyway, and they never got their horse."

Millie wondered what this Christmas would be like without their mother, but what happened on the rest of that day became lost to her, except that she didn't get a doll. That the family had eaten dinner with Ellen and Fred on Christmas day was highly likely. Yet, the relationship between Fred and Arthur had become strained in the last few years. One can assume that Effie's illness had affected Arthur's manner at work, but even though Fred had tried to do more than his share of work quietly and efficiently, Arthur had become more and more imperious to the point that, as in Moriarty, Fred felt demeaned. He had begun to think seriously about starting his own store.

Ellen had become frustrated by the problems in Arthur's household, primarily his inattention to his out-of-control children, as well as by the small tidbits Fred shared with her about work. She understood why everyone's feelings were so raw while Effie's health deteriorated and the bills mounted, but most of her attempts to contribute toward caring for the children, cooking, and cleaning, were openly rebuffed. Florence, especially, did not like Ellen's bossiness and became openly disrespectful to her. Harold followed suit. He simply ignored his aunt even when she was in the same room with him. Because of this and Arthur's lack of thanks, Ellen became more and more frustrated. She offered less and less of her time to the family, blaming Arthur for his lack of parental supervision. Even Crans was gaining a reputation in Milton for being his own version of Huckleberry Finn: unkempt, dirty, hungry, swiping things, and loitering here and there while Arthur appeared to be unwilling to do anything about it except whip the boy.

As Ellen's help lessened, Arthur began hiring a series of cooks and housekeepers, but each one lasted only a short while. Ellen filled in when she could, but Mildred was the only one of the children who was willing to put up with her aunt's brusqueness. Likewise, Ellen was very fond of Mildred, whom she invited over to her house where she could feed her and cluck over the little girl's clothing, which had become rattier and rattier even though Mildred tried to take care of it herself. Ellen tried to help Crans, too, but he was a stubborn child, suspicious of her motives, and remained aloof. He generally rebuffed Ellen's bossy attempts at cleaning him up, although he was happy to get an occasional sandwich or cookie from her. He didn't like having to wash his dirty hands before she'd allow him to eat some food.

And he certainly didn't like it when she scolded him. Eventually, by default, Ellen concentrated on Mildred, who was grateful for the attention.

When Ellen found out that Mildred had been suffering from a series of sore throats, she huffed over to the house and took Mildred to see the doctor. Mildred had had a tonsillectomy when she was six shortly after returning from her trip with Arthur to Missouri. That surgery had been performed in the family's dining room with Mildred lying on the dining room table. Effie had helped hold the little girl down while the doctor dripped some ether on a rag and placed it over her mouth and nose. When she was sedated, the doctor clipped out her tonsils. She was very ill afterwards, then gradually got better. However, in a few months her sore throats began to reoccur. Apparently the doctor had not gotten all the infected tonsil tissue removed on one side and it had begun to grow back.

When Ellen took Mildred to the doctor this time, the nine year-old was told to step out of her dress so the doctor could listen to her heart and lung sounds. That's when Ellen discovered Mildred's bloomers were held up with a big safety pin because the elastic had broken. Not only was Mildred embarrassed to reveal this lack of personal tidiness, Ellen was furious that no one in the household was seeing to the little girl's needs. Mildred didn't want Ellen to say anything to Arthur or Florence because she didn't want them to resent Ellen any more than they already did. Ellen fixed the elastic herself.

Mildred ended up having another tonsillectomy after which she was again very ill. This time she had no mother to comfort her. She vowed to never complain again about having a sore throat and Ellen made her promise to come over to her house more often so she could clean and mend her clothing and give her a good meal

Harold and Florence were glad when school resumed in the autumn of 1917. Harold was a good student and was serious about going to college. He began badgering his father for the things he thought all college-bound young people should have, a typewriter, for example. Arthur told him to earn the money himself if he wanted one. Harold also wanted a phonograph player so he could invite his teenage friends over to entertain them. Florence was definitely in favor of that! Once again, Arthur told him to get a job and earn the money. So Harold did. With his earnings he bought the phonograph first and was as proud as a peacock when he brought it home. Florence was thrilled, too. But Harold did not share his new possession with anyone and told everyone in the family not to touch it, including Florence. When he suspected that Florence had put on a record and listened to it in his absence, (which Mildred had seen her do, but Florence had denied doing), he took the diamond-tipped needle out of the playing arm of the record player and hid it. This infuriated Florence who, after looking for the needle without success, took a finger nail file and made a huge scratch on his favorite record.

And so it went for the next several months as their first year without a mother progressed: past the fall of 1917, through the winter and into the spring of 1918. All but Crans thrived in school, but for the most part, all the children were kept busier and life at home settled into a more modest drama in which they each learned to play their individual roles. The family quilt may have been frayed, but it held together.

7

Too Many Cooks

A new hat; burned food; rotten peaches

ARTHUR FINALLY HAD TO ACCEPT the obvious fact that his household was in vast disarray, so he began hiring a series of cooks and housekeepers, none of whom stayed very long. At first the cooks lasted a few months, but left after they could no longer stand the demands made upon them. Some of the cooks were even good at their work and during those times Mildred was happy to get a good meal. The housekeepers found themselves unable to keep the house tidy, but had no authority whatsoever to make demands upon the children, especially the teenagers.

Of them all, one young woman in particular was Mildred's favorite. Within a year or so after Effie's death Arthur had gone through most of the available cooks and housekeepers in Milton. Arthur heard about one young woman whom we will call Anna who was looking for work. She was from eastern Europe and had a thick accent. Arthur was desperate, so he hired her even though he could barely understand her. Anna was a hard worker, had a resilient demeanor, and was not afraid to holler back at any of the Milby children when their demands upon her exceeded reason. She was also a good cook and made the children use table manners if Arthur was not there to oversee. Florence took delight in trying to make life hard on her, but outwardly Anna held her ground.

What Mildred didn't realize was that Anna quickly saw that the younger children were clearly the underdogs and were being bullied by their older brother and sister. Crans' and Mildred's clothing was in wretched shape while Florence and Harold had no problem asking for money to buy what they felt they needed. Arthur may have thought that if the children didn't ask for something, they didn't need it. Years later Mildred told her daughter this story, mimicking the conversation as she remembered it:

"One noon when Dad came home from work for lunch Anna confronted him: "Mister Milby, you must give me money for take Mildred to the store for clothes." I had no idea this was going to happen. I sat there waiting for the explosion. Dad was completely unprepared for this request, looked up from his plate of food and stammered, "Why?" Anna replied, "Because Mildred has notting new, oney alt, and Florens and Haroll have much new and she need shoes and coat." To my surprise Dad reached for his wallet and forked over some bills. Anna grabbed the money and my hand and off we went. We got on the interurban street car in Milton and rode it into Walla Walla where Anna was not shy about buying me a new pair of shoes and a lovely coat with matching hat. There was a little left over so she even bought me some underwear and a new dress. I was in heaven and so proud! But when we got home we ran into a storm."

Florence flew at Anna. She demanded to see the purchases and when I showed her the hat she took it away from me and plopped it on her own head, saying, "I need a new hat more than you do!" and strutted around the room with it perched on her head. Anna stood there and waited for Florence to get over her snit, then said to her, "You have many nice tings but Mildred has none. Be nice to your little sister." Florence replied angrily flinging the hat off her head into a chair,

"SHE doesn't need a new hat and I DO!" Then she sat in the chair and crushed the hat, breaking off the little feather that was on it. I sucked in my breath while Anna became very angry. Florence realized she had overdone herself and got up and flounced out of the room. A few days later Anna quit. I never wore the hat because I didn't want Florence to see me wearing it. I don't remember what ever happened to it."

For the next several years a succession of cooks and housekeepers, most of them worse than the previous ones, filtered through the house. Florence was not shy in expressing her outrage at the women's inability to cook decent meals and Harold complained that he could not invite his friends over because the meals were so bad. Arthur had great forbearance in dealing with this matter because he had become aware that the word was out in Milton about how difficult the Milby children were. The final blow came when the last cook Arthur hired was a nearly blind 'widow-woman' who was desperate for work. She brought her fourteen year-old daughter with her to help her find things in the Milby kitchen. Nervous, she dropped a bowl and a plate and broke them, then she burned the meat for the first dinner she cooked. When the meal was served, Florence stood up abruptly, waved her arms, and ranted and raved in front of the woman who began to sob. Arthur shouted back at Florence, "If you think you can do any better then YOU cook!" and stormed out of the room. The unfortunate woman fled the house in tears without getting paid. Florence took up the challenge and did the cooking for several months, and did a good job of it, but she refused to do cleanup. Mildred was assigned this job.

When spring finally arrived in 1918 their world seemed to take on new life. It appeared that the War in Europe had turned in favor of the allies and would soon come to an end. The Milby family passed the one-year anniversary of Effie's death with forbearance and little said. Summer came and Harold got a job so he could buy a typewriter. He began to date a few girls in his class and Mildred regularly visited the homes of her friends and continued her 4-H club activities as well as piano and voice lessons. Crans faded into the wall-paper and was seldom noticed.

By mid-summer 1918 Harold had enough money to buy the type-writer of his dreams. He felt he would be well equipped to go off to college and was delighted with his new purchase. Once again, how-ever, he refused to let anyone in the house use his new toy. Florence pleaded; Harold was adamant. Florence got angry; Harold was reso-lute. Arthur refused to intervene. Florence accused Harold of be-ing selfish; Harold pointed out a few of her flaws. She was furious. He grinned at her and said, "No, Florence. I said NO!" So Florence began to plot revenge. One Saturday while Harold was away from the house, Florence walked through the neighborhood gathering up some dog droppings. She took the collection home and dropped them, then rubbed them into the keyboard and spring action area of Harold's typewriter with a soup spoon. When he came home he began to notice a very foul smell wafting from his bedroom. He fol-lowed the odor over to his typewriter where he discovered the sabo-tage. He completely blew his top, but Florence was not at home at the time.

The next day was a beautiful August Sunday. Florence donned her new chiffon dress and Mildred wore the new dress that she had gotten on her outing with Anna. They walked to the Methodist church, lingered afterward with their friends and then walked hap-pily home. When they entered the yard something hit Florence on the head. It was a rotten peach. Stunned, she looked in the direction from which it had come. She wasn't under the tree so it couldn't have dropped. Near the corner of the house was Harold with a big grin on his face and a box of peaches at his feet. SPLAT! Another rotten peach hit the skirt of her dress. She screamed, "STOP!" "STOP IT. You'll ruin my dress!" But Harold was well armed and had gathered mushy peaches that had fallen off their tree. He laughed and threw and laughed and threw. Florence continued to scream at him while she tried to dodge the next incoming missile. Then she realized it was too late. She had rotten peaches in her hair, on her face, on her beautiful chiffon dress, and on her shoes. She threw down her purse and charged Harold. Eventually she was able to launch a few peaches of her own and managed to rub some in Harold's hair. Mildred watched the whole battle from the safety of the side porch.

Surprisingly, the battle over the rotten peaches became turning point for Florence and Harold. Somehow they reached an accord and their intense battles ceased from then on. For the rest of their lives their relationship was "peachy keen." They were allies.

8

Battles at home and abroad

"They called the plague of 1918 influenza, but
it was like no influenza ever seen before."

— GINA KOLATA, FLU.

IN SEPTEMBER 1918 WHILE THE world began to hold its collective breath
about if or when Germany would surrender and The War to End All
Wars would finally end, newspapers began to report that a deadly
form of influenza that had already spread through both German and
Allied troops was now spreading in England, France and the United
States. The flu news item appeared in late summer buried within
newspaper miscellany as a sort of, "Oh, yes, and there's this..." bit
of information. Stealthily, like a slowly approaching weather system,
the reports worked their way forward into the more important news
sections where it was soon revealed that the illness had become more
widespread and frequently lethal.

It would be many years until forensic scientists would trace one
of the first outbreaks to a rural area in Spain in the early spring of
1918. The symptoms of that influenza outbreak had been unremark-
able initially and the illness was thought to have run its course within

a few months. While it had been highly contagious, it had not been unusually severe given the effects of the war on Europe. Access to normal fresh food supplies, such as fruits and vegetables, and medical assistance was limited in many regions. After a few months when warmer spring temperatures replaced winter weather, the influenza outbreak, true to form, apparently waned and medical personnel turned their attention back to matters at hand, namely the war and its effects. Yet only a few months later other influenza outbreaks unexpectedly began to appear in random areas of Europe. At first it was thought to be a different strain of influenza, but upon later laboratory investigation scientists discovered that the original flu virus of the previous winter had mutated and was not only more powerful, it was spreading exponentially.

This mutation of the influenza virus had a devastating effect on the people who fell ill to it. In addition to the very young and the very elderly who were the most vulnerable because of their weaker immune systems, an unusual number of adults who were in the prime of their lives and who should have been able to rebound from its symptoms began to die in unusual numbers often from a secondary severe pneumonia infection.

Once the influenza reached the United States, apparently arriving with U.S. troops who were returning home, it spread rapidly and reached little Milton, Oregon, just after Thanksgiving. Few Milton families escaped its ravages. Children, parents, grandparents, farmers, teachers, businessmen and women alike began to fall victim to this strain of flu virus, which had become far more virulent than it was first thought to be. Its victims became rapidly ill and were usually seriously ill for two or more weeks. After that, if they lived, most were in such a weakened condition they could not resume their normal activities for several weeks, even months, and often fell ill again.

The onset of symptoms began suddenly with a severe headache, then a cough, then disorientation. Upon taking the ill person's temperature, caregivers were astounded to discover the ill person who had been feeling fine only a few hours before now had a raging fever. By the time the person was sent to bed the damage was already done because the infected person had now passed the virus on to anyone who was near him or her. When their soaring temperatures finally began to subside, violent coughing and severe congestion persisted, exacerbating the ever-present headache. Shortly, lingering side effects frequently led to pneumonia and in some cases, heart failure. Because antibiotics had not yet been manufactured, aspirin, and cold compresses plus home remedies including chicken broth, mustard plasters, eucalyptus oil and oil of camphor compresses, and fluids were the most useful. Dehydration was frequent and further hampered the body's ability to defend itself. Once the worst had passed, those who survived continued to be debilitated by headaches, coughs, and fatigue for months. For some, a second battle occurred on the heels of the first: equally hard and equally devastating. Many mothers, grandmothers and aunts who had diligently tended their family members ended up following them to the grave four or six weeks later.

When the first few people died in Milton, many of them were in the prime of their lives giving further rise of alarm among its inhabitants. Those who should have been most resistant to the flu's ill effects were not.

In November, 1918, all four Milby children, ages 17, 15, 10, and 8, came down with the influenza and rapidly became seriously ill. So many people of all ages became ill that schools and businesses began closing down. Arthur, who never had a sniffle during that entire winter, kept his store open with Fred's help, but this meant leaving his ill children home alone. He couldn't find a woman to come in, nor would Ellen, who was afraid of catching it herself, come in the house. So Arthur dragged his children's mattresses down from the unheated upstairs bedrooms and arranged them on the living room floor near the coal heater. In the morning before work, he made them runny oatmeal and toast. Those who could eat, did. Then Arthur loaded coal into the heater and went off to work. At noon he came home, made the children some soup or toast, and refueled the stove. At five he came home again, made them something for dinner, stoked up the stove and went back to the store where he stayed until 8 p.m. Each child took care of himself or herself, coughing and sleeping through most of each day and night while their fever persisted. They lived like this for nearly three months as the flu ebbed, returned in full force, then ebbed again.

The flu raged on in Milton, overwhelming huge numbers of people. Funeral home personnel had to call on the same household two or three times to remove a second or third child, young adult or elder. Finally, since bedrooms were on the second story of most houses, they began wrapping the body in a sheet and lowering it by ropes out the second story bedroom window so the grieving family would not have to watch it being removed from the house. Other men stood below to receive the corpse and carry it to the funeral car. Munselle's Funeral Home became so short of helpers family members or friends had to assist. Funerals were arranged hastily and bodies were buried rapidly.

The Milby children were so weakened by their bouts of flu that it took them into late spring to recover. Christmas and Mildred's birthday came and went once more with little fanfare. The bout of flu had also caused Mildred's throat and ear infections to recur. She often awoke in the morning to discover that her hair and sometimes her face would be stuck to her pillowcase from the night's ear, nose and throat drainage. Her painful ear infections added to the discomfort of fever, headaches, chills, and coughs she already had from the flu. If she cried from the pain, Florence sometimes would drop warmed "sweet oil" in her ears to sooth them for a while.. When school finally started up again in the early spring of 1919, Mildred was feeling well enough to attend even though her headaches and ear infections persisted. Anything was better than staying at home. Crans maintained he was still too ill to attend school. Mildred learned to carry big wads of cotton in her pockets that she could stuff into her ears to catch the drainage. Some of the children kidded her about her matted hair and messy clothes, which made Mildred feel embarrassed and ashamed. She was eleven years old, thin, weak, and longed for her mother. Neither Mildred nor Crans knew then that the flu had undoubtedly left them each with a heart murmur.

Harold and Florence were glad to get back into the routine of school and being with their friends. Both the teens were very popular among their classmates. Harold studied hard and caught up in all of his classes. In one more year he would be ready to go to college. Florence, a high school sophomore, began seriously dating Donald Mason, a popular young athlete at McLoughlin High School. Mildred also caught up in her school work and happily began to practice the piano again. Crans never caught up. Never tried.

1918: Crans and Mildred Milby, ages eight and ten.

9

Moving Forward: 1919 - 1922

College; Courtships and marriages;
a birth; a death; more big changes

LIKE HIS CHILDREN, ARTHUR WAS relieved when the spring of 1919 arrived. The shadow of World War I had lifted. His children had survived what would later be called a pandemic. He personally had not suffered even a headache during that long winter while his children were so ill, and, while he was grateful for that, he was saddened by the number of his acquaintances or their family members who had succumbed. He had kept his store open six days a week throughout the long winter months. He paid off his bills one by one. Apart from the misery in his community and the illness of his children, he could not otherwise complain.

However, his relationship with Fred and Ellen continued to be noticeably strained. They kept their distance from him, but when they crossed paths at the store, they were quietly civil. Ellen could do little for Arthur's children who had toughed out the vagaries of the flu at home on their own except to provide them with an occasional pot of soup, meatloaf, applesauce, things she could make that she thought they might be able to eat without too much trouble and in containers which she could leave at their doorstep. Because he now had time with no sick wife to worry over or children who were desperately ill at home, Arthur expanded his interests by reaching out to make other Milton friends who soon began to fulfill his social needs. His two older children were popular in the community and were fairly self-sufficient. While he was constantly plagued by his youngest son's erratic behavior, he was not particularly worried about him. Boys will be boys. His youngest daughter was doing well in school and with her music. Having focused on Effie's illness and death for so long, paying her medical bills, providing for his four children, and trying to grow a business during the ten years they had lived in Milton, he was ready to move forward with his personal life. He was lonely.

Arthur began accepting his friends' invitations for dinner and card parties, which often took him to Walla Walla where his group of friends had expanded to include some of Walla Walla's elite citizens. Pleased with their father's increased social activities (which meant he was often absent in the evenings), Harold and Florence took full advantage of Arthur's social life by increasing their own and staying out late with their friends. Harold got a summer job and began saving for college, but found that his fondness for the latest fashions took precedence over putting aside much for school. Florence got a job in a local pharmacy, which provided money for her to spend on things that were important to her. Most of all, she was pleased to be able to ask for a flexible schedule of work hours which allowed her to watch her boyfriend Donald play baseball. Donald had a promising future as an athlete and as the months continued, their relationship became more serious. A year younger than Florence, Don would finish high school a year after Florence's graduation while she worked and then, hopefully, a semi-pro baseball team would snatch him up. Then when he was getting big money, they could marry.

Another year passed. Each family member had found their groove and stayed in it. Harold completed high school in the spring of 1920 and planned to leave for the University of Washington in the fall. Arthur was not at all certain he was in favor of Harold's grand plan, however. After all, Arthur had only gone through the eighth grade and was a well-respected and successful businessman in Milton. But Harold persisted. Admittedly, Arthur was proud of his son's good grades, popularity, and reputation for being a hard worker. He had chosen good friends and was well liked by their parents, some of whom were also Arthur's friends in Milton. Finally, Arthur agreed to fund Harold's dreams. Harold left for Seattle in September 1920, typewriter and phonograph in hand. Prohibition had come to the United States in January of that year, but on college campuses creativity about how to acquire "booze" became just another learning experience. ("The Noble Experiment" was repealed in 1933.)

In November 1920 the 19th Amendment to the United States Constitution was ratified. For the first time in the entire country all adult women received the right to vote. The presidential election was the first big test of universal suffrage and there was much jubilation among those who had advocated for equal rights for women. In Oregon, however, women had had the right to vote since 1912 when Mildred was four. She did not know if her mother had ever voted and so, for her, this momentous event had little significance at the time. Later, as an adult, she took pride in casting her ballot in every election.

The winter of 1920-1921 was fairly uneventful, except for Arthur's continued attempts to hire help in the household. It was another housekeeper and cook parade, here, then gone. Mildred was grateful when Florence filled in occasionally, and Mildred herself was learning to cook at Ellen's with her aunt's guidance. Florence was seldom at home during the day because of school and her work at the pharmacy. Her social life revolved around Donald and their friends. Harold had joined a fraternity at the "U" and was having a wonderful time while also earning solid grades. However, he was also spending his father's money freely in order, he maintained, to assure himself a place in Seattle's elite society. By the end of spring quarter his expenses amounted to far more than either he or Arthur had anticipated.

The flack hit the fan in the spring of 1921 when Arthur realized Harold's college bills would add up to just over one thousand dollars for the year. That's about $12,000 in 2014 dollars. When Harold returned home for the summer full of wonderful stories about college life and proud of his grades, he was unprepared for Arthur's incensed reception. Arthur raged at Harold for his lack of thrift. Undaunted, Harold told his father that Arthur was unrealistic about what a good education costs, and besides, he was making good contacts for his future. His father was beyond angry: there would be no more money for college; there was no way he was going to spend another dime on Harold's grand plan. If Harold was determined to go to college, he could get a job and pay for it himself. Harold was furious. Arthur was firm. Not a dime.

Determined to show his father that he was equal to the task, Harold enrolled in Walla Walla Business College. However, he could not support himself financially for long and began to look for work. His winning personality, reputation as a hard worker, his father's story of loss and hard work in his grocery business which included the repayment of all the money he owed from his wife's illness, set the family tone for Harold who found a good job with Mr. Mumford, an orchardist in the area. It wasn't long before Harold was dating his boss's daughter, Agnes.

There was another reason why Arthur was watching his money closely. His own social life had picked up and it required money to fund it. He definitely needed a new wardrobe. During the past year he had met and become interested in a Walla Walla elementary school teacher, Marian Marshall. She in turn became suitably impressed with the dapper widower. Their mutual friends rejoiced in matchmaking and many put together social events such as card parties, dinners and attending traveling vaudeville shows to which Arthur and Miss Marshall were both invited. Arthur developed a keen interest in playing bridge at which Marian was a skillful and competitive player.

Florence used her father's late nights to her own advantage and snuck out to events her father had forbidden her to go to, especially the ones where Donald Mason was certain to attend. On one occasion she took Mildred with her because she had promised her father (under duress) that she would look after Mildred and Crans all evening. Well, she did, in a way. Crans slipped out on his own to who knows where. She coaxed Mildred to put on her best dress and allow Florence to put make up on her. But when Mildred looked at her reflection in the mirror she was horrified at what she saw, so she rubbed much of it off which made Florence angry. Mildred felt that trying to make her look older only made her look like a floozy for she was still a flat chested, prepubescent thirteen year-old. Florence told her she didn't know what she was talking about and for heaven's sake at least act older! Mildred had been included in a few of Florence's parties at their own home, but had been required by Florence to stay out of the way while she helped host the events. She had no idea how to act or what to expect.

The girls snuck out through a window so the neighbors wouldn't see them, caught the interurban to College Place and attended a party complete with bootleg alcohol, loud music and dancing. Overwhelmed, Mildred wanted to go home. One fellow asked her to dance and when she said, "No thank you," he grabbed her anyway and twirled her around the room which made Florence laugh. Even though she must have sensed Mildred's unhappiness, Florence did not rescue her. When Mildred began to cry, the fellow let go of her in surprise and left her standing there. Florence became furious at her, and told her to quit being a baby because she was embarrassing Florence and her friends. There was no way Florence was going to take Mildred home until she herself was ready to go.

Mildred was left alone after that and sat off to one side of the room as the party continued on around her. They got home about 1:30 a.m., crawled through the window and got into bed without their father who had returned home from his own date hearing them.

Mildred spent the next few days wondering how she was going to tell Florence she wasn't going to go with her any more, but Florence never again brought up the subject. Florence was having a wonderful year. She gave a senior elocution recital that included musical selections by her thirteen year-old sister Mildred. She graduated from high school in May 1921. She was getting more hours at the pharmacy and she was in love.

Arthur decided that if he was going to successfully woo his woman friend Marian, he should sharpen up his own image because Marian clearly liked the refined life that her Walla Walla friends led, even if she was merely an elementary school teacher whose finances were limited. He decided to build a new, more modern store and borrowed from a local bank to do so. When he drove Marian by his home she seemed less than impressed with the farm house by the river, so he bought a house closer to the main street of Milton and moved the children and himself there. When he decided to ask her to marry him, he introduced Marian to his children who had dressed up for the occasion and were polite and respectful although it was a stretch for each of them. To a person, they took an immediate dislike to her. Both Florence and Mildred decided they couldn't stand Marian because of her pompous ways. Harold didn't care because he was rarely home and was falling in love himself. Eleven year-old Cranston wasn't home much either and cared even less, particularly after Florence had caught him sneaking out of the house just before Marian was supposed to arrive. Rubbed raw from Florence's scrubbing his filthy hands and face, and being made to put on clean clothes and pretend to be polite, his dislike of any stranger who caused this to happen was immediately assured. To him this woman friend of his father's would simply be a non-person or persona non grata. If he only knew...

Ellen had done her own research. She contacted her own Walla Walla acquaintances who reported that they did not think very highly of Miss Marshall who at her advanced spinsterhood age of thirty-three was said to be desperate to find a husband, and it was rumored that she had been manipulating social invitations so she could be near Arthur.

In the meantime, Arthur was thoroughly smitten with this cultured, well-dressed, outwardly popular social butterfly. He was immensely pleased to be included in events attended by Walla Walla's best. He was flattered by Marian's attention, and he didn't care whether Ellen, Fred, or his children liked her or not.

Marian had let him know she liked the finer things in life, so in addition to the new store and the new home, Arthur bought a new car, a complete set of china and crystal so that when they would entertain as husband and wife, they would be able to display the finest. He even hired a man to tear up the front yard of the new house, put in a concrete retaining wall and plant a double row of roses to greet his wife-to-be. Finally when he felt all was in order, he popped the question and she accepted. They planned to be married that same year, in March 1922, in Walla Walla.

Even though Arthur had again sunk deeply into debt, life held promise for him for the first time in years. For Fred, this was the last straw. With Ellen's complete support he decided to part ways with Arthur and opened up his own store down the street.

Another wedding was in the making. In early 1922 during Donald's senior year of high school, he and Florence were married. Their little girl, Donna Louise Mason, was born in July. Donald's parents were heartbroken that their son had married so young, but they had raised him with a high degree of integrity. He was adamant about marrying Florence, with whom he was deeply in love. The young couple moved in with his family while he finished high school. Apparently his marriage had ruined his chances for a professional baseball career, but he was able to finish his high school baseball season and hoped to play ball in the summer with a semi-pro team in the area. He also got a job while Florence continued at the pharmacy until she gave birth. Mrs. Mason agreed to care for the baby so Florence could go back to work as soon as she could after the baby's birth. Both young adults, realizing their dream of having Don become a professional baseball player was possibly ruined or at least sidelined, put their heads down and went to work. Unfortunately, shortly after Louise was born, Donald became very ill. A doctor was called, but it was too late to save Donald from a severe case of encephalitis. Donald lapsed into a coma and died less than three weeks after falling ill. His daughter was one month old. Florence and the Mason family were devastated. The Milbys were sad for Florence, but were apparently more focused on themselves and gave her little more than cursory support.

While Marian and Arthur were on their month-long honeymoon, life for Mildred and Crans continued uneventfully. They stayed by themselves. Ellen brought over casseroles and some of her popular desserts. Florence looked in on them occasionally, but she was now married, pregnant, and had a new life to focus on. Harold worked long hours and came and went as he pleased. He was well-liked by the Mumfords who had begun viewing him as a possible son in-law, one who could someday become involved in their farm. It was obvious that the young man was serious about their daughter. Harold slept at home, but was rarely there otherwise. Mildred had turned fourteen and was in the ninth grade. She had started French, excelled in her other subjects, and was in a small trio of girls who had begun singing at recitals, church programs, and social events. Her piano technique had also improved greatly through the lessons she got at the junior college and she was frequently asked to accompany other singers and instrumentalists. Her home making skills were increasing through her 4-H experiences and with Ellen's guidance.

In April when Arthur and his new bride returned from their honeymoon, it quickly became clear that changes in the household were on the horizon, and Marian would be the author of them.

1 0

Step Hen

March - August 1922
Making over the home; The beating

"Poor Crans, he just raised his own self up."

— MILDRED, AGE 94.

THE FIRST CLUES THAT MARIAN was planning to establish herself as a dominant force in the Milby household became apparent soon after she settled in. She hired a man to rip out the retaining wall and rose garden that Arthur had commissioned the previous year to impress her. Marian thought his design was plebeian and not in good taste. She had the roses dug up and the concrete hauled away, then replanted the roses to one side of the house where she said it would be a proper rose garden. Concurrently she began removing every item that reminded her of Effie's presence in "her" new home and stowed them in the attic. Harold quickly gathered up a few of his mother's paintings, which he gave to his girl friend Agnes, and Florence tucked away some of Effie's sketches and ink drawings, but everything else vanished from the living area.

To Mildred's relief, Marian was a reasonably good cook, but she performed no cleanup. That became Mildred's job. Mildred was also required to help with the more mundane tasks of meal preparation, and she was sharply rebuked when her tasks were not done to Marian's specific instructions. Harold, Mildred and Crans were instructed to be cleaned up and present at the table at specific times of day, but Harold often had to leave early for work, and likewise often missed dinnertime because of his work schedule or because he had been invited to supper at the Mumford's. Dinner time was set to be precisely at 5:30 so Arthur would have a hot supper waiting for him when he came home from work. Then he could return well-fed to his store before closing up at 8:00 pm. Florence and Donald were married by this time and were living with his parents. Harold was given a begrudging leeway because he was working, but the two younger children were not allowed any exceptions.

Of all the family members, Crans had the hardest time dealing with his new situation at home. At twelve he was clearly failing in school and had already repeated one grade. He took no interest in his studies whatsoever and frequently skipped school at midday or altogether. Where he went when he was truant no one knew. The further he fell behind, the less he tried to catch up. He began smoking. He also began getting into scraps at school, which were reported to his father. As a result, Crans got whippings. Crans would take on any boy, big or little, who gave him any grief and often had cuts and bruises to show for it. As the weather warmed up that spring Crans began staying away from home more and more, missing meals, then arriving dirty, tired, and openly defensive with anyone who scolded him, which Marian seemed to enjoy doing. Frequently when he came home late he snuck in through an unlocked window and crept up the stairs to his bed or slept in the barn in the hay in peace.

When the police began calling on Arthur at the store or at home informing him that they would be bringing the recalcitrant boy home to him because the boy had gotten into minor scrapes, Arthur's frustrations with his son became monumental. He was embarrassed to have such a disrespectful son running wildly in the town and in his home in front of his new wife. Marian wasn't any help. She couldn't stand the boy. What if their friends in Walla Walla heard about him? Arthur's attempts to beat sense into Crans increased. He would fetch his shaving strop from the bathroom and flog away at Crans, raising long welts on the boy's back. Crans learned that if he cried and begged his father to stop, Arthur thought he was sorry for his actions and that would end the beating. But Crans had no plans to change his ways; he just got better and better at eluding the police. Many of the people of Milton were sorry for the boy, but could do little about it except feed him when he dropped by his friends' homes. Ellen didn't like Crans's behavior either, but she was furious with Arthur about his treatment of him. Her attempts to give the boy advice, scolding him about his behavior, attempts to clean him up and feeding him only caused the boy to stay away from her, too.

After meeting Marian, most of Arthur's Milton friends, admittedly still loyal to Effie, took an immediate dislike to the woman, a circumstance to which Arthur was oblivious. Within months of their marriage Arthur and Marian's social life in Milton began to dry up to the point that Marian suggested that they should move to Walla Walla where the people had class and where they would be among their social equals. She maintained both would be happier there. Marian also insisted that she could not shop in Milton for the clothes that she needed, and that the stores in Walla Walla were more suitable to her. Arthur resisted, knowing he needed to keep his business strong in Milton so he could pay his current bills and the costs of having a new socially active wife.

To distract Arthur from his concern about the expensive clothes she continued to purchase for herself, Marian decided to use Mildred as her foil. She hired a seamstress to make Mildred a new dress. When the time came for her to present it to the fourteen-year-old, she made a big production of it to demonstrate to Arthur that she cared for Arthur's poor children whose current clothes were unsuitable. Mildred was delighted until she opened up the package and pulled out the dress. She was horrified to discover that the garment, made of gingham, was patterned after a child's dress, and was so short it did not reach Mildred's knees. The bodice was finished with smocking and ribbons...something an eight-year-old might wear. When she looked sadly at Marian to say her obligatory, "Thank you'" she saw only the woman's cruel smile. Marian knew exactly what she had done: she had found a way to belittle the girl who did not dare to act ungratefully. Then Marian told Arthur that the seamstress had tried to get her to use a different design, "but the woman doesn't know about style." Arthur was pleased with his new wife's efforts to benefit his daughter and was completely oblivious to the drama being played out in front of him. Mildred kept her mouth shut fearing severe punishment from her father if she said anything that could be construed as being ungrateful or disrespectful. Then Marian insisted that Mildred wear the dress to church and to one of her spring recitals. On each occasion Mildred was acutely embarrassed to be wearing a child's dress. Ellen even made fun of the dress in front of Marian, but it was Mildred who wanted to crawl away and hide.

A major turning point for Mildred came one day in mid-August. It began in the kitchen where Marian and Mildred were canning peaches. Neither Mildred nor Marian had wanted to preserve peaches on that hot day, but Arthur had pointed out that the remaining peaches on their tree would be lost if they weren't preserved. He had previously taken several boxes of peaches to the store to sell, but those that had remained were dead ripe. Mildred had no excuse to get out of helping Marian in the morning, but she did have a trio practice in the early afternoon. She had also canned peaches with her 4-H club and knew how it was done. In fact, their club had won first place and grand champion in the local county fair for their peach preservation project. This feat had earned the girls a trip to the Oregon State Fair in Salem later that month. Mildred was eagerly looking forward to the experience.

The last morning that Mildred was ever to live at home was hot and muggy both inside the Milby kitchen and outside. Pots of boiling water for blanching and canning simmered on the stove while outside there was not even a tiny wisp of breeze. Sterilized jars were standing in pans of hot water in the oven. Lids and rings were soaking in a pan of hot water on the counter. A twenty-pound sack of sugar stood on the floor and the juice from hand-squeezed fresh lemons was in a pitcher to the right of the stove where another pot of sweet syrup had been prepared. Marian continually picked at Mildred for not doing this or that correctly, and she stood in the middle of the kitchen floor with a spoon in her hand while Mildred blanched, peeled, halved, and pitted the fruit, stepping in only occasionally to help the girl peel and halve the peaches. Nothing Mildred did seemed to please the woman. When it was time to pack the peaches into the hot jars, Marian continued to harangue the girl to do better. Finally, Mildred snapped back at Marian, telling her she already knew how to can peaches and that she was doing it correctly. Marian exploded in fury and stalked out of the room. Mildred was stunned by the woman's eruption and knew she should have held her tongue. Since it appeared that Marian was not going to come back, Mildred placed the rack of filled quart jars in the water bath and finished the canning by herself.

When Arthur came home for his noon meal, he commented on the beautiful jars of peaches cooling on the kitchen counter which Marian immediately took credit for. Mildred did not refute Marian's comments because she knew it was more important to keep her mouth shut, but she was both tired and angry, and Marian had left the cleanup to her again. Arthur sat down at the table to receive his plate. After Mildred finished tidying up and turned to leave the kitchen, Marian suddenly began to weep and told Arthur in a plaintive voice how disrespectful his daughter had been to her while she was working so hard on canning the peaches that morning.

Without a word Arthur leapt up from the table, knocking his chair over and fetched his leather strop from the bathroom. He ordered

Mildred to come over to him and turn around. She walked to him slowly begging him with her eyes and wagging her head back and forth silently pleading to him to not to hit her. When she turned her back to him, he began to thrash her with the thick leather strop. When the first blow hit her, Mildred gasped. She grabbed for the door frame and hung on. Then she looked over at Marian who was sitting at the dining room table with a smirk on her face. Mildred knew at that moment she was doomed in that household, but she vowed to herself she would not give either her father or his wife the satisfaction of seeing or hearing her cry.

Arthur continued to beat Mildred until he ran out of breath and had to stop. Mildred turned to him slowly and looked him in the eye, her own eyes filling up with pain and disgust. Neither spoke. Turning, she left the room wordlessly and walked up the stairs as erect as she could while the two adults watched her in silence. She shut her bedroom door and collapsed on her bed. Burying her face in her pillow, she began to sob as quietly as she could. Her life was turning into hell on earth. What was to become of her?

Sometime later she remembered that she was supposed to be at her trio practice at two o'clock. Her back stung while she straightened her hair and smoothed her dress so she did was well as she could. She needed to get to her practice because the trio was going to sing for a community group in a few days. She crept down the stairs silently. Apparently, both her father and his wife had left. Mildred left the house quickly and walked to her voice teacher's house a few blocks away. She tried her best to act normally during the practice, but had difficulty singing her part with any enthusiasm. Her teacher asked if anything was wrong, and Mildred denied that there was, reasoning that if she told what happened, her father would be embarrassed and would have another reason to repeat his punishment. Her teacher did not press the issue. Mildred didn't realize that when she left the practice her dress was beginning to stick to her back where the welts had begun to ooze.

She walked aimlessly for several blocks trying to figure out what she should do. She had no idea, no plan. She covered one block then another. She couldn't return home, yet she had no place to go. She had no future at home, yet she had no future anywhere else. What would she do?

Realizing that she was near the little apartment that Florence had just rented after her husband's death, she decided to ask her older sister for advice, but when Mildred knocked on Florence's door, there was no answer. No help there either. As Mildred began to walk away, a voice called out brusquely to her from across the street.

"Mildred, what are you doing over there? Florence isn't home! Where have you been? Come over here and talk to me!"

Ashamed and downcast, Mildred walked slowly across the street to where her aunt Ellen was standing, broom in hand in the middle of sweeping the sidewalk in front of her own home.

"Why are you so gloomy? Look at me! What have you done?" Ellen demanded. Then Mildred looked up into her aunt's face and began to cry. Then she began to sob so hard she couldn't talk. She pulled away when Ellen reached out to take her by the arm, fearing her aunt would touch her wounds, and said, "Don't!" Then the story of canning peaches and her beating came pouring out.

Ellen was aghast. Just as Mildred finished telling her sad tale, Florence came up the street pushing a baby buggy. As she neared, she could see that Mildred was distressed.

"What's wrong with Mil?" Florence asked, thinking Ellen had been the one to make her cry.

Ellen snapped, "Mildred, you tell your sister what you just told me!"

By the time Mildred finished the retelling of her beating, Florence was furious. She made Mildred turn around so she and Ellen could look at her back. By this time, Mildred's dress was sticking to the oozing, angry lines that could now be seen through her dress. Florence turned the baby buggy around and shoved its handle into Ellen's hands, saying, "You take care of the baby. I'll be right back!" She turned on her heel and headed for town.

Ellen took Mildred and baby Louise into her house, and began to get the dress off Mildred by first applying wet cloths to the outside of the dress until she could pull the dress away from Mildred's wounds. Mildred cried quietly partly because of the discomfort, but also out of relief because now someone else knew her story and cared, and because she was afraid of what unknown horror might happen at home next. Ellen was frank with Mildred. "I don't know what's going to happen," Ellen said, but they both knew Mildred's life would never be the same.

When Florence got back, she merely reported that, "I told dad off!" Ellen heard later that Florence had literally stopped Arthur's world when she walked into his store and stood just inside the door. It was about 4:30 in the afternoon. There were several customers shopping. Arthur and his newly hired helper were behind the counter. Florence put one hand on her hip and pointed the other at her father and said in a loud voice, "Arthur Milby, the next time you beat one of your children half to death I am going to call the police!" The people in the store froze. Everyone knew Florence was not was talking about Crans because the boy had just left the store. Harold was working at Mumford's. Florence's comments landed like a bomb. By a process of elimination, they knew Arthur had beaten his youngest daughter, the obedient one, the shy one, the musical one! With nothing further needing to be said, Florence turned on her heel and marched back to Ellen's.

Mildred did not return to Arthur's home for sixteen years.

Reminiscing

Excerpt from Mildred's notebook

"August 24, 1999; Yakima, Washington, 10:30 P.M.

About this very time in Aug. 1922 was the beginning of my homelessness, seventy-seven years ago. I marvel now that I was able to come through the ordeal as unscarred as I was (I thought) at the time. However, I know now that I wasn't. All these many years I've been unconsciously praying to forget, to forgive and to try to become the person I wanted so much to be. I tried very hard. I am sure, though, that try as hard as I did there were choices I made which were always colored with negative thoughts. It takes a lifetime of trials and errors to find oneself or to feel one's worth and, most of all, _believe_ in it."*

*EXCERPT FROM MILDRED'S JOURNAL. WRITTEN at ge 91.

1 2

$\mathcal{B}anished$

Oregon State Fair; an unplanned diversion

IN HER LATER YEARS, MILDRED could recall only a few details from the week following her beating. Fifty years later when she began to share these childhood events with her children, she remembered only that she had never returned home after telling her Aunt Ellen and her sister Florence what had happened on that August day in 1922. Undoubtedly she was so emotionally and physically shocked, except for the event itself, she repressed her memory of the few days that followed. She surmised that she probably stayed with her aunt Ellen and uncle Fred where she was cared for and isolated from everyone else. Thus, as she began to heal, she was completely unaware of the tempest that had begun to gather; how she was the eye of the storm; how it gathered turbulence and how monumental the forces battling each other would become.

It was easy to assume that Marian would have been resolute in her version of what had led up to the beating and would not have backed down. She had few, if any, confidants in Milton, so she had no need to solidify her version of the story. Arthur, deeply enamored of Marian, had no reason believe his wife had lied. He never thought to seek his daughter's version of what had happened in the kitchen that morning, and so he stood his ground, too, unaware that the community had, on the wings of small town gossip, begun to form opinions about what else was going on the Milby household, since it was also generally known that Arthur routinely whipped Crans for the young boy's misdeeds. Arthur naively thought the matter was closed. He never dreamed others would make it their business or doubted that all would return to normal. He was irritated that Florence, and then Ellen, had interfered in his family's private matters and that Mildred was continuing to be disobedient by not coming home where she belonged. In his mind, perhaps, his daughter was seeking an ally in Ellen whom he knew had loved Mildred deeply from birth. He definitely knew that Ellen did not like Marian, and vice versa, but he had not expected Ellen to interfere so profoundly in his personal life.

Mildred was unaware how negative the dynamics between Arthur and Ellen had become. Fred, happy to no longer be under his brother's thumb, was now involved in his own store and kept his opinions to himself. Mildred only knew that she was temporarily protected from Marian. As for Arthur, he never suspected that he, a well-liked businessman in Milton, would become the focus of a hurricane-like condemnation. As the stories flew around Milton, emanating first from those who had witnessed Florence's public condemnation of Arthur for his abuse of Mildred, they also increased in details and suppositions – and Marian became the brunt of the discussion. Apparently, in their eyes, she should be equally condemned because she had done nothing to prevent Arthur from thrashing his daughter to such an extent that she had had to flee for protection. As the details of the event were embellished and passed around Milton, the storm grew and the decisions Arthur made next proved to be his eventual undoing. Mildred never dreamed that two weeks from the morning she was canning peaches in her father's kitchen, she would be cast away forever from her home, sister, brothers, aunt, friends and school.

One bright spot in all that upheaval was that by the end of the week following her beating, Mildred was healed enough to travel to Salem, the state capital of Oregon, to attend the Oregon State Fair with her 4-H Club and its leader. Perhaps the family, especially Ellen and Florence, believed it would be good for Mildred to get out of Milton for a while, so the 4-H trip was ideally timed.

Someone, Mildred never remembered who, collected some of her things from her room at Arthur's, packed a suitcase for her and gave her spending money for the trip. One can easily imagine diminutive Ellen as having huffily marched over to Arthur's demanding access to Mildred's belongings. The trip came off as planned and the five girls and their leader took the interurban to the railroad station in Walla Walla and climbed excitedly aboard the train to Pendleton. As the train chugged away from Walla Walla, Mildred was able to relax a little and join in the exuberant chatter of the other teenagers. From Pendleton they travelled west toward Portland where the group again changed trains to one heading south bound for California. Only when she leaned back in the seat and felt the pain of her wounds was she reminded of the conditions at home that she would have to face upon her return to Milton. She believed, erroneously, that no one in her 4-H group knew what had happened to her. No one said a word during the next five days about her having been beaten by her father.

Forty-five minutes after leaving Portland their train arrived in Salem where the girls and their advisor disembarked and began their adventure. The next few days at the fair with her 4-H leader and her friends were delightful. Mildred had never been anywhere where there were so many new sights and sounds and aromas all within walking distance. The girls' canned peaches project won a blue ribbon in the competition, and they felt proud of themselves. Subconsciously, Mildred even felt a sense of exoneration as proof that she really did know how to can peaches, despite Marian's opinion. In their free time the girls enjoyed walking through the exhibits, the horse barns, eating cotton candy, and even riding on the Ferris Wheel. When it was time to return to Milton, Mildred who had been very frugal with her money, had five dollars remaining. Little did she know how greatly she would soon need that money.

After the small group disembarked from the train in Portland on their way home, they had an hour or so to wait for their connection to Walla Walla. The girls enjoyed walking through the elegant train station watching others who were coming or going on trips or groups meeting others. Then when they gathered on the platform with their valises shortly before they were to board, Mildred's 4-H leader took her aside and delivered stunning news: Mildred would *not* be returning home with the group! The woman had been instructed by Arthur before they left Milton six days earlier to tell Mildred when they got to Portland on the return trip that he would arrive by train in Portland on the following day, and that Mildred was to meet him at the train station in the morning. Mildred was instructed to get a room at the YWCA in downtown Portland for the night. That said, her 4-H leader shooed the other girls who did not know what was going on onto the train and followed them aboard without looking back. She never asked Mildred if there was anything she needed or if she had any money.

Stunned, her feet glued to the platform, Mildred watched the train pull away with her leader and her friends on board. In those few moments, all the excitement and success of the 4-H adventure at the fair were shattered. It appeared to have been a sham all along, and her leader had known it and had played along with Arthur and Marian. Fourteen year-old Mildred's only other experience in a big city had been as a small child traveling with her parents who had taken care of all the arrangements. Now she was left by herself among total strangers in a large and busy metropolis. When the train disappeared around the curve of the track, she took a big breath, squared her thin shoulders and did the only thing she knew how to do: obey. She picked up her suitcase and walked out of the station and began walking south on the unfamiliar streets of downtown Portland.

Mildred found out that the YWCA was located near Portland's business district on the corner of Taylor Street and SW Broadway, about eighteen blocks south of the train station. After asking for directions a couple of times on her way, she eventually saw the large YWCA sign directing her to its front entrance. She registered and paid fifty cents for a bed for the night. The management had a place where she stored her small suitcase, and because she had nothing else to do, Mildred spent the afternoon walking up and down Portland's busy city sidewalks gazing in the windows of its department stores, mulling over this new development.

She tried to make sense of this latest turn of events in her life. Eventually she decided that this new situation was, in reality, a good thing. Surely her father was coming all this way to meet her so he could explain how sorry he was for what had happened that awful day a week ago. Surely he would tell her he loved her and that Marian had been wrong to lie about Mildred's behavior, which had led to his anger and his thrashing of her. Then she would tell him she loved him and even though she did not like Marian, she would try harder to be respectful of the woman. She would be firm in her statement to her father, however: she would never consider Marian to be her step 'mother' in any respect. She would acknowledge Marian as Arthur's wife and Mildred would, with effort, be respectful of that. Mildred would return home and be the good daughter her father expected her to be. Arthur surely would be pleased with Mildred's cooperation.

Having reasoned her way through the scenario that was undoubtedly going to play itself out when she met up with Arthur the next morning, Mildred continued sauntering through Portland's business district on that warm and sunny August day. In one clothing store window she spied a red wool sweater that was the prettiest thing she had ever seen. Its price was four dollars. Since she had paid for her room already, Mildred reasoned that she had enough to buy the sweater, so she did. She had never owned anything so lovely. Oh, wouldn't her friends be jealous! Caught up in the moment, she completely forgot about having enough money to buy dinner. Or breakfast! She did not realize that even though the YMCA served meals, they were not free. After paying for the sweater she had only fifty cents left!

For supper she spent twenty-five cents for a glass of milk and two pieces of buttered toast. She retrieved her suitcase and went upstairs to her room. There she found a dorm room with seven or eight small cots, one of which she chose after surveying the room. There were three women already there who had reserved beds for themselves. The women were quietly conversing, but Mildred was not acknowledged in any way after they all looked her up and down while she entered the room. She looked around, then walked over to a bed and sat down on it. She heard enough of their chatter to determine that two of the women were very coarse. She passed the evening lying on her bed listening to the conversation between the other women until she drifted off to sleep, dozing fitfully during the night as she repeatedly checked to make sure her suitcase remained untouched under the bed. One woman snored mercilessly.

In the morning she packed up her things, while the women slept on and went downstairs to the tiny dining area. There she used the last of her money, twenty-five cents, for a bowl of prunes and a glass of milk. She walked back to Portland's elegant railroad station, checked the incoming schedule to make certain the train from Pendleton would still arrive in the early afternoon, chose a bench, and sat down to wait for her father. Her excitement rose as the hours and minutes ticked by. She planned how she would describe all the things she and her 4-H girlfriends had done at the fair. She would show him her blue ribbon. She would ask how business was at the store. Finally, at the appropriate time she went out onto the platform to meet the train as it approached the station, eager to see her father.

When Arthur stepped off the train Mildred walked toward him with a smile on her face, but Arthur seemed to be preoccupied and made no attempt to greet her or converse with her. She asked if anything were wrong. His answer, "We're not going to Walla Walla, we're taking a different trip," was not what she ever imagined he would say.

Obviously, something else was on his mind. Now was not the time to tell him about the Salem Fair! She followed Arthur as he walked to a different platform where a conductor was standing by another train. After Arthur presented two tickets to him, the conductor gave them directions to their seats. Mildred still did not know where they were going. They sat in silence. Once the train began to move and they left the station, Arthur informed Mildred that she would not be returning to Milton at that time; in fact, not for a year! He had enrolled her in a private school, Laurelwood Academy, in western Oregon, and because of her actions in Milton, Mildred would stay there for the entire school year, including not coming home for holidays. There would be no negotiation. He also told her that this was costing him a great deal of money and that she should be thankful that he was doing this for her.

For the second day in a row, Mildred was completely blindsided. While they rode the train in silence for an hour or so, Mildred frantically mulled over this latest revelation. It didn't take her long to realize that she had been banished, not redeemed, and that her father had accepted Marian's false accusations against her as having been the truth. He was saving face. He was saving Marian's face. The young teenager was horrified. Once again, she found herself clenching her jaws, refusing to cry or plead with her father. She sat rigidly on the train's seat holding her chin up turning her face away from her father as she pretended to watch the farmlands roll by. In many ways, the emotional pain of what was happening to her on that train ride was far worse than the beating she had received two weeks earlier.

When the train arrived at the small Gaston, Oregon, railroad station, Arthur brusquely ushered her off the train. Mildred was surprised when Arthur claimed a small trunk she recognized as being from her home in Milton. "Marian packed your things for you," he said making it seem as if Marian had done her a favor. Her response was, "Oh." Arthur had no luggage. She waited for Arthur to lead her where it was that they were going.

Arthur walked to a truck parked near the station. Mildred followed. There he met a man he had hired to take them to Laurelwood Academy, which was situated several miles east of town. The man put her trunk and valise into the back of his truck and they climbed in, Mildred sitting small and quiet in the middle of the two men. She sat with her back straight a few inches from the seat back. The driver took in the strained air between father and daughter and was mute as the three of them rode through the rolling farmlands. Mildred's mind was full of questions, but she dared not ask them. After about half an hour the driver pointed up ahead and said, "That's the Academy up there." Through the windshield Mildred saw four or five large buildings on the side of a knoll about a mile away. The property around the buildings had been almost completely logged off except for a stand of evergreens next to one of the buildings. In the afternoon sunlight the white structures were startlingly brilliant. She thought to herself that despite the newness of the buildings, the campus was starkly forbidding. At least there was no fence.

The truck slowly wound its way up the long lane leading to the academy and came to a halt in front of a path which led to the building in the tall trees. Mildred soon learned that this was the school's administration office. The driver helped Arthur carry Mildred's trunk up the path and through the front door into a lobby where he deposited it. Then he muttered to Arthur, " I'll wait," and returned to his truck. Arthur set Mildred's suitcase on the wood floor next to the trunk. Mildred stood dumbfounded, thinking, "What's going to happen to me here? How much worse is this going to get?" Then Arthur told her that she would need to register, and "...they know you are coming." She looked at the sign over the inner door that said, "Office." To her surprise, she heard the screen door open and slap shut. Her father had left the room. She walked over to the doorway where she watched him walk down the steps and down the path to the truck's cab. She reasoned that he was going to pay the driver.

What she never imagined until Arthur climbed into the passenger seat of the truck and pulled the door shut behind him was that the truck would begin to retrace its path down the driveway without her and that her father was leaving her. He had not even said, "Goodbye." He had truly and completely abandoned her. Her despair was enormous.

That became the first of many future occasions at Laurelwood when tears of utter desolation pooled in her blue eyes and slid down her cheeks. In two weeks' time she had been cast adrift on a stormy sea, not once but twice. Her father had charted a course for her that had turned her away from the only harbor that she had ever known. Realizing that, she covered her face in despair and wept.

Laurelwood Academy 1922 Yearbook

1 3

Laurelwood

1922 – 1923

Alone in a crowd

As Mildred stood in the dim light of the administration building where her father had turned away and ebbed silently back into his own world, she could not begin to fathom what lay ahead of her in this new place, an island far from home. She felt truly adrift and was nauseous from having had nothing to eat except the bowl of prunes and glass of milk early that morning. The heat of the August day was oppressive; the air inside the lobby was still and heavy and sullen.

Her dress clung to her where she had perspired in the truck and was stuck uncomfortably in several places to her healing back so that if she moved one way or another the fabric pulled at or slid across her slowly healing welts. Yet in the muggy room she still began to shiver. Her eyes teared up as she crossed her arms and hugged them to her chest, hoping to stop the quivering and hoping to be courageous about what would happen next.

There was a small brown overstuffed couch against one wall. Its sagging, slightly askew pillows showed that it had suffered hard use. The crests of its armrests were shiny and threadbare. There were mahogany tables at each end of the sofa upon which creamy white porcelain lamps with light blue shades had been placed. Two worn overstuffed chairs with tatted lace antimacassars on each arm sat against the wall across from the door. Several leggy plants sat pathetically on the floor under a window whose lower sash had been opened slightly, but through which no breeze stirred. Framed photographs of people she did not recognize, and an original oil painting of a flowerpot on a table hung on the walls. Through the windows she could see a thirsty, struggling lawn sweeping gradually up to a wooded fringe in the distance. She stood rooted to the floor hugging herself, her grey-blue eyes sweeping the room, her body trembling.

Suddenly the office inner door opened. Startled, Mildred turned toward the sound. A woman whisked swiftly into the lobby and introduced herself pleasantly. "I'm sorry. I didn't hear you come in. Are you alone?" she asked looking around. Mildred nodded. One might assume that Mildred was not the first unwilling or lonely child to be enrolled at the school, but it was unusual for any new student not to be announced or to have someone help register and settle her in. "And you are...?" the woman asked. Mildred lifted her chin, looked directly into the woman's face and said quietly, "Mildred Lorraine Milby." "I thought your father was bringing you," the woman said with upraised eyebrows. "He left," Mildred replied flatly.

After acknowledging that Mildred had, indeed, been expected, the woman introduced herself and position, (the registrar of Laurelwood), she said, "You're early. Well, let's get you settled in," and picked up Mildred's small suitcase and led the girl outside. The woman and Mildred marched down a pathway and turned left toward a four-story building on a nearby knoll. It was, the woman explained, "Buena Vista," the girls' dormitory. On their way, the woman pointed out with pride two other buildings down the slope: The Adelphian Hall where music classes and chapel were held, and further down just off the main road, the Normal School in which the academic classes were held. The woman tried to make a little conversation, but Mildred found no reason to respond while she followed dutifully behind the registrar and provided no further information nor apparent interest in her surroundings. They ascended the stairs of Buena Vista, onto a small porch, and walked to a screened door and went through the open doorway. Once inside the building they crossed a small lobby, ascended a stairway and turned left down a hallway, their leather shoes striking the wooden floor like sticks on snare drums as they walked. "Echoes," Mildred thought. "There's no one here." The woman showed her to a small bedroom Mildred learned she was to share with another student who would be arriving in a few days, as would the rest of the students. Apologizing that she could not stay and help her settle in because she needed to return to her duties in the office, and adding that someone would bring her trunk and that supper would be served at 6, she left the girl alone to unpack.

The inside of Mildred's room was austere, but clean: bare floors, two beds, two small bureaus, one slender closet, a radiator under a window over which the lower half was covered with plain, shear curtains. The walls were bare and drab. Seventy-eight years later she wrote:

". that room at Laurelwood had bare floors. They were so cold! It's a wonder I didn't get splinters!" Mildred, age 92, Orchard Park, Yakima, 2000

Standing in the quiet solitude of her room, Mildred took a deep breath and considered her resources. She came up with a short list: she was fourteen years old and weighed about eighty-five pounds; she had spent the last of her money; she knew absolutely no one here; until Arthur changed his treatment of her, she believed she had the same options as an orphan. She walked to the window, parted the curtains and looked out at the winding road on which she and her father had travelled to this place from Gaston. She wondered how and when she could ever escape, or find a way to retrace her steps, or if she would ever regain the life that she had previously known. She knew this for a fact: she was loved by absolutely no one.

Deep in thought she was startled when a youth, not much older than she, came to the door dragging her trunk on a rug. "This yours?" he asked. She looked past him down the hall and did not answer. "Well?" he asked. Mildred just nodded her head and stepped aside. After he had left, she could hear his footsteps echoing down the empty hallway, then down the stairs. She opened her trunk. Staring down at her things she received another blow. She discovered that the trunk's contents revealed an unwritten message from Marian: her things had been wadded up and heaped randomly in the trunk. She removed two dresses, a winter coat, a few changes of underwear, all badly wrinkled; two pairs of shoes, two or three pairs of stockings, a selection, but not all, of her piano and voice music. She realized immediately how Arthur's wife must have enjoyed letting Mildred know how powerful she still was. Mildred had brought a few useful items with her when she had left for Salem just a week prior to her sudden arrival at Laurelwood, and of course, she had her lovely red sweater. However, she had learned her lesson about complaining, and she did not know what the rules were here. She resolved to make no remarks whatsoever about her lack of clothing to anyone for as long as she was there.

Mildred was to adhere to this decision for the next ten months as she switched back and forth between her two dresses. While she wore one dress, she cleaned and ironed the second. When the first dress became soiled, she exchanged it for the cleaner one, then laundered and ironed the first. And so it went. She received no further clothing that year. She learned precisely the difference between "wanting" and "needing." For the rest of her life she followed that as a guideline. Thereafter she made do with very few items of clothing, internally believing she did not deserve more because she knew how to make do with what she had. In this same manner, for the rest of her life she remained adamant about the proper care of her own and her family's clothing and refused to provide her children with anything frivolous or items that were not practical. Ever.

As Mildred got to know the Laurelwood campus she discovered it wasn't just the dormitory rooms that seemed lifeless; all the buildings on Laurelwood's campus seemed drab and prison-like to her. One afternoon sixty years later in a happier frame of mind she reflected that Laurelwood's school rooms were probably no different than the interiors of the public schools she had previously been attending. Having friends there had made them familiar to her and full of life. In Milton everywhere she turned were people and routines she knew, even the uncertainties of her home life. Here everything was unfamiliar, and because she was among the first of the students to arrive for the coming term, there was no lively chatter in the halls involving her, nor a roommate who welcomed her. At home she knew where to find things, how to get where she needed to be, and what she was supposed to accomplish. Here every activity was new to her and she had no voice in any of it.

Mildred was at Laurelwood from late August 1922 to mid-May 1923 during which time she completed her sophomore year of high school. From her first day there, almost everything about Laurelwood dismayed her. When asked a few years before her death she could not recall what had happened to that sweater,

Laurelwood: 1922 Yearbook
Left: Normal Building where academic classes were held;
Right: Adelphian Hall for music classes;
Background Center: Power Plant

Life at Laurelwood

"You may not control al the events that happen to you,
but you can decide not to be reduced by them..."

— MAYA ANGELOU*

DURING THE FIRST FEW MONTHS at Laurelwood Mildred did what she was told: got up, ate, went to class, went to chapel when she was supposed to. She had hoped for a friendly roommate, but apparently that was not to be. Mildred chose to keep to herself, and in doing so, further isolated herself at the school, focusing on her schoolwork and her job.

She had not been overly surprised to learn within a day or so of her arrival at the academy that in addition to the regular school routine, she would be required to work for her board and room. Her father, it was revealed, was paying only for her for tuition, books and piano lessons. This circumstance was also true for several other students who like Mildred were assigned to the laundry to which they reported at 7 a.m. five days a week. The girls were awakened at six after which they dressed and reported to the dining room where they were given a breakfast of a hot oatmeal, eggs, toast and milk. At the laundry room they were assigned one of several tasks: washing and ironing the schools' linens or other students' dirty clothing. Bluing was used to make the linens and white shirts and blouses a bright white. The sheets, men's and boys' shirts, and the women's and girls' white detachable collars were starched, (no spray-on starch in those years!) dried, dampened, rolled in towels, ironed and hung. Because her supervisor learned Mildred had learned how to darn stockings and small tears in clothing from her mother, Effie, many years earlier, she was also given the task of mending small holes or repairing hems.

The laundry girls were excused before noon. They returned to their rooms, quickly changed into their school dresses and went to the dining room for lunch, which often included a vegetable soup served with crackers or a sandwich, sometimes a fruit, and milk. In the afternoon she attended classes, which finished at 4:30 or 5 p.m. Her subjects were: Study of the New Testament, English II, Physiology, Algebra, and a music elective. When the music director learned Mildred was skilled at the piano, she was often asked to accompany the small chorus. She offered no extra information about herself and did what was asked of her quietly and obediently, all the while despising her circumstances.

After their afternoon classes, students had a brief hour of free time, which they could use for club meetings or elective classes after which they met in the dining hall for supper. No meat was served because this was a Seventh Day Adventist school. Most of its students were members of this faith and did not miss meat at their meals. Mildred, on the other hand, was used to having meat at least once a day and often more, and oh, how she missed a good slice of bacon or ham at breakfast! After supper the students reported to chapel where they participated in a prayer service. Mildred tried to avoid going to the chapel for evening prayers, saying, " I don't need to. I am a Methodist," but someone would always be sent back to fetch her. She then dutifully sat through the services (the girls seated on one side and boys on the other) without actually participating or, in fact, listening to what was being said. She preferred to remain in her room studying, but she was not given that choice. After the service ended, the rest of the evening was spent studying and working on assignments. On Saturdays there was a long chapel service in the morning and quiet time spent in their rooms in the afternoons followed by the usual evening prayer service. In good weather they were encouraged to walk out on the school grounds. On Sunday afternoons students had more free time during which they studied and gathered in areas of their dormitories, which were like small living rooms. On pleasant days in the fall students organized games out on the lawn: croquet, softball, dodge ball and the like. Mildred watched and usually did not join in.

Within a few months, as the crisp autumn days gave way to the cold and damp of a typical western Oregon winter, Mildred developed a serious case of depression. She did not seek any social interaction throughout the fall or winter. If people spoke to her, she would respond, but she rarely initiated any conversation other than to ask for information. She spent most of her free time in her room, which itself was gloomy. At ninety-two, remembering those emotions, Mildred wrote in her notebook,

"Oh, I was so cold in that room! I could never seem to warm up"

For relief when she could find a piano that was not being used, she practiced alone and content in one of the music rooms, but she always felt her music skill suffered that year.

Because she had no money, Mildred could not buy stamps or stationery. Thus, she did not have a way to write letters to her sister Florence, her aunt Ellen, or her friends in Milton. She received few letters from home. She waited hopefully each day to hear from anyone, but it was several months before Arthur gave out her address so others could write her. Her friends knew better than to ask Marian for a way to correspond with their friend. Mildred was ecstatic when she received her first letter, but after reading it she realized Arthur had painted a very different picture about how he had escorted her to Laurelwood, the school itself, and why she would be going to school there. Someone sent her some spending money so she was eventually able to buy envelopes and stamps from the school office, but as eager as she was to start up a correspondence, she found she had little to say other than to describe the school, which she did as dispassionately as possible. She did not want anyone to let Arthur know how painfully lonely she was, or how inadequate the school was because he would tell Marian, and that would be another victory for the woman. The only person she yearned to hear from but did not during the first eight months at Laurelwood was her father.

Always a good student, Mildred was distressed by the poor quality of teaching at Laurelwood. Her education in Milton had been exceptional because of her access to excellent opportunities offered in conjunction with the small college there. Other courses that she took at Laurelwood were second year Latin, English, Home Economics, math, history, and music. Her father continued to pay extra for music lessons for her for a while and she enjoyed them and was grateful to be able to have them. However, at mid-year, as Arthur's business began to fail in Milton, he informed the school he could no longer afford to pay for Mildred's music lessons. Her piano teacher did not want Mildred to stop so she continued to give her lessons if Mildred would sit with her two sons two times a week while they practiced. Mildred agreed to this arrangement.

In defense of Laurelwood, it was a relatively new school and was just getting on its educational legs, but Mildred didn't recognize that as a reasonable or legitimate attribute of the school at the time. Laurelwood's teachers were often young and relatively inexperienced. One can surmise that they were chosen because of their adherence to the Seventh Day Adventist faith. Mission work, taking the faith to other countries, has been a tenet since the inception of the faith in the 1800s, so not only were these younger staff members getting their first experience as teachers, they were in training to take this experience to other areas to further spread the faith. The older high school students were also encouraged to consider going forward from high school to do mission work. Also on the staff were several older teachers whom Mildred felt were better at their jobs than the younger ones and she was glad to have them on occasion even though they were dry and stern. Eventually she was drawn to one or two of the younger teachers because they were kinder and more enthusiastic about their work even though they had much to learn about teaching strategy. They were quicker to openly recognize good work. Their occasional compliments gave Mildred hope.

Eventually, Mildred heard from her aunt Mary Ellen Fisher Lucas, an older sister of her late mother's. The Lucas family lived a short distance north of Laurelwood in Forest Grove, Oregon. Mary Ellen invited Mildred to come to spend a weekend with them. Mildred was delighted to get off the grounds of the school and gladly accepted. She got a ride into Gaston and took the train to Forest Grove where Mary Ellen met her at the station. (When asked eighty years later, Mildred could not remember where she got the money to pay for the ticket and she surmised her aunt had probably paid for it.) At ninety-two, reflecting upon the two or three excursions she made to Forest Grove that year, Mildred wrote,

"My Aunt Mary Ellen was a dear to me. She was so sweet. That's when I was down in Laurelwood. They lived in Forest Grove which was about a half an hour's ride from Laurelwood. The rest of mother's family moved to California while I was in Laurelwood. I would take the train to Forest Grove and stay at Aunt Mary Ellen's. I'd go over there and she'd ask me what I'd like to eat and say,". would you like some meat?", and I'd say I would, so she'd go to the store and get me some and fix it. Boy that tasted good! They wouldn't eat any but I did. She could make the best buttered toast. She'd toast it and butter it on both sides and put it in the warming oven. I could have it all day long. She had lost her husband, and she moved to her daughter Carrie May Wyant's in California the next year." Orchard Park, Yakima, 2000.

Prior to attending Laurelwood, Mildred had not really known this aunt, but that year she enjoyed her visits with Mary Ellen and her daughter Carrie, and Carrie's young daughters Bernice and Fern Wyant whom she later kept track of until they died. Mary Ellen, like all the Fisher women, was a wonderful cook and Mildred was pleased to be allowed to help her prepare the meals. She pretended that Mary Ellen was her mother and this was how it felt for mother and daughter to be together. The kindness that Mary Ellen showed her by taking off her apron and going to the store to buy meat to prepare for her niece's dinner was the first example of family kindness Mildred had experienced since her aunt Ellen and Florence had stood up for her in Milton. Mary Ellen admonished Mildred to eat better at the school for Mildred was very thin.

Mildred' trips to spend the day at the Lucas family's home were her only visits with family that year. Since she tried all her life after Laurelwood to erase it from her memory, she did not specifically remember what she did or where she was on Thanksgiving, Christmas, or Easter that year, but figures those were the occasions when she was invited to the Lucas's. She spoke fondly of her aunt Mary Ellen:

I think aunt Mary Ellen saved my life. She was very kind to me." and "She made rugs. She'd cut up all the rags she could get ahold of and make them into a rug and sell them. Those she made on her loom with a great big thing...it was a shuttle.... and she'd change the pedals with her feet and change the direction. She'd make them any length or width people would want. And she'd make wool braided rugs. They'd have to sew the braids into big circles. It's hard on your fingers...." Mildred, age 92, Orchard Park, Yakima, 2000.

By springtime Mildred's wall of self-preservation had softened and she allowed herself to become friendly with several girls and boys whose company she began to enjoy. One of their favorite activities on a Sunday afternoon was to climb the ridges behind Laurelwood and look down over the farmlands below. They hiked farther than they were allowed to on several occasions and when they were caught, they were forbidden to go on walks for a few weeks. Somehow they managed to sneak off a few more times. These outings were carefree and Mildred enjoyed them immensely. One young man took a shine to Mildred who was now fifteen (once again having her birthday pass unnoticed by her family), but Mildred had no intention of becoming interested in anyone who was a Seventh Day Adventist. She knew it was not fair to blame the school or the faith for her unhappiness, but she could never shake the negative feeling about anything related to Laurelwood for the remainder of her life.

As spring approached Mildred began to wonder what would happen to her when the institution closed for the summer. She greatly feared being the only student left at Laurelwood for the summer when all the other students returned to their homes. Even the ones whose parents were doing mission work overseas had places to go for the summer. Then she found out that Mary Ellen was moving to California. Then a letter from her father arrived. At first she was eager to open it, hopeful that enough time had passed for her father's anger and the reason for her beating to be diminished. Her grades were excellent. She had been an obedient daughter. Although a reluctant enrollee at the school, she had been compliant for the most part. She had worked hard in the laundry. She dared hope that she would be allowed to return home. But the contents of the letter dashed her hopes.

Arthur's letter informed her succinctly of three important details affecting his teenaged daughter: (1) her grandmother Martha Albertson Fisher had died on May 3rd in Athena, Oregon, while living with her son Scott and his wife Florence. (Martha was also Mary Ellen Lucas's mother, but Mary Ellen had not sent word to her about Martha's death.) Martha was buried in the Milton Cemetery. Mildred paused after reading this first bit of news, which made her curious. Why had her grandmother been buried in Milton when her husband, David Fisher was buried in Brownsville, Oregon, on the other side of the state? Reading on, (2) Arthur informed Mildred that she would not be returning to Milton at the end of the school year. Instead, she was being sent to live in Athena, Oregon, with the Fishers. Furthermore, (3) since her schooling at Laurelwood had cost her father so much money, she would not be returning to Laurelwood in the fall, but would attend school in Athena. She would also continue working for her board at the Fishers and he would send them money each month for her room. In the letter was a train ticket. The letter was in her father's handwriting, but all she heard was Marian's voice.

It was mixed news for the fifteen year-old. Thankfully her prayers were answered about not having to spend another year at Laurelwood. She did, however, know enough about the Fishers to be apprehensive. Florence Fisher was known for her temper and imperious disposition. Their daughter Charlotte, another of Mildred's Fisher cousins who was two or three years younger than Mildred, was not only fiery-tempered like her mother, but in Mildred's opinion, she was a spoiled brat. Florence's husband, Scott Fisher, Effie's youngest brother, was known for his lack of ability to hold a job for very long. What was her father getting her into now?

It was in this frame of mind that Mildred packed up her things a few weeks later and caught the train at Gaston for Portland. There she transferred to the train going to Pendleton, remembering how stunned she had been twice in this very same railroad station the summer before. In Pendleton she transferred to the Athena route. Mildred mused about The Greek goddess Athena being the goddess of wisdom and creativity in mythology. Could this be a sign that her life was going to get better?

"No tears are shed that God does not notice. There is no smile that He does not mark."

Some of the work activities at Laurelwood in the1921-1922 school year. In the bottom left photo Mildred is the small dark figure standing in the middle holding a sheet of the type she helped launder and iron as a part of her job in the laundry each morning..

1 5

Arthur's Fall From Grace

"Like sparks that from the coals of fire do fly..."

— THE PILGRIM'S PROGRESS: THE AUTHOR'S
APOLOGY FOR HIS BOOK, 1964 PRINTING

WHILE MILDRED STRUGGLED TO FIND her way at Laurelwood, and because she was not in communication with anyone in Milton, she had no idea that a storm was brewing there. Immediately after Florence's public admonishment of her father for having beaten his youngest daughter, sketchy details of that outburst had spread from household to household, and business to business. As with most rumors, many of the details were missing or not accurate. The first few details Ellen heard were from Mildred herself and were limited to Mildred's rendition of the incident at home. Florence's description of her confrontation of Arthur was short and sweet: she had told her father off. During the week that Mildred stayed at Fred and Ellen's, Mildred and Ellen did not discuss the incident much although Mildred was asked to repeat what had happened to her to Fred and Ellen made a few comments about Marian's apparent approval of Arthur's actions.

The last Ellen saw of Mildred for more than nine months was when the teenager took the interurban to Walla Walla with her 4-H group on their way to the Oregon State Fair in Salem. Ellen and Fred had no inkling about what decisions would be made by Arthur and Marian in the interim before Mildred was supposed to return home a week later. Undoubtedly prompted by Marian, Arthur had been busy.

Arthur's other children, none of whom were present during Arthur's thrashing of Mildred, knew nothing more than the part about canning peaches and the beating. The 4-H leader knew only the part about Arthur's instructions to her to leave Mildred in Portland while she and the other girls finished their trip from Salem home to Milton. The woman had, however, heard the early rumors flitting about town before they left. But as gossip spun its ever-increasing web of truths and untruths in Milton, enough supposed details were added that the story refused to die. Then when it was revealed that Mildred had been sent away to school, the tempest was renewed and questions asked. The crux of the story was that Arthur had beaten his younger daughter for some reason involving Marian and had sent his daughter away to some private school too far away for her to come home and too far away for her to reveal her version of what had happened. Evidently she had done something terrible and was an embarrassment to Arthur.

"Poor" Arthur, with so much to be sad about (the death of his first wife; a son who was becoming a delinquent; and his older daughter having to get married), was now burdened with his younger daughter's misdeeds when all he wanted to do was make his business a success and enjoy the company of his new spouse, Marian. But there must be more to the story, people thought, and Marian who was not popular in the community, had to be somehow further involved. To what extent no one seemed to know. Florence kept mum. Harold knew nothing and refused to discuss it. Crans was too young and too uninvolved with his family to be asked outright. The issue that made people curious was that those who were acquainted with Mildred knew her to be quiet, courteous, compliant and an excellent student and musician. So what *had* happened in the home to cause Arthur to beat her?

Next, the town wags could only guess what kind of "school" Mildred had been sent to because Arthur was close-mouthed about it.

It was several months before he revealed Laurelwood's name and that it was supported financially by many of Effie's Seventh Day Adventist relatives. Conversations with Effie's sister Ida who lived in College Place a few miles away from Milton had possibly brought Laurelwood to Arthur's attention. Arthur had then probably contacted Effie's older brother George Fisher and learned from him that Laurelwood had a good reputation, was seeking additional students, and how to arrange for the girl to go there. Rather than face Mildred's return to Milton after the Oregon State Fair, and Marian's disapproval of the girl, Arthur felt sending her away would be the best for all concerned: it would give the community time to let the story die down, would provide Mildred with good schooling, and would keep his daughter out of his wife's hair. Furthermore, Mildred was half way there and the school's fall term was about to begin. Plus, with Mildred not present in Milton, he would not have to answer questions about having beaten his daughter, an act he never admitted. Things would die down, surely. And because there had been no complaint made to the police, no legal action was ever taken.

In the next few months Arthur had not been particularly worried when the business receipts of his Economy Grocery Store on Main Street began to diminish noticeably. Marian did not seem to mind when people who passed her on the sidewalk either did not greet her, or gave a perfunctory response to her greetings to them. Apparently she believed it was further proof that the citizens of Milton were socially unskilled and, therefore, socially unacceptable to her. In fact, she did mind. Just as she had suspected before marrying Arthur, Milton was not a place she could or would adjust to. It was beneath her.

Initially, Marian's early card parties in Milton had been attended eagerly by Arthur's friends. Her efforts to impress them with tales of their socialite friends and events in Walla Walla, however, did not yield good results. Many found her to be haughty and opinionated. Arthur, still smitten by her, did not notice his friends' reactions until they began to return their regrets to her invitations with greater and greater frequency. Then it became known that the Milbys had been overlooked for several dinner and bridge parties at several of Arthur's friends'. Ellen and Fred were omitted from Marian's guest lists because Ellen, sharp-tongued as usual, was openly critical of her new sister in-law. Marian increased her complaints to Arthur about his friends, but he defended them and would not hear her protests about their lack of social etiquette. Marian continued to press Arthur to attend as many social activities in Walla Walla as she could muster invitations to.

Little could Arthur have predicted that his poor judgment in dealing with Mildred's supposed transgressions would have such a drastic affect on his once stellar reputation. Many of his faithful customers began shopping down at the street at Fred's grocery store at 910 S. Main just north of the Talbert Building. It took only few months of reduced income for Arthur to struggle to pay his bills on time. He was in debt at the bank for his loan on the purchase of building supplies to build his new store building plus the house he had bought to impress Marian; his new car was not paid for; he was obligated to pay for Mildred's tuition at Laurelwood; and Marian continued her shopping sprees and social engagements regardless of Arthur's suggestion that they pull back on expenses for a few months. Marian believed to do so would only present ammunition to her critics. When the subject of Arthur arose with Ellen and her friends Ellen made no bones about how she felt about Marian's influence on her brother in-law. To what degree Ellen's opinions fanned the flames among Arthur's friends, his customers and his creditors, one can only surmise. After all, what had happened to Mildred was as if it had happened to Ellen's own child, and while she deeply resented Arthur's behavior, she was powerless to help Mildred except with her tongue. According to Arthur his daughter was attending a very good private school in western Oregon and was happy there. According to Ellen, Arthur was being led by the nose by his new wife who was jealous of his children.

Still Arthur continued to be oblivious to the direction the tide was taking him. He did nothing outwardly to change his or Marian's ways and if anything, doubted that such a personal and private event could affect him both publicly and professionally for very long. Milton was a very small town where rumors and secrets spread easily and rapidly. He continued to believe that surely once this new topic of interest had peaked, the rumors about the Milby family would die down, be forgotten, and all would return to normal. Arthur was content to wait it out. Fred's reputation as a kind and considerate man earned him many of Arthur's customers. He also kept his opinions to himself while Ellen gossiped enough for them both. By year's end Arthur was looking for a life preserver. By springtime Arthur realized he was beginning to drown.

If Marian would not reduce her spending, one way Arthur could economize was to quit paying tuition to Laurelwood for Mildred's schooling. Since the girl certainly would be unwelcome back in his and Marian's home in Milton where she would probably upset his wife, she would have to be sent somewhere more economical. At Laurelwood while Mildred was wondering what would happen to her over the summer, she never dreamed that Arthur had begun to blame her for being the root cause of his growing financial crisis. While Marian fanned these flames for their financial woes on his daughter, Arthur was trying to save his business, his marriage and his reputation.

In the end, three events changed the course of Arthur's life: Mildred did not return to Laurelwood the next fall. Instead she was sent to live with her Fisher relatives in Athena while she completed her junior year of high school and worked for her board. This was Arthur's meek attempt at throwing his daughter a life preserver. But while Mildred was very happy to leave Laurelwood behind, her upcoming future with the Fisher family in Athena was another enigma for her.

Secondly, the bank threatened to begin foreclosure proceedings on Arthur's store. This was a very difficult time both personally and professionally for Arthur because the bank manager was a close friend of his, and it had been at his personal intervention that the bank had held back their demands for payments from Arthur any sooner.

Finally, Arthur agreed to put the store and the house up for sale if the bank would back off foreclosure proceedings for up to a year to give Arthur time to solve his financial woes. By agreeing to this, the bank added interest to the amount owed. Apparently Arthur did not ask Fred and Ellen for help. Perhaps he didn't want to endure the indignity of being denied. Eventually Arthur lost everything in Milton; Marian got her way and they moved to Walla Walla.

During the next year Arthur was able to sell the store and his business, got an offer on the house, and paid the bank what he owed them and finished paying for the car. For Arthur, this was a very bitter pill to swallow. For Marian it was candy. They found an apartment in Walla Walla and Arthur found a job there in a men's clothing store selling children's shoes.

And how did this series of events affect the other three Milby offspring? Although almost completely separate from Arthur and Marian's household, Harold began to discover quickly that his father's financial troubles affected him as well. Shortly after Mildred had entered Laurelwood, he had become engaged to his employer's daughter Agnes. It was a good move on his part. He was well-liked by the family, he had proved to be an able and hard worker, he was financially astute, socially adept, and he had learned much about being an orchardist. He was the kind of person they were looking for to marry their daughter. Harold could see good money down the road if he kept at the grindstone and was able to join the family business. However, when the rumors about Arthur's financial problems were coupled with the gossip about Mildred's beating, Harold's future father in-law finally confronted the young man about what he had heard. Since Harold was not privy to anything that went on in the Milby household, he knew as little or as much as anyone else, but clearly his future was being threatened. He kept his head down and worked even harder to prove himself. Several months later his fiancee's father withdrew his permission for the young couple to marry, and shortly thereafter he fired Harold.

Harold was furious. Apparently he could not hold back his fiery temper and said some things that completed burning the bridges to this family he had aspired to join. When this relationship was severed, Harold left abruptly, and in doing so did not reclaim several of his mother's paintings he had given to the family as gifts. He did not take rejection lightly. He soon found a job with Pacific Power and Light Company in the Walla Walla district office. He was focused on success, worked diligently, and quickly became a young man on the rise. PP & L would prove to be Harold's lifetime career spanning more than forty years as he rose up the ladder in the company. Most of all, this job became his ticket out of Milton.

Florence continued to work in Milton. She also got extra work in Hermiston, Oregon, at a pharmacy. Hermiston was less than fifty miles southwest of Milton. She had an aptitude for retail and her employers found that not only was she a hard worker, she had a good head for business, was intuitive about what products to order, and was a sharp sales woman. Her late husband's mother continued to help with the baby.

In the meantime, what about Crans, the child in the shadows? Trouble was Crans's frequent playmate. He continued to be truant from school and fell behind his classmates again. He began running away on a regular basis and when he showed up somewhere down the road panhandling for food or was found by the police and returned home, the cycle of Arthur's abuse of him continued. While Arthur was under mounting pressure financially and personally, he was trying to beat some sense into the boy. Marian continued to watch from the sidelines and not interfere, except to inflame Arthur about his son. Crans, frustrated by the negative reactions of adults both at home and at school and guided by his propensity to confront everything that stood in his way by lashing out at it, was bent on going through life the only way he knew how: with his fists. It would only be a matter of time until Crans, like Mildred, would surely be gone from Milton for good.

1 6

Athena

1923-1924

*Athena is the Greek goddess of war, wisdom, civilization,
strength, strategy, crafts,justice, and skill. She is a shrewd
judge of people, and did not like being crossed. Two of her
symbols are the owl and the olive tree. (Wikipedia)*

ATHENA, OREGON, IS TUCKED AWAY in the northeast corner of Umatilla
County, just south of the Washington-Oregon border. It is about
fourteen miles southwest of Milton-Freewater and seventeen miles
northeast of Pendleton. Today it is a small rural town of 1,200 or so
residents with two or three main streets and a few cross streets. Since
its origins in the mid1880s as a stage stop, then later a railroad stop,
between Pendleton, Oregon, and Walla Walla, Washington, Athena
grew to include a modest complement of small businesses, schools,
grocery stores, churches, bars, gas stations, a post office, a park, and
residences. In 1923, it was a small, rural town.

Umatilla County was a key location from 1776 to 1877 while the
Pacific Northwest was being settled. Prior to the mid-1850s, many
small tribes of Native Americans related to the larger Flathead
and Nez Perce nations freely roamed the Oregon Territory, now
encompassing the states of Washington, Oregon, Idaho, and parts

of Montana and Wyoming, where they gleaned a good life from its abundant resources in the rolling hills and prairies, and in the Wallowa Mountains to the east which were part of the current Selway-Bitterroot Range of the northern Rocky Mountains. Before settlers discovered the rich soil in the prairie-like land now called the "Palouse" they usually passed through the Athena area settling in a region where the deep river bottom lands were perfect for farming in what is now southwest Washington State. The Lewis and Clark Expedition used part of the old Nez Perce Trail to the north over Lolo Pass, and in the 1830s Marcus Whitman established his mission, Wailatpu ("place of the rye grass") in the lowlands near the present city of Walla Walla and vigorously attempted to bring Protestant Christianity to the Indians. However, after a few years there, an outbreak of measles among the settlers resulted in the deaths of many Native Americans. Fear and confusion among the Cayuse tribe in the area propelled them to rise up and massacre Whitman, his wife Narcissa, their adopted children, and twelve other white settlers in the area.

Aggravating the situation was the apparent animosity between the zealous Protestants and the mission work being done by Catholic priests who had preceded them in the area. The pot of distrust between Catholics, Protestants and Native Americans continued to be stirred long after the massacre, and it was in this atmosphere that the U.S. military was called upon in 1865 after the end of the Civil War to force the small "non-treaty" band of Nez Perce led by Chief Joseph to move off its beloved land onto a reservation far away from the settlers.

Today, that stately Wallowa Mountain Range to the east embraces Athena across rolling wheat lands and mixed agricultural farm lands through which in 1877, only forty-five years before Mildred arrived there, Chief Joseph and his ravaged band of Nez Perce Indians fled from the U.S. Cavalry as they tried to reach sanctuary in Canada. The northwestern portion of the Wallowas that can be seen from

Athena are also called the Blue Mountains because of their stunning deep blue-gray color. It was to these beautiful mountains with their cool, clear air that Effie Milby had retreated in the heat-filled summers of 1914 and 1915 when her health began to decline rapidly. Ninety years later, of Mildred's few happy memories from her childhood, she recalled those two carefree occasions when her mother had packed up her children and fled to a small, rented cabin in the "Blues" during the most oppressive summer weeks in Milton. This had been a happy time for all the children who didn't realize at the time how desperately ill their mother was.

And so it was in May 1923 that Mildred Milby, fifteen, travelled to Athena under much different circumstances. She was alienated from her immediate family, yet was dependent upon them. Now she was about to settle within a few miles of them, but would not be allowed to interact with them. Within days of moving into the Fisher household tension was apparent. Florence and Scott Fisher had a stormy relationship that kept the household on edge. Their ten year-old daughter Charlotte was a feisty and demanding only child. Florence's brother Charles Putnam and a boarder, Frank Long also lived with them. Mildred's arrival meant Mr. Long had to find other lodgings, and to supplement that loss of income Mildred was assigned a share of the dusting and mopping, washing, ironing, and preparation of meals as payment for her board. Because Scott Fisher did not have steady work, it was necessary for Florence to take in additional washing and ironing from other households. Mildred's laundry room skills, which she had honed at Laurelwood, were a benefit to Florence as well as Mildred's ability to assume much of the upkeep of the home. Florence Fisher was a no-nonsense cook whose meals were tasty, but not elaborate. The portions were measured precisely and nothing was wasted. Mildred learned a great deal from her aunt and was grateful to have meat included regularly in her diet once again. Florence was not afraid of hard work and was clearly the moving force in the household.

Scott had held several types of jobs, even trying to study medicine at one time. Ever the self-focused optimist, Scott had trouble with the mundane aspects of life and believed prosperity would eventually come his way without having to work too hard for it. Several people called him "doctor" Scott, because of his initial hope of becoming a doctor, but the only occupation that helped him support his family was carpentry. Charlotte Fisher's responsibilities in the household were few and often given to Mildred to complete. Younger than her cousin by several years, Charlotte was not inclined to do housework or schoolwork. She was, however, proficient at pouting.

When school started in the fall Mildred entered her junior year of high school and Charlotte began fifth grade. Mildred was surprised to discover that she liked school in Athena, even though she soon discovered she had fallen behind while at Laurelwood. She applied herself and was easily able to not only catch up, but rise to the top of her class and to participate in several school activities such as choir and the girls' basketball team. Mildred's success only made her relationship with Charlotte more strained because Charlotte, although smart enough, was a lackluster student who was more interested in her friends than her studies. She knew that her mother was too busy trying to make ends meet or was too tired to press her daughter into doing what she didn't want to if she held out long enough. Despite the frequent squabbles, Mildred was fairly content in Athena even though her father never wrote or called. She had learned to not expect to hear from him and struggled with the possibility that he did not love her any more, despite her continued attempts to declare her allegiance to him.

On Mildred's sixteenth birthday, she was surprised to receive a little gift from Florence. With it was a note:

"Here is a little gift for one of the dearest girls I know. It is an expression of the endless love that is held for you in my heart. I hope you will enjoy it and have many more birthdays each one bringing you a little more happiness to you than the last. From Aunt Florence. Feb 2, 1924."

Mildred was surprised by the gift (a necklace, she recalled, seventy years later), but the tone of the note meant a lot to her. She was not accustomed to hearing caring words from her sharp-tongued aunt, and she did not remember hearing anything from her family on her sixteenth birthday. Florence's note was among Mildred's possessions at the time of her death.

Another surprise on that chilly February day was a visit to Athena by several of her Milton friends who had baked a cake and brought it along with some little gifts to surprise her. Mildred, not realizing her friends were coming, had gone to visit some other friends in the country. She was devastated when she got home and found the cake and gifts and saw that her Milton friends had left.

As the year progressed, Charles Putnam moved out. Shortly after, Florence and Scott's marriage began to unravel. It became apparent that few people in Athena were willing hire Scott to do their carpentry because that small town's grapevine had begun spreading the news that he had a predilection for 'dallying with the ladies,' married or not. Not having a regular job gave him plenty of free time to make "house calls." Florence, ever vigilant, put him to work when she realized he had time on his hands. He remodeled their house, adding a front porch and making repairs inside to the extent that it became a truly charming little home. His work was good. However, by spring there was no work at all for him in Athena, so he decided to seek opportunities in Seattle, and abruptly left town.

Florence stewed about Scott's absence as well as his lack of correspondence. She was working hard to support the girls, and Arthur's payments for Mildred's room had dried up, too, as his Milton financial difficulties increased. When Florence did hear from Scott he was vague about his jobs, seemed to enjoy being in Seattle, wanted to remain there, but didn't think he was settled enough for Florence to move there.

Florence had her own ideas. When school ended that spring with no further news from Scott, she put the house up for sale, and sold it quickly. After checking with Arthur who was not willing to have Mildred return to Milton, Florence packed up the household, the cash from the sale, and moved the three of them to Seattle. Once again Mildred was on the move.

Seattle

1924-1926: high school and ties

FLORENCE MOVED THE GIRLS AND herself to a rental house on Seattle's Capitol Hill. She banked the money from the sale of the Athena house after using a small amount of it to set up the household. Financially stable for the time being, they were comfortable. Her first job was to locate Scott, and when she found him, she laid down the law. He moved back in with them and began to help financially. Mildred began working for both her room and board at the Fisher's, and with jobs provided by Florence who took in outside laundry and sewing, the young girl was able to contribute her share while adjusting to life in a large city.

Broadway High School, at Broadway and Pine Street, was only a few blocks from their house. Mildred enrolled there for her senior year. This would be the fourth high school Mildred had attended. She had some difficulty collecting her various school records, but was thrilled at the quality of her classes. She took another year of French, and added English, debate, history, and mathematics. She also was able to take more piano lessons and voice lessons and became a popular accompanist at recitals. She also found a job playing for services at a nearby Christian Church for which she was paid one dollar per Sunday.

She began to wear a little makeup and on one occasion her French teacher quietly said to her, "Mademoiselle Milby, you have too much bloom on today." Even though she was embarrassed, she thought it was funny, and used a smaller amount of makeup more proficiently by paying attention to how other high school girls wore their own makeup. Senior play tryouts were held in the fall and Mildred auditioned for one of the leads. However, because she was so tiny, she was cast as the little sister to the main character. To her dismay she was required to sit on her "big brother's" lap for an entire scene. This actor was a very well known student at Broadway High, and Mildred was acutely embarrassed to have to sit on his lap in front of everyone.

While Mildred worked hard and excelled in her schoolwork as well as meeting her obligations to Florence for her room and board, the marriage of her aunt and uncle continued to fall apart. Not wishing to deplete her savings from the Athena house sale, Florence got a job at a tie factory in downtown Seattle and began working long hours. Both girls were able to manage for themselves after school. Scott worked only occasionally, spent time away from the house, and began to voice his dissatisfaction with their marriage openly. Florence knew if they parted permanently, she would have to give him half the proceeds from the Athena house sale, so she continued to put up with his erratic behavior over the winter. As the tension in the house increased, she became increasingly cross with Mildred and Charlotte.

Meanwhile, in Milton, Mildred's sister Florence had begun to have some health problems. She wrote Mildred that she had been referred to a doctor in Tacoma for "female" surgery and would be coming to Seattle with her daughter Louise. She hoped to stay with the Fishers. Florence Fisher, however, was not too pleased to have her niece and child arrive, and for how long, she wondered. Never thinking she would be asked to pay to stay with a relative, Florence Milby Mason could not afford to pay room and board because she had to reserve all her money for her medical expenses. Mildred and her sister had a lovely visit for a couple of days and Mildred was thrilled to see little Louise, who was a charming child. Florence Fisher counted every penny it took to run the house and announced one day that she couldn't afford to have Mildred's sister and niece stay any longer, and they were especially not welcome for a long recuperation stay after surgery. In addition, she informed the sisters that Louise would not be welcome there either while her mother recovered from her surgery.

Embarrassed, Florence Mason called some of her late husband's relatives who lived near Tacoma and explained her predicament. They kindly offered to have Florence and Louise stay with them for as long as it took. Deeply disappointed, Mildred sadly said goodbye to her sister the next day. Since her sister did not know how to use the streetcar system, Mildred went with Florence and Louise to the King Street train station to help get them on the right train. Florence Fisher did not even say goodbye to them.

On February 13th and 14th, 1925, Broadway High School's Boys' and Girls' Glee Clubs put on "The Fencing Master," a comic opera in three acts. At the last minute Mildred was chosen to replace one of the fencing students who had not come to enough practices. She had to learn the fencing moves as well as the dancing choreography of the scenes in just a few short days. She had a wonderful time! Her friend Margery Brandt was a dancer in the play and the two friends attended the cast party after the opera's final performance. Finally, Mildred could say truthfully that she loved school, her friends and her life.

As graduation approached, Florence Fisher borrowed a lovely dress for Mildred to wear at the ceremony and helped her buy new shoes. However, a few weeks before the ceremony Mildred was notified by the principal that she might not graduate because she did not have any physical education classes on her transcript. After a flurry of letters back and forth to her previous principals, the Athena principal wrote to the Broadway principal that Mildred's participation in girls' basketball served as her physical education requirement at his school. With this consideration, Mildred cleared the final hurdle.

Her happiest moment came when it was announced that Mildred 'Louise' Milby would graduate in the top ten percent of her Broadway High School class of three hundred.

Mildred had high hopes of going to college and dreamt of being the second Milby to attend the University of Washington, which was easily accessible by bus from the Fisher home on Capitol Hill. Financially, however, it was well out of her reach. She knew that her father would never consider helping her, not only because of their estrangement, but also because she had heard from her sister about his financial woes. Florence Fisher procured a job for her at the tie factory. A few days after her high school graduation, Mildred began her first day in the working world.

Florence also informed Mildred that since she would not be home to take care of the household chores and therefore complete her financial obligation to her aunt, she would be required to pay one dollar per day for room and board. It cost Mildred ten cents each way on the bus to and from work, so each week her expenses were $8.00. Her beginning salary was twenty-five cents an hour, times eight hours a day, times five days a week which amounted to $10.00 per week or forty dollars a month, plus she earned $4.00 per month for playing for the church. If she saved every penny and bought nothing for herself she would have only $12.00 to put aside for college at the end of each month. This was not going to be enough.

Mildred worked diligently at the tie factory and proved to be a hard worker. Within a couple of months her pay was increased to thirty-five cents an hour, which helped increase her savings. But Mildred also had a desire to do something socially, so she joined a young women's business club, which required monthly fees. She enjoyed the group's activities and found herself becoming more self-confident. She also found herself taking on more responsibility at the tie factory, but not getting paid for her extra effort. One day her supervisor asked her to take over another woman's job carrying heavy bolts of cloth from one area of the workroom to the cutting tables in addition to the job she had. The other woman had been working there for some time and had a much higher salary. Mildred thought it over for a minute or two then told her boss she wouldn't take on the harder job unless he paid her fifty cents an hour! He was so surprised he agreed to her terms. From then on Mildred was able to have a little social life as well as save for college.

By the spring of 1926, Florence Fisher had had it with Scott who had resumed his habit of rarely being at home. Nor could he be depended upon to contribute any money for the family. She went to the bank and withdrew Scott's half of the proceeds from their Athena house, and handed it to him one evening when he came home. She told him to pack his things and get out, and that she was going to divorce him. He didn't seem to mind at all. A month or so later Florence informed Charlotte and Mildred that the divorce would soon be final, that she was going to go into the real estate business, and that she was moving to Tacoma by summer's end. She looked Mildred in the eye and told her niece that Mildred would not be coming with them.

Mildred knew her hope of attending the University of Washington was now dashed. By the end of summer she figured she would have saved about $250 from her job at the tie factory and her music job at the church. She had also picked up a couple of piano students and that money had also gone into her savings. Nevertheless, she knew $250 would not be enough even to attend a smaller school. When some parishioners at the Christian Church found out that Mildred wanted to go to college, and impressed with Mildred's efforts to bring good music into their services, they offered her a scholarship of $250 if she would attend the Christian Church's new college, Spokane University, in eastern Washington. Grateful and surprised, sad to leave the Seattle area and its many post-high school opportunities, and disappointed in her relatives once again, Mildred accepted the scholarship and applied to the college. Together with the scholarship and the money she had saved, Mildred had slightly more than

$500, which was enough to give her a start, especially if she could find work in Spokane to supplement her income.

Mildred quit her job at the tie factory when aunt Florence and Charlotte left for Tacoma in late August. Florence seemed happy to be rid of her niece and Charlotte did not seem to care. Mildred took one last trip to downtown Seattle to King Street station and boarded the train for Milton to stay at Ellen's and Fred's until the fall semester at Spokane University began. Once again, Mildred was on the move.

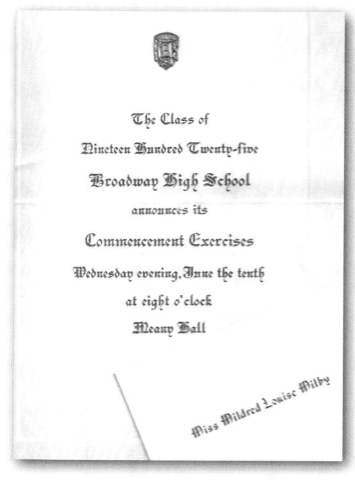

One Last Farewell to Milton

Remembering the good times; finding an empty attic

MILDRED STAYED FOR A WEEK in Milton with her aunt and uncle. Both Ellen and Fred had given her a warm hug on her first day there. Over iced tea and coffee she enjoyed long conversations with her aunt to whom she happily described her life in Seattle. Mildred helped Ellen with the meals, but beyond that Ellen treated her like a guest and pampered her. She even made her famous sweet & tart lemon sherbet dessert, which tasted delicious on those hot and humid August days. They talked a little about Effie and various members of the Fisher family, but skirted the topic of Arthur and Marian.

Each day Mildred visited old friends and walked the familiar streets of the town she had loved a lifetime ago. Many of her friends were now married or had left with their families for the cool forests of the Blue Mountains or Wallowa Valley. Nothing much had changed visually. She walked slowly past McLoughlin High School and the beautiful Junior College building where she had spent many happy hours in what seemed like another lifetime. She walked downtown past her father's former grocery store now standing empty with a "for rent" sign in its front window. Down the block she paused in front of, then walked into Fred's store. She enjoyed the pungent smells and colorful displays she found there in the high-ceilinged, long, narrow room: newly harvested onions and potatoes in their bins, boxes of sun-ripened tomatoes and the last of the summer's peaches and apricots whose heavy, sweet fragrances wafted in the air. The sight of them reminded her of the infamous peach fight between Harold and Florence. On the store's left, lining the wall were twelve-foot high shelves full of meticulously arranged canned goods, preserved fruits and evaporated milk. On the tops of the shelves stood those familiar bottles of Dr. somebody's Liniment, boxes of dried figs, and Kennedy's Cough Syrup. In front of the shelves was a three-sided window case in which customers could find plugs of tobacco, boxes of cigars, beef jerky, and jack knives. A gallon jar of candy sat on top. Mildred wondered if they were still ten for a penny. At the far end of the counter gleaming and ready to be fed sat Fred's newest modern acquisition, an intricately decorated cash register. Beside it was the usual stack of catalogues.

As she left, she turned to wave and smile at Fred who was helping a customer. He pointed to the big crock sitting near the front of the store and said, "Better take one of those." She lifted the brick off the plate that served as the lid, and set it on the floor. Then she unhooked the fork that was hanging on the lip of the vessel, lifted up the plate, and speared a giant dill pickle, shaking it slightly and letting it drip for a moment before she replaced the lid and brick. She waved it at him with a smile and walked out the front door. It was like eating spiced candy when she bent over and bit into the crunchy pickle letting some drips fall on the sidewalk, then shaking it slightly to let more juice drip away from her dress. This was the way it had been so many years ago and the moment caressed her like a favorite shawl. "*What good people Fred and Ellen are,*" she thought to herself. She was so lucky to have them in her life, and the truth of the matter was that she was relieved to be able to walk around Milton without having to worry about seeing Marian or her father who was now employed at Gardner & Co in Walla Walla. They had moved on and thankfully, she had also.

That spring Mildred had received a letter from her sister Florence in which she reported that the sale of Arthur's Milton house had fallen through, but Ellen had just told her another sale was pending. Most of the furniture had been removed, but apparently Arthur had not taken all the memorabilia. Mildred walked over to the house in the hope that she would be able to find a few of her mother's paintings and drawings, maybe one or two of Effie's's dresses, and perhaps some of Mildred's own toys in the attic where they had been relegated when Marian moved in. As she approached the house a neighbor came out with an armload of washing to hang on her line and exclaimed, "Why, Mildred Milby! What are YOU doing here?" Putting down the clothes she came across the yard and the two women, each delighted to see the other, began to chat. When Mildred related the highlights of her last four years, her graduation from high school with honors, working a year in Seattle, and was now going to attend college in Spokane, the woman seemed thrilled for her.

"So what *are* you doing here?" she asked. "I would think this would be the *last* place you would want to see!"

Mildred replied, "Actually, I was hoping to find a few of my mother's things. I have nothing to remember her by."

The woman blanched. She looked away, then said. "Oh, Mildred. Life is so sad sometimes. You don't know, do you?"

"Know what?"

"I suppose I will be the one to tell you," she sighed. She gathered her thoughts, then shrugged, tightened her lips into a thin line, and began, "Of course you know that Arthur and Marian have moved to Walla Walla?"

"Yes," Mildred answered, puzzled and stone-faced.

"Just before they moved, Marian cleaned out the house...things she didn't want to take with her. She called Florence to come over and get a few things of hers that were in the house. I don't know about Harold or Crans. So Florence came over one day and left with a few things on her arm. She had Louise with her so she couldn't carry much. I waved to her and she waved back but she didn't come over to say, 'hello.' It didn't look like Marian and she were speaking to each other either because Marian came out of the house while Florence was inside, then went in the back door after Florence came out the front. At any rate, after she left, Marian started hauling things out of the house and started making a big pile in the driveway beside the house. It made me so curious! You know, on the dirt. After a while the pile got big and I could see that there were children's toys in the pile...a doll buggy...some small books. You know. But mostly it looked like clothing, and some square boards. I walked over and asked her what she was doing, thinking I should probably help her (I didn't really want to), because she was huffing and puffing and was all perspirey."

"So when I asked her what she was doing, she just snapped at me!" the neighbor said as she began to mimic Marian's starchy reply. "I am cleaning out the attic. There is nothing there that we want! "

"I can tell you, Mildred, I became alarmed because when I got close to where Marian was, I recognized some of Effie's beautiful dresses and her art work and children's toys. There were stacks of sheet music and music books. So I went back home and called Florence."

"Florence," I said, "I think Marian is getting rid of all your mother's things--her paintings and her clothes. If you want anything of hers, you'd better get over here!"

"By the time Florence got there, Marian had thrown kerosene on the pile and lit it. It made a huge fire. Florence ran up close and grabbed a few of her mother's drawings, but little else. She turned toward the house and shouted something at Marian who had run into the house and was looking out the kitchen window, and then Florence left. When the fire burned down and cooled, Marian raked the ashes into a pile, put them into a washtub and carried them out back. She piled the twisted metal of the baby buggy frame on top of it. By the time she got through, there was little to show that there had been a fire there that day, and Marian went inside to clean up before returning to Walla Walla, I suppose. My heart broke for Effie, Mildred. I didn't know you didn't have anything of your mother's. I could have saved something for you if I had thought about it. I was so sad thinking about Effie that day. She didn't deserve to be treated that way. She was a good woman. I'm surprised Ellen didn't tell you."

Mildred was speechless and teary. No one had told her, not even her own sister or her aunt Ellen. Why? So now she had learned that Florence had some of Effie's drawings and paintings. Was she going to hide them from Mildred always? Ellen had the dog picture Effie had given them for Fred and Ellen's wedding. But the dog picture was hidden away in their basement because Ellen didn't like it. Harold had taken, then given away, several of their mother's paintings to his former fiancee. Did he have any left? Undoubtedly Crans was out of the picture, but was there anything of her mother's left for her? Could Marian truly be such an evil person and Arthur not know it? Or worse, even care? Did he not love his children a little bit, or the memory of their mother who had borne his four children?

Worst of all for Mildred was Marian's resurgent presence in her life as well as her spitefully subtle acts against her siblings as well. From the very first moment of her marriage to Arthur, Marian had seemed bent on eradicating every bit of minutia that was a reminder of Effie. First, she destroyed the trust between Arthur and his children and erected a physical, if not psychological barrier between them and him. Next she destroyed every physical item in the house that Effie had created or loved. To Mildred Marian was a scheming, self-serving, hypocritical, hateful woman. Yet Arthur loved her. Did he respect her? How was that even possible?

Mildred could not bring herself to enter the unlocked house to see for herself that the attic was empty. She thanked the woman for her forthrightness and walked home slowly to the Milbys', mulling over what she had just learned. At home Ellen could tell that Mildred's mood had completely changed from the light-hearted manner in which she had left earlier in the day. Instead of asking her what was wrong, Ellen took one look at the young woman, turned on her heel and walked into the kitchen. She must have guessed that Mildred had been asking questions. Mildred who had looked for solace from her aunt knew there would be none now or probably ever.

19

Leaving Milton Behind

*"...I took the one less traveled by,
And that has made all the difference."*

— ROBERT FROST

THEN THE WEEK CAME TO an end. By Mildred's last night in Milton she had begun to turn a very important corner in her life. She was rested, she had had a good visit with her aunt and uncle, and she had begun to let go of her painful childhood memories. True, she had been wounded by the bad news about the loss of her mother's personal belongings and her own favorite toys, but realizing she could not do anything to change that now, she was ready to start her new life as a college student. The next day she would leave for Spokane and hopefully begin a new life.

When Mildred returned home from her walk around Milton that afternoon Ellen had guessed that her niece had talked to someone about her early years in Milton. Just before dinner they discussed what Mildred had found out briefly, but in Ellen's abrupt way, she passed it off as "What's done is done. No use crying over spilt milk." Ellen's comments, however, only made Mildred's pain rise to the surface again. She expected Ellen to be an ally. It wasn't easy for her to let go of the loss of her mother's things or forget the way it had happened. Sighing, Millie accepted the apparent Milby *modus operandi* of producing yet another blow from out of the blue. She kept reminding herself that she was about to embark on a new journey she herself had chosen, not anyone else.

After supper, Fred, Ellen and Mildred went outside to sit on the shady front porch where there was a light breeze cooling down the heat of the day. Ellen and Fred had been quiet during the meal. Mildred thought perhaps they were sad that she was leaving and felt badly that Mildred had been so hurt by more news about one more spiteful act of Marian's. What she didn't expect was that her aunt and uncle were about to launch a completely new assault on her.

They sat and fanned themselves and began to chat in the usual fashion: It's certainly been very hot; Mildred spoke of seeing many old friends and the pleasure of visiting Fred's store; the dinner was delicious; I'm going to miss your good food and company, etc. Then abruptly Ellen and Fred began a many-pronged attack.

"Why are you even thinking about going to college?"

"There is no need for you to go to college."

"None of our family has ever needed a college education."

"Your uncle Fred is doing well; he only had a few years of high school."

"Florence and Harold are doing well."

"A young woman in your circumstances should get a job and earn her own living."

"You can meet people your own age here, meet someone to marry you and you can settle down and have a family. You are making a big mistake going to college."

"It's money you don't have."

Mildred was stunned by the severity of their comments. Then Ellen added sternly, " Some people think you are trying to be better than them."

There it was: the reason Fred and Ellen were angry with her. They thought that a young woman without any financial resources who was adamant about going to college was trying to rise above the other members of her family who were already successful in their own lives despite their lack of schooling and any hardships they may have endured. (*"Well, you can exclude Crans from that picture!"* Mildred thought to herself.)

Mildred sat in silence while she listened to the two people she dearly loved berate her for having the audacity to try for a college education. Clearly they thought their beliefs would cause her to change her mind, and, after all, she "owed" them obedience. Mildred's stomach began to churn and her thoughts began to run wild. No one had thought anything negative when Harold went off to the University of Washington, but they were certainly thinking that about her now. It didn't matter to Fred and Ellen that Mildred wanted to become a teacher. In their day, capable young women often became teachers before they had even graduated from high school! If she had chosen to go to a two-year "normal school", such as the one in Ellensburg to get a teaching certificate, would they be any less critical? Of course a teacher's certificate at Ellensburg would be much less costly than going to a private college like Spokane University for four years. According to Ellen and Fred the school she'd chosen was wrong. Her goals were wrong. She was unappreciative of what her family had done for her since her mother died. Having to work for her board and room while going to high school had not hurt her. Look how well she'd done! She needed to stay in Milton and get a job and settle down.

And so the conversation, which had begun so sweetly, evolved into a monumental barrage aimed at their niece. Mildred began to counter every point with facts but was met with resistance and emotional counterpoint. Mildred was shocked. Another of her dreams began to shatter. She had been completely blindsided. Were they even proud of her for graduating with honors from Broadway High School? Apparently not! Still she held her ground and told them every dime of the money she was using she had earned by her own hard work and she wanted to take advantage of the scholarship money she had been given. Fred stood up abruptly, pointed his finger at her, and said sternly, "You have no business going there!" Disgusted and silent, he marched into the house and went to bed. Ellen continued the onslaught. Like a scorned woman with a dagger she continued to cut at Mildred viciously. Unprepared for this onslaught, Mildred was reduced to weeping and silence.

Sensing Ellen was finally nearing the end of her tirade, Mildred became an anarchist. She sat up straight, looked directly at her angry aunt and said quietly, "I am still going," Ellen paused for a moment, looked at Mildred with no facial expression, but blazing anger in her eyes, said nothing, got up from the porch swing, walked to the door of the house and went in, closing the door firmly behind her. In stunned silence Mildred sat on the porch swing, hands in her lap, eyes staring at the porch railing and replayed the conversation, thinking: "*Surely they had dreams when they were young? Surely they must understand that getting a college degree is my dream? Why are they really so opposed to college for me? I have always felt their love for me. What is different now?*" This was not at all what she had anticipated when she had left Seattle. Earlier in the week she had even dared hope that Ellen and Fred might surprise her and help her a little financially. How naive she had been!

Spent emotionally, Mildred sat on the swing in the darkness and sobbed quietly for several minutes. It was nearly eleven o'clock. She should just go to bed. Maybe they would feel differently in the morning. Just as she was about to get up to go into the house, she heard a "click." Someone inside the house had locked the door! She was locked out! Surely she was wrong. She got up and tried the knob and pushed on the door with her shoulder. It stood fast. Stunned, Mildred leaned her forehead on the door with one hand against its warm surface and the other in a clenched fist at her side and began to weep anew. She thought of her first moments at Laurelwood when she realized that her father had abandoned her there. It was as if someone had just died. Again. Her heart was leaden. Mildred turned quietly and faced the closed door with hands on her face thinking, *"What on earth is going on here? Why do I keep doing the wrong thing? Why are they treating me like this? Where will I sleep tonight?"*

After a few minutes she turned and stepped off the front porch and began walking. She walked up and down most of the dark sidewalks of Milton that night, weeping and blowing into her handkerchief, and trying figure out how her life had gone so terribly wrong yet again, and trying to decide what to do next. Should she go against the two people she loved dearly and whom she considered her second parents? Should she continue with her plans to go to college and by doing so lose their love and affection? Should she bend to their wishes and get a job in Milton and find someone to marry as they wished? No! Never! She could not bear to think of staying in Milton, the very place where her misery had started.

Even if she could stay for a while with Ellen and Fred, she now believed they didn't think much of her or her aspirations or trust that she could make wise decisions for herself. She couldn't go to Walla Walla and face an unplanned meeting with her father's wife. She couldn't go back to Seattle because even if she could get her old job back, she couldn't afford to live there on a tie factory worker's pay. She couldn't go to her sister Florence's, who only recently had returned from Tacoma to Hermiston where she was about to become engaged to a pharmacist there and begin a new life with him. Harold was out of the question. Crans, sixteen, had run away again and was working for a farmer in the Palouse. It was too late in the evening to go to one of her Milton High School friend's. When she walked by their dark houses she could not bring herself to knock on their door, and if she did, all of Milton would know the continuing saga of the Milby family's troubles before supper the next day. Did she have any other options?

Eventually, Mildred's footsteps brought her back to Ellen's and Fred's front porch. Softly she tried the door. Still locked. She sat down on the swing, bent over with her elbows on her lap and her face in her hands and began to weep soundlessly again. The swing creaked a little. Realizing there was no other place for her to go, she knew she would have to curl up on the swing and sleep there for the night. Then she heard a soft "click." Was that the door being unlocked? Listening, she heard no other sounds except those of a town fast asleep: a dog barking in the distance; a car passing; a door shutting. She waited and listened. It was quiet in the house.

Then she got up and walked over to the front door and turned the knob. The door opened. Mildred stepped inside into the empty living room. Whoever had unlocked the door had returned to their bedroom without waiting to speak to her. Still unsure of her status with her aunt and uncle, she closed and locked the door behind her, walked silently to her room, lay down on the bed in her street clothing, and fell into an exhausted sleep on top of the covers.

In the morning, the air in the kitchen was heavy with tension. Ellen had little to say even to Fred as they went through their daily breakfast rituals. Without saying goodbye, he left to open up his store. Mildred dragged her small trunk to the front door and put it outside for the man she had hired to help her get it to the interurban. She put her suitcase and purse by the front door, turned to her aunt, gave her a hug and said, "Thank you for all you have done for me." And she meant it. For all the many times Ellen had mothered her over the years, Mildred was profoundly grateful. Ellen glanced up at her then looked away. Her aunt did not hug her back, but stood there as if waiting for Mildred to admit her sins and give in to her wishes. Ironically, it may have been Ellen's own stubbornness that had taught Mildred over the years how to persevere. The girl picked up her purse and suitcase and went out on the porch to wait for the truck driver.

Mildred arrived at the Milton interurban station in time to make the connection to Walla Walla. There, she walked through the steps of the next leg of her journey in a daze. She arranged for the

stationmaster to put her trunk on the train, reexamined her previously purchased ticket and found a seat in the correct car. Once
again she was beginning a journey to an unknown place without the
love and support of anyone she knew. It was as if Milton was still trying to beat her down and to live she had to flee.

The Union Pacific train chugged northward out of Milton and
slowly wound its way first to Walla Walla then north through the eastern Palouse's rolling wheat lands stopping at nearly every little town
through which it passed: Prescott, Starbuck, Hay, LaCrosse, Winona,
Endicott, and Diamond. In Colfax because the two railroad companies' tracks were a different gauge and did not meet, she changed
to the Northern Pacific Railroad and continued northward. Huge
rolling acreages of newly harvested golden wheat stubble as far as
her eye could see flew by her window. As the train travelled through
Garfield, Farmington, Tekoa, Latah, Seltice, Fairfield, and Rockford,
the large grain fields gradually morphed into smaller, more diverse farms, rocky bluffs, and forested hills. The state line between
Washington and Idaho lay only a few miles to the east, but the beauty
of this diverse country did not impress Mildred that day. In fact,
she looked through the window, but barely saw it as the train rocked
rhythmically northward. Flashes of event-filled memories from the
last ten years of her life raced through her mind as she tried to make
sense of them. She wept. She sighed. She took deep breaths and let
them out slowly. If there were other passengers in her car, she never
noticed them and they left her alone. Beginning with the death of
her mother, so many of her childhood dreams had been dashed. Was
this a train ride to another disaster?

Mildred's journey that day ended in Dishman, Washington, the
closest stop to Spokane University. The small college was located on
a hill few miles south and east of Spokane. The little white clapboard
station was located in the bend of the tracks just after it turned west
toward Spokane from its north-south path to and from Colfax. The
trip had taken a good part of the day and would have been pleasant

enough had it not been for the heaviness in Mildred's heart and the fairly rough ride over the two rail systems on that hot August day. She had been too depressed to buy anything to eat in Colfax. She might have enjoyed the scenery or the variety of people in the cars with her had she not been reliving the highs and lows of her life and wondering what she was heading into. As it was, she had to separate what she had learned and experienced in Milton in the previous week and try to tuck it away with the other tattered bits and pieces she had stowed in her mind so she could concentrate on a plan to survive the difficult years she knew lay ahead of her.

Once off the train, and with her trunk and suitcase sitting on the platform, Mildred realized she could not see any college buildings in sight near the station nor in the surrounding ponderosa pine forests. Surprised, she had no idea in what direction the college was located or how she would get herself and her baggage there. She asked the stationmaster who had some vague idea that Spokane University was "...that way (east) only a mile or so and up that hill (south) although I've never seen it...," so she asked and got permission to leave her trunk there and promised to have someone pick it up later.

Suitcase and purse in hand, the resolute young woman began to walk. The sun had begun to dip behind the tops of the forested hills that cast ever-lengthening shadows in the repressive August afternoon. Tiny dust devils swirled up lazily from each purposeful step, powdering her worn shoes as she followed the road where she hoped to find the door to a life she had dared to dream of, to a place she'd never seen: some place where she could step into a future she could scarcely imagine.

Spokane University

1926-1930: College and The Great Depression

Veritas est Lux

MILDRED'S FIRST VIEW OF SPOKANE University was from a distance and at first glance not very impressive. She had no idea what to expect and had little to compare it to any other college other than the stately buildings of the University of Washington in Seattle. Spokane "U" was a place that she had chosen sight unseen, where she would promise to pay more money than she had, and where she was prepared to dedicate the next four uncertain years of her life.

As she trudged the mile and a half up the hill from the railroad station her suitcase seemed to grow heavier and heavier as if it was taking on its own passengers all heading for 'the promised land." Like the dust swirling around her feet with each plodding step, thoughts flitted against the dry corners of her mind. *Was this the right day? What if the stationmaster was wrong and the school wasn't there? Or, maybe she had misinterpreted his directions and followed the wrong road? What would she do then? What had she been she thinking? Why hadn't she just given in to Ellen and Fred's advice? That would have been so much simpler in the long run. And, speaking of a "long run," would happiness ever find her? Would she ever know what true happiness was or recognize it when it surrounded her? Was she trying to become something or* someone that was "above" her family and eventually alienate them instead of honoring them?

Remembering another trip four years earlier when she was fourteen and was on her way to another school on the side of another country hill she had never seen before, Mildred wondered if this journey would ultimately prove to be any different. Spokane University was another religious institution. *They, too, like Laurelwood, prepared young people for a lifetime of service to spread the faith of their church. Would she be the only one not interested in that kind of education? How different could they be, really? Like Laurelwood, this school had only been in operation for a few years. Would their instructors be learned and talented like those she had dreamed of finding at the University of Washington? She didn't care what the place looked like, she just wanted to get there.*

Deep in thought she was almost startled when she looked up the hill and saw edifices of red brick and wood on the crest of the hill among the tall Ponderosa pines. The buildings were too large to be private homes and looked too prestigious to be anything other than an institution. Maybe, just maybe, this was the place. True enough, after an hour or so of walking and shifting her heavy suitcase from one hand to the other, she had found it! Exhausted emotionally and physically, she stopped thinking about her arrival at Laurelwood in 1922 and realized how different her circumstances had been then. There she had no say about her life. Here she would. She had to admit she had only enough money to pay for the first year of school, and had no foreseeable financial help, but for the most part, she was in charge of her own destiny. She was determined to end the old story and begin a new one.

And she did.

During her freshman year at Spokane University Mildred lived in Redford Hall, the women's dormitory, where she met several young women who would be her dear friends for many years. It took a while for Mildred to stop smarting from her disappointment at not getting to attend the University of Washington. Also weighing on her were the abrupt dismissal of her dreams by her aunt Florence in Seattle and the severe criticism of her by her beloved aunt Ellen and uncle Fred. However, keeping in mind Ellen's advice-- "Don't cry over spilt milk!" -- Mildred tried to make the best of her newest challenge.

Mildred poured herself into college life as well as her studies. She wanted to experience it to the fullest. Once settled in, Mildred found a job working a few hours a day in the college office for thirty-five cents an hour. Mildred kept that job for four years, even in 1929 and 1930 after the Depression began, when her pay was reduced to ten cents an hour and her hours were cut back. That money all went back to Spokane University to pay for fees they had allowed her to charge while her money (and nearly everyone else's) was scarce. Anything was better than nothing and there were plenty of students who would gladly have taken her place at the job. She enjoyed her classes and her grades were strong. She wrote her aunt and uncle short letters about her life at Spokane University, her classes and how happy she was there. By early spring 1927 Ellen appeared to have mellowed. She sent Mildred a valentine letter from her Milton home at 308 Mill Street in which she wrote:

Dearest Mil:-
I surely intended to send you a valentine but when there are no little folks around one forgets - am looking forward to Easter -
Love from Aunt Ellen

There followed a handwritten poem which she (probably) had copied from somewhere:

A Valentine
This little valentine I send
Not rich or quaint or lettered well
But just a homely verse self-penned
That may for lack of better tell
Why you, I hope, already know

Because I said it long ago,
I love you, - I love you
Again I say I love you.
I loved you when you were so small
You could not love me back at all;
And then when you were larger grown
I made for you a golden throne,
And at your feet I humbly poured
A wealth of homage; I adored
The girl that you had come to be,
A pretty girl, my friends agree.
And now that you are older still
You, who my fondest hopes fulfilled,
I say again - I love you
I love you dear, I love you.

Mildred kept her aunt's letter for the rest of her life. Even though it was difficult for Ellen to admit that she regretted how she and Fred had ridiculed Mildred for daring to dream about having an education beyond high school, it meant the world to Mildred to know her aunt still loved her. Ellen was always the only woman who had been most like the mother she had lost so early in her life.

By the end of her freshman year in 1927, Mildred was one of eight listed on the Honor Roll out of one hundred forty students. However, reality had also set in. She and several of her friends realized that they could no longer afford to live in the dormitory, so she and three other girls rented a large upstairs bedroom of the Callicoat family who lived near the university. The young women had a two-burner hot plate on which they made small meals. When they splurged, they sometimes ate in the university commons. Besides one dollar per week Mildred paid for the room, she earned her remaining portion of the room rent by teaching piano to Mrs. Callicoat and her two children. This proved to be very satisfactory for the next three years.

Two of her roommates were sisters from a wheat farming family in the Palouse. Their mother was very kind to Mildred, often giving her outright small gifts of money. The third roommate was Vergie Smith from Sandpoint, Idaho. Vergie became Mildred's best friend at Spokane University. On a few occasions Vergie invited Mildred to come home with her for a weekend in Sandpoint. Usually Vergie's father made the trip by car to Spokane and drove the girls each way. Mildred loved these outings, which gave her the experience of interacting with an intact, loving family. Once or twice the girls went by train, but this proved to be a huge financial hardship for Mildred, so occasionally she turned down Vergie's invitation saying she had studies, practicing, or office work to do.

During her junior and senior years Mildred picked up several more piano students including a family who lived near downtown Spokane. Although it cost money to take the streetcar to the family's home and back, Mildred enjoyed interacting with the family and taught piano to the mother as well as her two children. This friendship proved later to be a valuable one for Mildred. Although the children were loath to practice and their lessons showed it, they were delightful children. Often Mildred would be invited to stay for dinner following the lessons and she gratefully accepted.

Mildred also played piano occasionally for a Congregational Church on Sprague Avenue in downtown Spokane. She also had begun looking for a church to find as her own faith home. She visited several, then found St. John's Episcopal Church in downtown Spokane, which was the temporary seat of the Missionary Diocese of Spokane while a cathedral, The Cathedral of St. John the Evangelist, was being built on the lower side of the South Hill overlooking Spokane. The Bishop, aptly named Bishop Cross, was inspiring to her. At the end of her life it was to this same lovely cathedral that Mildred, then in her nineties, came to enjoy the rich Anglican liturgy and full mass with choir and carillon on Easter Sundays and other special occasions.

While Mildred poured herself into her studies, her music, and any job she could find, she also poured herself into the activities of Spokane University. In her Spokane University Scrapbook she appears in many pictures with others who presented a program or activity. With baton and streamers she is a "Stepper"; in a group of young women in overalls she writes about herself and five others "They thot (sic) we were boys!"; she appears in her bloomers and sailor top with her girls' basketball team "The Champs".

Her other friends in addition to Vergie Smith, were Margaret Grove, Marie Reece, Rosalie Roehr, and Grace Johnson. Mildred briefly had a boyfriend nick-named "Hod" and another named Carl E. She and her friends posed for Leo Ostreicher who later became a well-known Spokane photographer. She appeared in a production called "The Festival of the Little Lanterns", and was in a Delphian Theatrical program, She joined the Pep Girls (called "The Little Peppers") and appeared in a Pep Girl program where in one scene she danced to the Sailor's Hornpipe in a sailor suit, and in another scene she was a nurse who sang a duet, "If I Had You" with Vergie Smith dressed as a man. She was elected secretary-treasurer of the Spokane University Drama Club. With her friends she went on winter outings to Liberty Lake and Mount Spokane, Newman and Twin Lakes in the summer, and took a 600-mile trip to Canada in the summer of 1928. Her friends all called her "Millie."

Also in April 1928, she was selected to attend the Intercollegiate Associated Women Students Western Conference held on the campus of the University of Washington, the college of her dreams. She was provided with a room in the Alpha Gamma Delta sorority house on 21st Avenue in which ironically many years later her daughter and granddaughter became members. On the last evening before the conference ended, she and her fellow delegates attended a formal banquet in the Spanish Ballroom of the Olympic Hotel in downtown Seattle where she dined on "broiled chicken, peas, potatoes parmentiere, salad de saison, fancy coupe, cakes, and cafe noir." During the dinner the delegates were serenaded by a string quartet, a vocal soloist and a violinist. The irony of this experience was not lost on Millie who, in her borrowed dress, soaked up every tiny nuance of that evening. Less than one and a half years previously she had lived only a couple of miles up the hill from that luxurious Olympic Hotel. In those completely different circumstances, she had been about to be ejected from the house where she paid for her own room and board by doing housework and working in a tie factory.

In the summer of 1929 Millie and two friends attended the summer session at the University of Washington to pick up some music and English credits. Ellen and Fred Milby sent her $50.00 to pay toward the $72.00 tuition. In her scrapbook she is shown on the steps of Suzzola Library, sitting on the edge of Frosh Pond, near the Columns, and by Meany Auditorium. She had to borrow the money to attend the six week session, but at last, she could say she had finally taken classes at the "U."

In January 1930, Mildred took the train to Tacoma to visit her aunt Florence Fisher who hosted a little party for her. Appearing in the Tacoma Ledger and the Tacoma Times were articles in the social columns which announced:

> *Mrs. Florence Putnam Fisher entertained with a bridge party Saturday evening at her apartment at the Broadmoor, in honor of Miss Mildred L. Milby, who was home from the University of Spokane. Guests were Rose B. Harrison, Violet Erickson, Hortense Erickson, Charlotte Fisher, and the honor guest, Miss Milby. (Tacoma Ledger 1-7-30)*

Mildred was amused at the term "home" in the article, but realized she had no other place she really considered "home."

Later that spring of 1930, Carl E., a junior from Tacoma, appeared to be interested in Mildred as more of a girlfriend than a member of their larger group of friends. Several couples had begun dating seriously and were talking about marriage, and as graduation neared most of the women were hoping to establish a relationship with a fellow because the United States was deep in the throes of the Depression and jobs for women were very scarce. In March Carl invited Millie to join him on a three-day visit to his parents in Tacoma and to attend a dance there with him. Mildred had no money at all and tried to get out of the invitation, but Carl persisted. Mildred borrowed a dress, which turned out to be completely unsuitable because Carl had neglected to tell her the dance was a formal affair. They made the trip by car, possibly Carl's, and arrived late Friday.

It was clear to Mildred that Mrs. E. took an immediate and open dislike to her and the rest of the weekend went downhill from there. Carl's mother was openly critical of Mildred who had had her fill of overbearing adults while growing up. To Mildred, who was simply pleased to "have a boyfriend" at all, the shock of being ridiculed by Carl's mother was unsettling. It appeared that of the previous candidates Carl had presented to his mother, there had been none who was able to meet Mrs. E's requisites as a wife for her son, and very quickly Mildred determined that the last thing on earth she would choose for herself would be to have this woman as a mother in-law. Apparently Millie's lack of money and family support were red flags to Carl's mother, and she dwelled on these things constantly and in front of the two collegians. Millie tried to be respectful while being grilled by Carl's mother, and even her experience with aunt Ellen's banty hen's go-for-the-throat manner of questioning, it was still difficult to keep the edge out of her replies. The dance was a disaster and Millie couldn't wait to get back to Spokane, nor did she care that she had failed this test. Carl did not pursue her further. This experience taught Mildred she was not ready for serious dating. She was focused on getting a teaching job. She had contacted the Westmore Teacher's Agency in Spokane from whom she received a list of available teaching positions throughout the State of Washington, and began to write her inquiry letters.

A full week of activities preceded graduation. There were many meetings, recitals, banquets and a baccalaureate to attend. On June 4, 1930, the night before she graduated, she attended Shakespeare's *Twelfth Night* performed by the Expression Department of Spokane University. The next day, June 5th, at 10:30 a.m. she and her sixteen fellow seniors in caps and gowns marched on the lawn in front of Science Hall on the Spokane University campus, surrounded by their friends and families and received their degrees. On the program Mildred who still could not bring herself to list Milton, Oregon, as her home, chose Tacoma out of the blue even though she had never lived there. Her degree was an A. B. in Public School Music from Spokane University's College of Fine Arts. Mildred was the Salutatorian of her class and gave a speech. During the ceremony she also sang in a women's trio that included her friend, Vergie Smith. As expected, there was no contingent from her family there to honor her.

Millie did hear from several of her friends and relatives, however, in response to her having sent out announcements that she would graduate. In her college scrapbook Mildred saved a note from her aunt Florence Fisher, which ironically read,

> *"My darling Mildred, May this little gift of love record only sunny minutes & hours - not just for to day (sic) your graduation but always. Aunt Florence and Charlotte. "June 4, 1930."*

The card's envelope had a Weisfield and Goldberg Jewelers sticker on it, so one can assume that Florence had sent Mildred jewelry. Considering the difficult three years Mildred had had while living with the Fishers, she was touched. Ellen and Fred also sent Mildred a gift, a dress, and a card that read,

> *"Congratulations and lots of love, Aunt Ellen and Uncle Fred."*

Mrs. Munselle, Effie's best friend in Milton, sent her a purse. The Callicoats, her landlords, gave her "step ins" (underwear), several people gave her jewelry, and her friend Marjorie Brandt from Broadway High School sent her "beads." A few cards may have included monetary gifts, and a couple of notes mentioned that they hoped that their help during her college years had helped ease her burdens. Since Mildred owed the college money at the time of her graduation, the money she received at graduation time went directly to the college. Until the last day of college Millie's friends were still trying to "set her up" with a young man. In her scrapbook Millie saved a note from a Mrs. Minnick, which read,

"Dear Mr. Emerson, (Fenn Emerson, also a senior) We would be pleased to have you take dinner with us next Sat. Eve May 31st Kindly bring Miss Milby with you altho she isn't invited. Mrs. Minnick".

Millie and Fenn were friends, but not interested romantically with each other at that time. Nevertheless, Fenn contacted Mildred and asked her to accompany him. Good-naturedly they went as a couple to the Minnicks. After all, it was a free meal and she liked the Minnick family. Years later she enjoyed telling the story about being asked to go on a date to a dinner to which she was "...not invited."

Shortly before graduation Mildred received a letter from a Mr. Max Steinke, chairman of the Ewan, Washington, school board. He offered her a job teaching music and English in the town's high school. Her salary would be $1,350. for the nine-month school year. She accepted. She borrowed another seven or eight hundred dollars and bought a well-used roadster with four bald tires. The day after graduation, just as she had done at Laurelwood, she took stock of her resources. Cons: She owed the college money, she owed friends money, she owed the car dealership money, she had given back the dresses she had borrowed, and she weighed only eighty-nine pounds.

Pros: She had a college degree, she had friends, she had a car, she had a job in the profession she had chosen for herself, and by being thrifty she would be able to pay back her loans in one or two years. Happiness melted all over her like butter on a warm biscuit.

And once again, she was on the move....

Millie, left, with Spokane University Pep Girls' "the Steppers" 1928

2 1

Interlude

Summer, 1930

MILDRED BADE SPOKANE GOODBYE A few days after her graduation. She packed up her roadster and headed for Cloverdale, Oregon. She ignored the bald tires except when she had to put air in them every hundred or so miles. She looked forward to a long visit with her sister Florence and Florence's new husband, Merrill Groshong. Groshong was the pharmacist Florence had met in Hermiston a year or so after Don's death. At that time Merrill, who had recently completed pharmacy school and was still a bachelor, was filling in temporarily for the owner who was recovering from an illness. With Florence's good business and marketing instincts adding to Merrill's expertise as a pharmacist, the Hermiston pharmacy had begun to flourish and Merrill began to look in earnest for his own store. Neither Merrill nor Florence had sought to begin in such a small town as Cloverdale, which is about twenty-five miles south of Tillamook, Oregon, on the Pacific Ocean, but the price was right and the opportunity could not be passed up. Florence and Merrill married and added two more daughters to their family in quick succession.

Mildred was exhausted when she arrived in Cloverdale, but so was Florence who had gone back to work at the store almost immediately after giving birth to each of her Groshong daughters, Jean and Connie. So while Florence and Merrill worked at the store, Mildred stayed in their home and took over the housework, meals, laundry, ironing, and care of Florence's three little girls, Louise, six; Jean, two; and Connie, the newborn. Gradually they formed a routine that was beneficial to all. Best of all, Mildred did not have to pay room and board, but she worked long and hard hours for Florence who was thrilled with the arrangement. The sisters had a good visit that summer. Rarely did they speak of their difficult experiences in Milton. Florence was proud of Mildred and told her so. Mildred was pleased that Florence had found another good man to marry even though Merrill had a sharp tongue, quick temper, and definitely ruled the roost. Millie was amused that Merrill (like few others!) could easily stand up to Florence when she wanted her way. He, too, liked "Mil" (as Florence always called her sister), and the three little girls liked her, too.

The two sisters caught up on the news of their two brothers. Harold had married a delightful young woman named Arah Spoon from Goldendale, was still doing well with his job at P. P. & L. (Pacific Power and Light Company), and was living in The Dalles, Oregon. For Crans, there was a different scenario. After Mildred's abrupt absence from home in 1922, Crans had realized that his days with Arthur and Marian were also numbered. He was truant and in trouble with the police so often that he knew he would soon be in jail if he didn't get away from Milton. One day when he was about sixteen he hopped a train (again) and headed for Florence's in Cloverdale. This time he got there without being caught en route. Florence said he could live with her and Merrill only if he went to school and tried to pull himself together. This he agreed to do, but he was so far behind his chronological peers academically that he was placed in the eighth grade, many grades below where he should have been. He did moderately well for a while, still chafing at the rigid routine of the school, even though his grades began to improve. In one year he was able to move up two grades, but then he hit a wall. At the age of seventeen he fell head over heels in love.

There was a dark-haired, shy young girl in one of his classes who took his breath away. Maizie Margaret Thayer was about Crans's age, new to the school, and like Crans, was not included in the other students' social gatherings, she for her aloofness (which was in reality extreme shyness) and her Native American heritage. Crans openly demonstrated his "edge," the guy with a chip on his shoulder. In a small town if you weren't "in," you were "out." Crans thought Maizie was the most beautiful girl he had ever seen and began to try to form a friendship with her. At first she seemed wary of him just as she was everybody else, but gradually they began spending more time together until it became clear that they were an "item" and that was fine with their classmates. Crans now had a good reason to stay in school.

Maizie was living with her mother, Hazel, who had gone through a bitter divorce with Maizie's father, Marshall, after a difficult marriage. Maizie was a gifted artist who had been noticed by the district's art teacher who had already started encouraging Maizie to attend art school after high school. Maizie also had a very mature grasp of literature despite her general dislike of reading. She understood many of the subtle references that sometimes had to be explained to her classmates, and if she could be persuaded to answer a question or offer an opinion in class (rarely), her teachers were startled by Maizie's insight, her ability to cut to the nub. Maizie was a complacent student at best. Although excelling in art and literature, Maizie only went through the motions in her other subjects because she was not interested in them, saw no benefit to them, and did not waste her time worrying about them. Though Maizie was a gentle person, she was stubborn beyond belief.

When Maizie was seventeen and Crans was eighteen Maizie got pregnant and the two decided to marry. Since the likelihood of ever finishing high school was now dim, the couple initially lived with Maizie's mother, who was down on her luck. She made it clear she couldn't afford to feed them. Florence and Merrill were furious with him. Without skills or education Crans had little or no luck finding work in Cloverdale especially since the Great Depression had settled in. Jobs were scarce and for an uneducated, unskilled boy, there were few opportunities to get steady work. They decided to move to Walla Walla where Crans had family, but the Milbys had nothing to offer them except a brief place to stay until their son, Marshall Cranston Milby, was born October 30, 1929. Shortly after the baby's birth and because it was too late in the season to get a field job in the area, Crans and Maizie decided to move on to Hope, Idaho, where Maizie's father was supposed to be working for the railroad. Perhaps prospects would be better there. It was not to be. They struggled through the winter months living with Maizie's father, an alcoholic, who was out of work himself. Crans made a futile search for any kind of job, but was largely unsuccessful. In early spring when it was still cold and dreary Marshall Thayer told them he could not support them any longer and they would have to leave. So they did. They pooled just enough money to buy train tickets to Walla Walla where Crans was sure he could find work among the people he knew and work one did not have to have a high school education to obtain. Surely he could find work as a field laborer. Complicating matters further, Maizie was pregnant again.

On their way through Spokane and while they were waiting for their connection to Walla Walla, Crans called Millie from the train station and asked if she could lend them some money. Millie was horrified, not only to hear how down on his luck Crans was, but that she did not have spare money to give him. She herself was dependent upon the small sums her friends' parents often loaned or gave her. She also realized that she could not jeopardize her chance at finishing her own education by giving them money she herself had borrowed. Nevertheless, she took the streetcar into Spokane to the train station and met them. For the rest of her life she was never ever able to erase the picture in her mind of the teenagers and their small infant wrapped in coats as thin as onion skins huddling together in the train station on that day going who knew where with their lives.

Their story was full of lost hopes and missed opportunities, and yet they did not seem to despair. Maizie, her black hair hanging free like a mantilla down her shoulders and back, was a plump girl-woman. She was pleased with her child, and was aglow with adoration while she nursed the baby during their visit. Then, when the baby slept, she laid him on her shoulder, warming him with her body heat and covering him with a blanket. Crans held her hand while he and his sister talked. Maizie barely said two words during the visit, but years later she admitted in a surprisingly candid conversation with Mildred in Pendleton that she had been afraid of Mildred that day because Mildred seemed so self-assured and well-dressed at the time. When Millie heard that, she asked Maizie if she knew that she also had no money at that time and was borrowing money to stay in school. After a moment Maizie looked directly at Mildred and said softly, "No, but you had a place to sleep, you had food, and a job." In their eyes Mildred had seemed wealthy.

There in the train station Crans looked wistful, but he did not complain. He was rumpled, but clearly loved Maizie and the baby. The young couple admitted they were hungry. Maizie's father had not only *not* tried to help them, he had made them turn over what money they had, drank up part of it, and sent them away when they had nothing more to give him. Crans still hoped "things" would get better, but behind his eyes he also had the look of a person who was afraid of falling over a cliff. He was still a boy, but living a man's life. As their train arrived and they began to board, Mildred gave Crans five dollars in change and bills. She kept a streetcar token and some small change to get back to the college. Her brother had no idea how many jobs Mildred had worked to keep herself in school, or for that matter, why she would even want to be in school, but he was grateful for what she gave him because it meant they could eat for another day or so. Once again, Mildred stood near some train tracks with her heart broken watching someone she cared for disappear from her life.

Many years later, when brother and sister were again talking about their hard times, Crans chuckled and told Mildred that despite her tiny size she had always been the tough one in their family. He had had no idea how hard her life had been leading up to that day in the Spokane train station. Despite his knowledge that shortly after their father's marriage to Marian, Mildred had been beaten by Arthur and had left home for good, Crans thought he had been the only Milby child to suffer true hardship.

By the time Mildred had graduated from Spokane University in 1930, Crans and Maizie were living in Pendleton. Their second son, Delwyn Lloyd, was born November 14, 1930, during Mildred's first year of teaching at Ewan. Crans had learned to keep his temper under control at work, and by often holding two jobs at a time and being a hard and reliable laborer, he eventually rose from working in the fields to driving a truck and was soon able to support his family although finances were always an issue. A daughter, Sharon Rose, was born a few years later.

So in Cloverdale that summer of 1930 the sisters wept together and laughed through their tears to remind each other that Ellen would tell them not to 'cry over spilt milk.' "How many times has that milk jug tipped over?" Florence asked, shaking her head. "You just have to do what you know is right," Mildred replied. Despite everything, neither sister ever blamed their father downright for what happened to them, but they were always saddened by Arthur's complete lovesick blindness regarding Marian's vindictiveness toward his children and his choice to believe whatever the woman told him.

By the end of summer, Millie had washed and ironed a truckload of little girls' starched dresses with ruffles, pleats, and tucks. Florence's girls always had beautifully ironed dresses for every occasion that summer and she begged her sister to stay on, but, of course, Mildred would not even consider it.

A place called Ewan beckoned.

Ewan: Three Years in the Palouse

1930-1933: Ewan, Washington

"Oh beautiful for spacious skies,
for amber waves of grain..."

— KATHERINE LEE BATES, 1895

ROCK LAKE IS SITUATED IN a long and narrow depression between low basalt cliffs in eastern Washington's Whitman County. The area around Rock Lake was the last dwelling place of Chief Kamiakin of the Yakama Indian Nation who farmed near there until his death in 1877. One hundred and thirty-plus years later much of the immediate landscape around the lake remains virtually unchanged. In the spring a brilliant blue sky blankets the area while clouds tumble and boil overhead. Brisk breezes ruffle the surface of the dark blue lake bordered by random basalt rock outcroppings and clumps of long, wild grasses. Stretching farther than the eye can see in any direction now are thousands of acres of grain fields that wave like lush green carpets soon to become a golden surf.

In 1903 an entrepreneur so taken by the beauty, isolation, and economic potential of the area, built a hotel there to attract tourists. It was soon joined by a store. Both owners drew their water from Rock Lake by bucket and pulley. In 1904 the completion of the Chicago, Milwaukie and St. Paul Railroad line brought more people who formed the community of Rock Lake near the foot of the lake. By 1907 Rock Lake had its first post office and soon boasted a butcher shop, a livery stable, a harness shop, and a building that was a dance hall for six days each week and on the seventh day hosted church services and school. After one or two years, however, inhabitants of the town disliked both the town's location below the railroad's high wooden trestle and the distance to the railroad depot which was located a mile or so south of the Lake. The Milwaukie Railroad Co. had built the depot in the more lush and flatter valley bisected by Cottonwood Creek because it would provide a more accessible route for their customers. In 1911, a tract of farmland about three and a half miles south of Rock Lake was purchased from Mr. and Mrs. Charlie Ewan (originally pronounced in the Scottish way "yoo-wenn"). The Ewans agreed to the sale if the new town were to be named after them. The townspeople agreed, except that they wanted the accent of the name to be on the "E" and the last syllable pronounced as it was spelled, "wan."

The property was subdivided into lots and orchard plots, then sold at auction September 16, 1911. Several of Rock Lake's buildings were then moved on skids or torn down and rebuilt on the new sites, and on May 18, 1912 the town was renamed Ewan. It soon included two hotels (one with a dance floor overhead), a variety store, a hardware store, a general store (Western Mercantile Co.) a butcher shop, a barber shop, a pool room, a lumber yard, a garage, a harness shop, a branch of the Terhune Bank, a doctor, a post office and switch board, a community hall, and a brand new brick school house.

Like most Eastern Washington farming communities that grew up around rail sidings where area farmers could transport their grain, cattle, alfalfa, sheep, and lumber products to markets, and have supplies such as wheat and corn seed and machinery shipped to them, Ewan was born out of opportunity, only to struggle twenty-five years later to keep itself alive in the throes of vacillating weather, the Great Depression, economic instability, and two world wars.

One hundred years later, the unincorporated community of Ewan is bisected by State Highway 23. It is nestled between volcanic scab lands and the rolling Palouse hills. To strangers Ewan may seem to be merely a place to pass through on the way to somewhere else. Only a few remaining houses can be seen along the pavement. Three features stand out: The white spire of the Nazarene Church, a white community hall, and two large grain elevators that testify to Ewan's brief heyday. The elevators sit by the tracks on the side of the hill overlooking the town and dominate the skyline as the road descends onto the shallow valley floor. A few miles to the east, after Highway 23 rises up into the rolling wheat-covered hills of the northern Palouse, is the tiny town of St. John, which remains happily alive today and in which all the area schools have been consolidated.

On the short trip from one side of the valley to the other, the highway crosses the only other main road, Rock Lake Road, at the center of what remains of the town. In the north, this road originates where I-90 meets Cheney, bisects Ewan, and continues southward through a narrow valley carved by Cottonwood Creek and Cherry Creek, until several miles further where it meets highway 26 near La Crosse and Pampa.

The Ewan School, a large brick building for grades eight through twelve was completed in 1913 and demonstrated the promise that a community would soon thrive and grow there, and that a comprehensive education would be available for its children. Community members formed a school district, elected a board of directors who hired a staff of six men and women to teach and coach every subject and activity. Music had not been offered until Miss Milby arrived in 1930. She was determined to change that mind set.

Upon arrival in Ewan a week or so before the first week of school, Mildred's first two items of business were to find a room to rent, and check in with Mr. Max Steinke, chairman of the school board who lived on his wheat farm east of town toward St. John. She discovered that there were no rooms available in the small town, and she couldn't afford to live in either hotel. When she met with Mr. Steinke, he told her that a bedroom had been reserved for her in a widow's home. She would be expected to pay $30 per month for her room and board, which included two meals per day. ("Reasonable," Mildred thought). However, when she arrived at the correct address, Mildred discovered that her landlady was nearly blind, advanced in age, noticeably senile, arthritic, and in Mildred's opinion, somewhat paranoid. Within a few months, and discounting many of the mediocre meals Mildred had consumed in Spokane University's Commons out of necessity, the only thing that "filled" Mildred in Ewan was indignation about the quality of her suppers at the "widow lady's." Most of all, she was appalled by the amount of burned surface she was obliged to scrape off her meat because the woman liked her own meat "well done." When Mildred offered to help cook, the woman adamantly refused. There was nothing Mildred could do about it.

Shortly after school began, Mildred set about improving the musical opportunities and experiences of her students. Most students lived on farms many miles from the school out in the vast rolling wheat lands of the Palouse and had had few opportunities to enjoy enrichment in the arts. She started a Girls Glee Club in which every high school girl but one joined. Because buses were ready and waiting at school's end to take them on their long rides home, that time was not a good practice option. They practiced whenever they could find a common time, before school or during the noon lunch hour. For their recital in the spring, each girl wore a homemade gingham dress sharing one pattern that went from house to house until all the dresses were finished. Both the dresses and the recital were a huge success.

After she advertised that she would accept students for piano lessons, several students and one or two parents signed up. She taught piano after school using the school's old upright, which she insisted the school get tuned. In the spring she persuaded the Glee Club to put on a little operetta, and with girls taking male parts, they put together a program. The whole thing lasted forty-five minutes and ended with enthusiastic applause and cheers from the audience who began demanding they do the whole production again. The cast and Mildred were exhausted, so they couldn't fathom doing it all over, but they were pleased to be asked to do so. Miss Milby's value to Ewan High School had been established.

During her first academic year besides pouring herself into the curriculum and activities at Ewan High School, Mildred was determined to pay back some of her loans as soon as her salary checks began to come in. During her college years she had kept careful records. Her account book shows the following: On January 16, 1931, she repaid a loan to a Mr. George B. Woodward of Walla Walla, which with 7% interest amounted to $160.50. On April 11, 1931, she repaid a loan due June 1 to Spokane University, which with 8% interest amounted to $64.96. On March 1st, she repaid $30.00 to Mr. W.R. Emerson, whose son Fenn Emerson had, as she put it, "dumped" her in their senior year just when she had begun to get interested in him. They had, however, remained friends. Mr. Emerson of Nezperce, Idaho, had on three separate occasions slipped her a ten-dollar bill during her senior year. She repaid her voice and piano teachers, Mrs. Gladys Bittinger and Mrs. More, for lessons she had taken during her senior year. She even paid a $25.00 pledge she had made (during her senior year when she had absolutely no money at all and didn't have the slightest idea where she would get any) to Spokane University for their capital fund drive.

But what to do about Mrs. Reece, the mother of her friend Marie? During Mildred's senior year Mrs. Reece had written her a check for $125. Mildred wrote a notation by that amount: "*... at the time I was not to pay it back. Was part of the money they usually gave their church.*" Mildred would tell her daughter sixty years later that it still embarrassed her that she never paid the Reeces back, but should have.

Mildred had also kept exact records of the money people had sent her as gifts during her high school and college years. Ellen and Fred had begun sending a little money to help her out while she was in Seattle in high school. In August 1925 just after she'd started working at the tie factory, they gave her $2.00 cash. Later that fall they sent her $13.00 so she could have her "...teeth fixed." Beginning in August 1926 right after their terrible disagreement the night before Mildred left for college, (apparently having had a change of heart, but never an apology for their comments to her) they sent her small amounts of money she always used for specific needs such as "shoes," "train fare," "pajamas," "dress," etc. Over the five years (1926 - 1930) following her graduation from high school Mildred recorded that Ellen and Fred had given her a total of $217.70 including money to attend 1927 summer school in Seattle.

Likewise, her aunt Florence Fisher, whose financial situation had improved after she shed herself of her husband Scott, began sending Mildred checks for small amounts to help her out in her senior year at Spokane University. Mildred was even able to use part of Florence's money to pay off the Woodward note. But in early 1931 after Mildred had begun her job in Ewan, Florence Fisher contacted her in desperation as the bottom had fallen out of her real estate job in Tacoma. Not only was Scott not contributing anything to support his daughter Charlotte, he would disappear for months at a time. Grateful that Florence had provided a place for her to live, despite its hardships, Mildred sent Florence Fisher small amounts of money that added up to $305.

As Florence Groshong's life became more stable she, too, helped Mildred. Her aid usually came in the form of supplies from the drug stores where she worked, such as toothpaste, school paper, soap, a pair of silk hose, fruit, medicine and sometimes a few dollars. While staying at the Groshongs the summer after her college graduation Florence had also slipped Mildred five or ten dollars every now and then. Arthur had not contributed anything for her support since the first few months she was in Seattle at the Fishers.

As Mildred's first teaching year came to a close in May 1931, she noticed that she had lost weight. She was thinner, cranky, and tired. She made an appointment with Mr. Steinke and told him, "If the school board cannot find me a room where the landlady is not trying to poison me, I will have to find a job somewhere else!" Steinke, who had reluctantly agreed to be the school board president a few years earlier, preferred to spend his time farming instead of getting sidetracked by the idiosyncrasies inherent in running a school district. Mildred's board and room dilemma was one of those issues he would have liked to avoid, but worse was finding another teacher to replace her. Thus, he told her that she should, indeed, return the next August. During the summer the school board would have had time to work out a different, more suitable arrangement for her.

When Mildred returned to Ewan in August 1931 after another summer in Cloverdale she discovered that Mr. Steinke had made a bargain with Mrs. Steinke. As soon as their daughter went off to college at Eastern, Mildred could rent her bedroom, but only if she complied with one condition: Mildred was required to gain weight! The Steinkes had a milk cow, and nearly everything Millie ate at the Steinkes for the next two years had cream in it: her cereal, her coffee, desserts, casseroles, gravy, and glass after glass of rich, creamy milk. Every meal was heaven!

The next two years were truly rewarding for Mildred except for two major things: She had little social life, and due to the Depression, the school district was unable to pay her salary for several months at a time. To improve her social life, Millie joined the Eaton Grange, which farmers had refurbished from the old Alki School at Rock Lake. She also began attending the United Brethren Church. For some reason she couldn't warm up to the format of the church's services. The congregation was pleasant, but something was missing. While she enjoyed the Grange gatherings, dances, and potluck dinners, most of the attendees were married couples. Her best friend on the faculty was Minnie Pierson was married and had two children. Nor was Millie attracted to either of the two wheat farmer bachelors who belonged to the grange. After one attempt at a date to attend a grange dance, she turned down any further offers. She could not see herself in the role of farmer's wife living miles and miles from the nearest neighbor or town. She was still young enough to find someone, but a likely prospect near Ewan did not appear to be probable.

The Depression years had caused most people's financial well-being to become very sluggish. Mildred trusted her employer, as well as the people of Ewan who did everything they could to keep both their school district and themselves solvent. Warned in advance that the school district was experiencing a money flow problem, Mildred was not too alarmed when she began receiving "warrants" instead of an actual salary check. Warrants were essentially guarantees that the entity issuing them were legally obligating themselves to provide actual money in a reasonable amount of time, and banks accepted warrants on faith from their reliable customers, such as the school district. However, the warrants could not be converted into actual currency until the issuer had deposited money to cover them. Customers who had balances in their checking accounts that were backed by warrants could likewise pay their bills with their own warrants, but no one could operate completely on warrants. Eventually, when the flow of money began to trickle back into the economy, the warrants were replaced by actual cash and bills could be paid in full.

Complicating the money flow problem and her lack of much social life, Mildred also experienced some health problems in her third year of teaching. By late fall she was experiencing a steady pain in her abdomen. She took a day off of work, drove herself to Spokane and consulted a doctor whose examination revealed that she had a growth on one ovary and that it needed to be removed immediately. The bad news was that the surgery was major and that she would need two to three months to recover. This was difficult for her to absorb, but nothing could be done to prevent the inevitable. She contacted one of her Spokane University friends, Margaret Grove Starling, who agreed to come to Ewan to teach Mildred's classes until Mildred could return to work. Mildred decided to postpone the surgery until December when she would be able to use the two-week Christmas break as a part of her convalescence time.

On December 7, 1932, Mildred, now in nearly constant pain and weak from sleepless nights and little appetite, packed a small suitcase, caught a bus to Spokane and walked from the downtown station to Deaconess Hospital to check herself in. The next day Dr. H. E. Wheeler whose office was in the Fernwell Building in Spokane removed the tumor-impacted ovary. Dr. Wheeler's fee for the surgery was $150.00, and for her two-week stay in Deaconess her bill was $79.95. She paid twenty dollars to the hospital when she checked in and was told that if she paid the remainder by February 1, 1933, the balance would be only $50.00. She noted in her account book that she had to pay the fifty dollars by warrant, and she sent it to them on January 26, 1933. She paid Dr. Wheeler her last ten dollars when she checked out of the hospital on December 20th, and by April 1933 she had paid the remainder by warrant. Mildred was able to stay on in Spokane at the home on Pacific Avenue with the family whose children she had taught piano lessons. She stayed there one more week while she got her strength back. The family would not allow her to pay them anything for their hospitality.

She also needed to pay her friend Margaret for substituting for her classes. They agreed on $6.07 per day, and for the 17 days Margaret taught her classes and stayed at the Steinkes, Mildred paid her $103.20 less $17.00 for the dollar per day board and room at the Steinkes which Mildred paid. Margaret had loaned $10.00 to Mildred, part of which Mildred paid off by giving Margaret a typewriter she had bought earlier. Although going back to work after Christmas was difficult, Mildred got through the first month, then the next. By spring she was feeling fine. By May 1933 Mildred was squared financially with Margaret and was able to exchange real money for her warrants. Just when she thought she was free and clear, she had a blowout on one of her car's tires which forced her to purchase a complete set of tires for $100 when the mechanic refused to let her leave the garage repair shop with only one good tire because he maintained anyone who looked could "see clear through the other three." She also had been putting money aside for a grand trip she had begun to plan with the Starlings.

By the spring of 1933 Mildred had decided that, for as much as she was fond of the people of Ewan, she had to leave if she was ever going to have a personal life. She sent letters of inquiry to several school districts throughout Washington and received two offers. When she submitted her resignation to Mr. Steinke and the school board, she was extremely sad. Both Mr. and Mrs. Steinke tried to talk her out of it, but Mildred would not yield.

On her last evening at the Steinke's, Mrs. Steinke made a huge feast with everything except the ham slathered in cream: creamed new peas and onions; scalloped potatoes au gratin; yeast bread rolls with butter; banana cream pie; coffee with cream. Now good friends, they had been honest with each other: the Steinkes were adamant about wanting her to stay, while Mildred was resolute about needing a job where she had an opportunity to find family life. That night after she had packed her suitcases, she made a list of her resources:

Cons: She had barely saved any money from her job because she had had to pay back her college loans, finish paying for her car and a set of new tires, pay for a surgery, and save for her trip;. She would miss the friendly people in this little community and her students who had blossomed under her guidance; The new job wouldn't pay as well as her job had in Ewan.

Pros: She had three years teaching experience plus glowing recommendations; she owned a 1925 Chevrolet Roadster with four new tires free and clear; she had few bills left to pay; she now required two suitcases to hold her things; and she had a job offer from the Sunnyside School District to teach English, typing, and music, even though she had agreed to receive a salary that was half of what she had received in Ewan.

The next morning, a fine day in June 1933, with Mrs. Steinke's wash flapping on the line under a canopy of huge white clouds tumbling across a brilliant blue Palouse sky, Mildred said her goodbyes to her friends. As she headed out of town she wondered, *"Do I know what I'm doing?"* But then she smiled when she remembered that when she told the Steinkes goodbye and thanked them again, she had been able to tell these kindly people that, in the two years she ate cream at every meal, she had gained two pounds!

And down the road she went...

Ewan High School Yearbook 1932. Mildred Milby, center.

2 3

Sunnyside

August 1933 to June1934
The high school burns down; a wedding; a quilt

AFTER SPENDING THE REST OF the summer in Cloverdale, Mildred loaded up her little roadster and headed north for Sunnyside, Washington. Located in the middle of the Yakima River Basin in south central Washington State, Sunnyside had proven early on to be an ideal location for cattle and sheep ranches as well as diverse farming operations. Sunnyside, surrounded by thousands of acres of fertile volcanic soil and rich lake-bottom sediment, was near a river, had good roads for travel, and was ideally situated to become a thoroughfare for commerce.

The Yakima Valley is a long, relatively flat area that follows the Yakima River as it winds southward from Selah in the northwest, past the county seat Yakima, continuing past Grandview, and Prosser the county seat of Benton County, all the way to the Columbia River into which it empties near the confluence of the Snake River near the current Tri Cities (Kennewick, Pasco, and Richland). On a northwest to southeast diagonal the valley is bordered by low ridges of the sagebrush-covered Rattlesnake Mountains on the north and the Horse Heaven Hills on the south. The valley was sculpted when ice dams near Glacial Lake Missoula ruptured several times between 15,000 and 13,000 years ago flooding and scouring western Montana, northern Idaho, eastern Washington and southward into western Oregon.

West of the Yakima Valley lies the Cascade Mountain Range sculpted eons ago by volcanic activity, principally Mountains Rainier, Adams, and St. Helens and cracks in the earth's crust whose eruptions and upheavals of strata created finger-like hills which the more recent Missoula Glacial Ice Dam Floods both eroded and moved tons of earth throughout the valley. A sandy volcanic soil base was laid on top of rich layers of lake deposits left from the flood waters. This rich soil continues to support diverse crops including asparagus, alfalfa, corn, beets, mint, tomatoes and other truck farm vegetables, as well as fruit orchards, abundant grasslands for cattle and sheep, plus hops, and vineyards. The four-season climate is well-matched to some of the world's finest wine-producing areas. The valley was originally a haven for herds of elk, deer, and antelope that grazed on open bunch grass lands dotted with sagebrush along the Yakima and Snake Rivers until the advent of the cowboy. Sunnyside is proud of its heritage as having provided prime grazing lands for Ben Snipes and his wranglers in the late 1800s and early 1900s.

Founded in 1893 and incorporated in 1902, Sunnyside's first farmers were sturdy German Baptists. Sunnyside's early developers had foreseen that the hot desert-like summers and cold winters plus its sandy, rich soil would be perfect for farmlands if water were more available. Walter Granger, an engineer, convinced the Northern Pacific Railroad Company to help build a diversion canal just south of Union Gap, on the Yakima River. With water accessible through a system of canals, tens of thousands of acres were opened up and potential farmers poured into the valley. This was the final blow to the Yakama Indians, who were forced onto a large reservation near the town of Toppenish.

When Mildred arrived in Sunnyside in the late summer of 1933, she was greeted by a thriving town ten times the size of Ewan.

Surrounded by prospering farms, it was a busy community. Here was potential for a full life! To her dismay, however, she soon learned that the high school had burned down over the summer. Its replacement was just then being started on the one-block square property on Edison Avenue between 9th and 10th Streets. High school classes were to be held all over town that year: in church basements, in an empty grocery store, and in some empty classrooms in two elementary schools. Mildred learned that she would be teaching English in one part of the empty grocery store and would share the room with two or three other teachers and their classrooms that were divided by temporary walls that did not extend to the high ceiling and noise would prove to be an unfortunate and steady distraction.

Mildred found a bedroom to rent not too far from the downtown area where her classroom would be. She was somewhat in shock over her circumstances as the school year began because this was a much larger town and school district, and due to the complete devastation of the high school, there was little opportunity for the entire staff to meet or interact. Nevertheless, the superintendent and school board worked diligently to make the best of a difficult situation and within a few weeks of the start of school a passable routine was established. To supplement her income Mildred advertised for piano students. Since the school piano had burned up in the fire, she was given permission to use the piano in the parish hall of Holy Trinity Episcopal Church on the corner of Edison Avenue and Fourth Street.

A month or so into the fall, Mildred attended a dance at one of the several granges in the area. There she met a young bachelor, Lloyd Smith, who worked at the post office. Lloyd, thirty-two, was called "Red" by his friends because of his naturally curly auburn hair. Although he took the brunt of kidding from his bachelor friends, Lloyd and Mildred soon began dating regularly. By spring they were engaged.

Seven years older than Mildred, Lloyd Francis Smith had been born in Missouri in 1901 and was the oldest of five children of Turner

Williamson Smith and Cecilia Rebecca Steadley Smith. Turner had been in poor health for many years and had failed three times to make a go of farming: twice in Missouri and the last after the family had been lured to Sunnyside in 1920 by his brother Hugh Smith, a successful farmer in the area. Lloyd had graduated from Sunnyside High School in 1922 at the age of twenty-one because he had had to drop out of school so often to help his father farm. After one year of college at Ellensburg Normal School, he had given up his dream of a college education because he could not afford it. For several years thereafter he attempted to "read for the bar" with help from a local attorney, but after two failed attempts at passing the qualifying exam, he abandoned that pursuit and concentrated on his job as a clerk in the post office.

Mildred found Lloyd to be sincere, honest, and hard working, all the attributes she was looking for in a man. He had been a baseball player in high school and had taught himself to play the violin so well that he played in a dance band to earn money while attending college. To her delight, he had vowed never to be a farmer after living through the desperate times his family had experienced for so many years. He had kept his job throughout the Depression and was well liked in the community.

Once they began discussing marriage, the problem of choosing a church home arose. Lloyd's mother Cecilia was a devout Catholic and had raised all her children in her faith. His father, a protestant, did not attend church and was content to have his wife take over that responsibility. However, before moving to Sunnyside when Lloyd was a teenager, he had approached his parish priest in Davenport, Iowa, where the family lived at the time and asked for some clarification about one or two of the Roman Catholic tenets. The priest became incensed at Lloyd's audacity to question the church and angrily berated him. Lloyd was surprised by the priest's reaction because he had meant well and had been thinking deeply about his faith. A day or so later the priest called on Cecilia and informed her that she had to do a better job of teaching her son about the church and needed to show greater respect for God's chosen religious representative. Embarrassed, Cecilia confronted Lloyd who was offended and hurt by both her and the priest's reproach. He reacted bitterly toward the church, saying he could no longer be a Catholic if a member of that faith could not ask about the practices of the church and had to accept everything blindly. From that day forward Lloyd never participated in any Catholic rite, leaving his mother heartbroken.

Mildred, whose own religious experiences had not been especially positive, still believed that attending church was important for a family. She suggested that they visit a few of the local churches together to see if they could agree on one. For Lloyd, the Methodist church service was bland, but he liked the hymns. The Baptists and Congregationalists startled him with their lively interaction and long, haranguing sermons. Then they attended Holy Trinity Episcopal Church, a small mission church on the west side of town where Mildred had been teaching piano lessons in the parish hall. Mildred was familiar with the services because she had attended St. John's in Spokane during her college years, and enjoyed the formality, the prose found in the 1928 prayer book, and the richness of the hymns. For Lloyd, the service was exactly like the Catholic service except that it was in English and the sermons emphasized God's love more than how much everyone had sinned even before they were old enough to know better. They also both liked the priest, Rev. Gordon Graser, a soft-spoken, kind man who, when approached by them in the spring of 1934 after a few months of attending services, agreed to marry them after he met with them for counseling.

The couple set a wedding date for early June, but Rev. Graser had promised his own family that he would take them on a long-awaited vacation during that very time. Since the Graser family was headed for the Blue Mountains east of Walla Walla, the priest agreed to drive to St. Paul's Episcopal Church in Walla Walla on June 3, 1934, to perform the wedding. This would be convenient for Ellen and Fred who still lived in nearby Milton, but everyone else would have to travel to attend.

In the meantime word got out in Sunnyside that Mildred and Lloyd were a serious couple. Mildred was nearly overwhelmed by the attention she began receiving from her new Sunnyside friends, Lloyd's bachelor friends and many of her students. She was the honored guest at two ladies' parties that were duly reported in the Sunnyside Times and the Walla Walla Union-Bulletin. Students in two of her classes passed around pieces of notebook paper and signed their names:

We the undersigned sincerely congratulate Miss Milby and "Red" Smith

(followed by thirty-one signatures)

and

We the class of English IV Period III hope you enjoy life when not a pedagogue (followed by twenty-six signatures among which was that of Hiroshi Furukawa who was later to be one of the troops in the famed 442nd Infantry Division in Europe in WW II, and who after returning stateside after the war, became an M.D., returned to Sunnyside and became the Smith family doctor)

A few days after school let out in May, Mildred took the bus to Milton where she stayed with her aunt and uncle. Lloyd wrote her from Sunnyside on May 31, 1934:

Hello Honey: This is my list hurriedly made, as I haven't [sic] much time - have been rather busy all day; but didn't want to delay this until tomorrow. I will be up late tonight and must get up about six in the morning as they want my car decorated for the parade. I suppose you are also busy, honey but take it easy - there is always a tomorrow; I already miss you honey and can hardly wait until I see you. Give my kindest regards to all but keep all my love for yourself. Lloyd

Included in the letter was Lloyd's list of friends to whom they would later send an announcement of their marriage.

It was to be a small wedding with only family members in attendance. Mildred's sister Florence was her matron of honor and Florence's daughter, Connie Joyce Groshong, four, was her flower girl. Friends from Milton provided music: "Ave Maria" by a violin and piano duo and two vocal solos, "Because" and "Beloved it is Morn." Neither Harold nor Crans came. Lloyd asked his brother Victor to be his best man, and invited his parents and three sisters to attend. Cecilia was heartbroken at Lloyd's choice of church, blaming Mildred. She declined to attend, citing the need to stay with Turner who truthfully was not well. Of Lloyd's three sisters, Pearl Golob, Louise Allen, and Angela McKibben, only Pearl and Louise came and left immediately following the brief ceremony. Ellen and Fred were in attendance as was Mrs. Munselle of Milton who had been Mildred's late mother Effie's dearest friend.

Mildred did not invite Arthur, because she was afraid he would bring Marian. So the small group of ten or so people gathered in the rector's office while Rev. Graser read the short service. They could not be married in the sanctuary of the church because although both had been baptized, neither Mildred nor Lloyd were members of the church yet. Uninvited and unannounced, Arthur appeared and stood in the doorway of the rector's office with his hat in his hand just as the ceremony began. He was ignored by all. As soon as it was over, he turned and left. Mildred and Arthur did not speak to one another that day.

Following the ceremony a reception was held at Ellen and Fred's. As usual, Ellen had prepared a lovely spread including small sandwiches, mints, punch, a wedding cake and her famous lemon sherbet.

It was not until the party was over when Mildred and Lloyd were leaving that Ellen noticed she had never lit the candles on the buffet table and she was horrified by her faux pas. For years she berated herself that she had failed to light the candles at Mildred's wedding reception until senility finally tucked that error away in a far and dim corner of her mind. Mildred never cared.

Mildred and Lloyd's Wedding day, June 6, 1934
With their flower girl, Connie Joyce Groshong

Mildred and Lloyd enjoyed a week's honeymoon along the Oregon coast. They ferried across the Columbia River at Astoria and spent several days with Florence and Merrill in Cloverdale, OR. On the way home they visited Harold and Arah in The Dalles, Oregon. When they arrived home in Sunnyside and entered the two-bedroom house Lloyd had bought on the southeast corner of 8th Street and Grant Avenue, they discovered that Cecilia had left them a present. On their bed was a lovely quilt with a "wedding ring" design. Its blue and white intertwining circles on a white background had been completely hand-stitched by her. Regardless of Cecilia's heartbreak over Lloyd's failure to get married in the Catholic Church, it was truly a mother's gift of love. The quilt remains in the family to this day.

The first Decade

Family; World War II; a new house;

THE LITTLE HOUSE AT 704 South 8th Street in Sunnyside was a delight for Mildred, spare as it was. It had about 1,000 square feet and was typically designed. A large covered porch was on the front side of the house, which faced west where it was delightful to sit on hot summer evenings. The front room was fairly small but featured a fireplace (with a faulty draft) on the south end with built-in bookshelves on either side. On the west wall was a window seat under three casement windows looking out over the porch. Two bedrooms separated by a bathroom were on the north side of the house. One could walk through a door from the living room into one bedroom, through it to get to the bathroom, and through another door to reach the second bedroom. The south side of the house was divided into the fireplace end of the living room, a dining room, and kitchen. An archway supported by two dark stained square columns atop a half wall framed the entry into the dining room from the living room. The dining room featured a bay window on the south side with diamond-shaped panes. The floor was covered with brown linoleum and a heat register was in the floor near the doorway into the kitchen.

The kitchen had a trash burner and a small electric stove on the left and a place for a small drop leaf table under a double casement window on the right. On the east end of the room was a doorway leading to a small pantry, which had a grooved countertop that- slanted downward into a shallow sink for washing dishes. On the opposite wall were floor-to-ceiling cupboards separated by another counter top. A narrow window looked out over the small back yard.

The back door opened onto a small screened porch, which was a good place to store a broom, mops, a bucket and containers of onions, carrots and potatoes in the winter. Through the screen door and down a couple of steps was a sidewalk leading to the cellar.

The cellar, typical for homes built at that time was essentially a dirt dug-out. Two wooden cellar doors were built on a downward slant leading away from the house's foundation. They opened lengthwise in the middle revealing concrete steps down to a door which opened into a room lit only by one electric bulb in a socket hung from between the joists from which there also hung a pull string to turn the light on and off. The air was always very cool and smelled and felt damp there. Wooden shelves stood on three walls. Anything that remained in the cellar was soon covered with a layer of fine dust. It was also a perfect environment for spiders. On one occasion Mildred and Lloyd had to leave the house while it was being fumigated for black widow spiders. But for Mildred who had been living out of bedrooms for eleven years, it was a delight to have a whole house to make into her own.

They had very little furniture at first. Lloyd brought with him secondhand everything including an oak upright piano, which delighted Mildred because it meant that she could continue to teach piano lessons, but now it would be from her own home. With the few things that came with the house--a table, dishes, some pots and pans, a couple of kitchen chairs and an overstuffed chair in the living room--Lloyd's sparse bachelor furniture gave them just enough to get by.

Lloyd and Mildred enjoyed attending various social events in Sunnyside during their courting year and the first year of their marriage. It was a new life for Mildred who would smile shyly when she recalled attending dances and dinners at the various grange halls throughout the lower Yakima Valley. On one occasion they attended a dance at the Waneta Grange Hall south of Sunnyside during which Lloyd's friends had done a good job getting him a little schnockered. The room was hot and full, the music was loud, and cigarette smoke hung in the air. A group of the men took turns going out back to take a nip when the band took a break. Lloyd disappeared out the back door two or three times, but Mildred didn't think much of it while she visited with their friends until Lloyd came in with a silly grin on his face, climbed up and stood on a chair and announced with a silly grin on his face, "I would like to make a speesh!" Mildred could never remember what Lloyd said next, but she remembered the roar of laughter that followed his pronouncement.

By the time Mildred and Lloyd sat for their formal wedding picture in November 1934, Mildred was pregnant with their first child, a girl who was born May 22, 1935, whom Mildred named Vergie Ellen Smith in tribute to her best friend from college and her aunt Ellen who had been "...the closest thing to a mother I ever had..." Mildred had resigned her teaching position when she and Lloyd had married, but she substituted occasionally at the new high school, an imposing brick building with two floors and a basement.

Despite very severe economic conditions as the United States struggled to emerge from the Depression, Sunnyside citizens willingly obligated themselves to build this school. After her marriage Mildred was sorry to not have a full-time job, but for the first time since she was fourteen, she did not have to work for her room and board. By substituting at the high school, giving piano lessons, and occasionally filling in as organist at Holy Trinity Episcopal Church where she pumped the little reed organ to its glory, Mildred earned enough money to pay for their groceries while Lloyd's salary paid for the remainder and supported their car. To Lloyd's delight he discovered Mildred was adamant about keeping within their budget and was good at doing so.

For the first three years of their marriage Mildred kept a record in her journal of every penny they spent. For example, for two adults and a baby:

January 1936:
  Food - 28.46
  House Expenses - 22.06
  House Investments and Improvements - 32.13
  Insurance (life insurance for Turner and Lloyd) 32.13
  Car (gas and oil) - 3.91
  Miscellaneous (paper, cleaners, doctor, magazine, etc) 78.03
  for a grand total of $176.5 for the month.

Mildred had sold her little roadster after she had arrived in Sunnyside, not only because she was low on money, but also because she could walk wherever she needed to be. By putting this money into their joint account, she had also helped to fund the gas and some meals for their honeymoon with money left over.

Lloyd was very protective of Mildred. One night shortly after they had gone to sleep Mildred thought she heard someone going through their things in the living room. "Lloyd!" she hissed, shaking him and waking him up. "Lloyd! There's someone in the house!" LLoyd jumped up and fished his pistol out of the closet and began to load a bullet in it. But he was so excited he couldn't get the bullet into the chamber, so he squeezed the gun to steady it. And that's when he shot a hole in the floor. Millie shrieked and they both recoiled backward onto the bed. The baby slept on. After the initial shock of the gun blast, they tiptoed through the house peeking in every room and out every window, but no one was there. Lloyd got a lecture on how to store his gun properly from his shaken wife many times in the years to come.

The baby consumed most of Mildred's energy for the first year. Mildred had a hard time keeping any weight on. The baby was very colicky and Mildred was too thin to nurse, so after several weeks of trying Mildred began to make formula for the baby. Even then the infant was colicky. Finally her doctor told her to buy lactic acid at the pharmacy and to add it to the regular whole milk, which she should cook at a low boil for five minutes. This made a big difference and soon both mother and daughter were gaining weight. Mildred suspended music lessons for several months and stopped substituting at the high school. She was also trying to make friends with Lloyd's family, especially Cecilia, whom she truly came to love, telling her she had really never had a mother and would like for Cecilia to be hers. She always called her "Mother Smith." Cecilia was now having to care for Turner around the clock. His poor health had completely incapacitated him. On August 10, 1937, Turner passed away after a long and painful decline.

Even in their grief the family was relieved that Turner was no longer suffering. Cecilia was completely exhausted, nearly ill. The Lloyd Smith family settled into a routine, content with living within their means and relatively isolated in their rural American life, far from world problems. But as the United States slowly emerged from the Depression in the mid- to late nineteen thirties, news from Europe became increasingly ominous. In Germany overt "state actions" against the Jews and other minorities were being reported. Germany showed signs of political restlessness and seemed inclined to renew its aggression against its neighbors even after it had been soundly defeated in World War I, the "War to End All Wars" that had ended only twenty years previously. Adolf Hitler in his *sturm und drang* (storm and urging) speeches was inciting Germans to rise up against its ineffective leaders as well as "impure" minorities, had become politically powerful in the country.

Cecilia remembered that her own father Anton Steudle had fled Germany in the mid-eighteen hundreds at age nineteen for this very reason: abhorrence of aggression leading to war. Having served one tour in the German army, he had become incensed when he had been redrafted six weeks after returning home to Baden-Baden. Once again in the late 1930s in the gathering storm promulgated by Hitler, Germany prepared to march on Poland. While interested and aware of these events, Mildred felt secure from the political unrest in Europe and concentrated on her family and a new pregnancy.

Her second pregnancy did not proceed well. Just caring for her daughter Vergie Ellen, managing the household, and being exhausted from this new pregnancy was almost more than she could handle. Her physician, Dr. Schutz, told her she had an abnormally high albumin count, which was dangerous to both her and her unborn baby. He instructed Mildred to severely limit what foods she ate, and being so thin to start with, Mildred was left with little reserve at the end of each day. For the last five months of her pregnancy Mildred was allowed one glass of milk and a few non-starchy vegetables each day; no meat, no eggs, no fat, no flour, no sugar. Determined to carry the child to term, and expecting a boy this time because the child was so active, Mildred and Lloyd decided to name the child Robert Lloyd Smith: Robert after Lloyd's grandfather, William Robert Smith, a Civil War veteran.

Two weeks before Mildred was due to give birth, Lloyd and Mildred drove to Milton. Ellen had agreed to take care of Vergie Ellen for a month, but the little girl was not at all happy to be left in Milton with people she hardly knew. When the Smiths' robust baby daughter was born on May 10, 1938, they were so surprised that it wasn't a boy that they could think of no new names, so Robert Lloyd became Roberta Mildred. At last, Mildred could consume a regular diet. Her first meal at home "...was a dish of cold peas right out of the frig".

The new baby, like her older sister, was colicky. Once again, Mildred tried to nurse the infant, but it was to no avail. As the baby began to lose weight, Mildred knew that if she returned to using boiled milk with lactic acid, the baby should be able to tolerate the milk better. And so she did, and so the baby did. When Mildred and Lloyd returned to Milton to gather up their oldest daughter in time for her third birthday, they brought a new doll and a new title for the big sister who, every day for a month after her nap at Ellen and Fred's, had gone out to the front yard and sat on her little red chair to wait for her mama to come to get her. Then when her father and mother arrived at the Milby's, Vergie Ellen was indignant. Taking an Aunt Ellen pose with hands on hips and tone of voice, she said, "Wy, for heffin's sake did you tape so long?" After she had patted the baby on the head she wanted nothing more to do with her new sister and took her new doll for a walk.

Six weeks after Roberta was born, Mildred received a surprise call from her father's wife, Marian, who told Mildred that Arthur was very ill with septicemia, an infection in the bloodstream. Once the infection reached his brain, he would not survive. The doctor had given him only a few days to live. Arthur wanted to see his daughter while he could still speak and had insisted Marian call Mildred. It had been sixteen years since Mildred had been in her father's home and Mildred had no desire to return there as long as Marian was in the house. She had a six-week-old baby and a three-year-old to take care of. However, still needing some kind of closure with her father, Mildred called her mother in-law, Cecilia Smith, who agreed to come immediately to take care of the girls while Mildred hurried to Arthur's bedside.

Mildred stayed in Walla Walla with Arthur and Marian for several days expecting Arthur to die at any moment. His comment was, "Mil, I'm glad to see you." Her reply was, "Well, here I am, dad." Then a few days after her arrival he began to rally and the doctor told the two women Arthur would survive. Since there were no antibiotics at that time, this was truly an amazing outcome. The two women spoke very little to each other, but they were civil. Arthur did not say anything of substance to Mildred except, "Thanks for coming," when she left.

While conditions in Europe continued to deteriorate, the Smith family continued to thrive. Six months after Roberta's birth, and after Mildred had returned from Arthur's sick bed, Lloyd and Mildred moved into their new house, which Lloyd had had built at 811 East Edison Avenue, just a block and a half from the post office and three blocks from the center of town. He found a renter for the 8th Street house. The cost of the new two-story house had been a whopping five thousand dollars. Exhausted during her pregnancy and then recovering from Roberta's birth, Mildred had had little to say about the design of the house (later regretting this). Caring for two small children and her husband was all she could manage for the next year or so. Within a few months of moving in, Lloyd learned that his widowed mother Cecilia was completely insolvent. Having used up all the money they had on Turner's lingering illnesses, she could not pay her rent. So Lloyd asked the renter of his 8th St. house to move out so that his mother could move in there. Cecilia loved that little house, was grateful to be debt-free. She remained there for thirty-two years until shortly before her death in 1969.

By 1941 the Lloyd Smith family was healthy and happy. Mildred began teaching piano lessons again. Lloyd had nearly finished building a double garage with a small apartment above it in the back of their property next to the alley. He often went out to the garage to work for an hour or so after coming home from the Post Office. On one occasion he happened to look over his shoulder at the ladder that was leaning against the roof over the garage. What he saw shocked him. There, peering over the edge of the roof was a very blond head and two blue eyes. Three-year-old Bobbie had followed him up the ladder to the second floor! Getting down was interesting and both parents thereafter always checked to see where their adventuresome daughter was when Lloyd picked up his hammer.

Eventually, there was no ignoring the events in Europe. Lloyd's brother Victor joined the Merchant Marines. The United States was pressured into helping supply the British while they tried to ward off

Hitler's Nazi army from gaining further toeholds both in Europe and in the United Kingdom. President Roosevelt and the U.S. Congress continued to hold back from going to war even as their allies pleaded for support. Then the U.S. got the news that Hitler had been courting the Japanese government to become their ally, too. World affairs were looking ominous. On December 7, 1941, when Japan bombed the U.S. naval port in Pearl Harbor in the Territory of Hawaii, the United States could no longer keep out of the war.

The war in Europe and now in the Pacific brought trade with other countries to a minimum. Bananas and oranges became scarce in grocery stores. As with everyone else, the Smith family was issued ration books for meat, sugar, flour, rubber tires, and gasoline. Alcohol was even rationed. Each household member, including babies, was eligible to have one ration booklet. By spring 1942, joining a crusade throughout the 48 states to help keep nutritious food on the table, Mildred planted a large "Victory" garden. She canned many quarts of vegetables and fruits and often traded with other families to increase the variety of supplies they had and stored them in a fruit room that Lloyd partitioned off in the basement.

Civil authorities divided Sunnyside into sections and chose block wardens to help supervise "black out" procedures every night in each section of the town. Street lights were turned off in the early evening, and people were instructed to close their shades, blinds and curtains so that if Japanese bombers flew overhead they wouldn't be able to see the community below. In cities and towns all over America including Sunnyside women met in homes, churches and Red Cross offices to knit scarves and gloves for the fighting men and women, and roll long strips of linens for bandages to be sent to the wounded. Children were taught how to peel off the layer of tin foil in gum wrappers and roll it into balls. The balls were collected and sent to factories, where they were melted down and used to make medals, snaps and other items needed by the military. Parents and children alike made rubber band and string rolls and took them to collection centers. Then in late spring 1942 Mildred discovered she was pregnant again.

Thomas Milby Smith was born in a snowstorm and nearly in a snow bank on January 29, 1943. Lloyd got the car stuck in a snow drift in front of the house and during the rocking back and forth of the car to get it unstuck, Mildred nearly gave birth then and there all the while giving Lloyd a thorough tongue lashing. They arrived at the nursing home (a regular house run by a nurse where women were taken to give birth in towns where there were no hospitals) just in time for the baby to be born. The doctor, called away from his dinner, arrived just in time to catch the baby while Lloyd stood there in his overcoat, holding his hat in his hand too shocked to leave the room. When Dr. Schutz announced that the baby was a boy, everybody cried, including Lloyd. Mildred and baby Tommy remained in the nursing home for a week. The two little Smith sisters, ages seven and four, spent the week at their Smith aunt Pearl and uncle John Golob's farm. On February 2nd, Mildred's birthday, Lloyd brought the girls to the nursing home to see their mother and their new brother. First they stopped by the bedroom where the babies slept in their basinets. Lloyd told the girls to find which baby was their brother, but they chose the wrong one! He made them keep choosing until through a process of elimination, they picked the fifth and last baby. How could you choose when they all looked alike? When they went to see their mother, Lloyd told Mildred, "The girls chose the wrong baby, so should we take that one home?" Mildred replied, "I don't think so, but girls, which baby do you want?" Vergie Ellen answered huffily, "We want the right one!"

Tommy Smith was a bright-eyed little guy from the day he was born. Like his sister Vergie, he had their father's dark brown eyes and brown, (later) curly hair. He thrived on his boiled milk and lactic acid formula, and when he wanted his bottle, everyone knew it! Mildred often had a basket of laundry in the kitchen and on many occasions she dumped the howling baby in it while she warmed his milk. This was to be a foreshadowing of Tommy's many future inter-actions with food.

Easter Sunday 1943

2 5

First Vacation

The beginning of a Smith tradition

IN ADDITION TO THE BIRTH of Tommy, the summer of 1943 included another major event for the Smith family: they took a vacation! One of the citizens who frequented the Sunnyside Post Office happened to strike up a conversation with Lloyd about fishing. Lloyd, who had not had time to fish for many years, expressed a desire to find a good spot to try it again. The client mentioned that he and his family had found a resort in northern Idaho that just fit the bill: a superb place for families, cozy rustic cabins, and excellent fishing both in the lake and in nearby streams. Lloyd was intrigued and wondered if he and Mildred could manage a trip that far away with gas rationing, thinning tires and three small children. Their last trip together had been their honeymoon nine years previously.

Lloyd contacted Ike Elkins at his Elkins Resort on Priest Lake, Idaho, and made reservations for a week's stay in the forthcoming July. They invited Lloyd's mother Cecilia to come along with them and off they went: three adults and three children firmly packed into a two-door Plymouth. The three adults rode in the front seat. In the back seat, Mildred had put a collapsed baby buggy on top of folded blankets. Six-month-old Tommy rode in the buggy. The two girls rode with their feet propped up on more blankets and food boxes.

Suitcases, warm coats and perishable food items were stowed in the small car trunk. Into the last inches few inches of space Mildred stuffed cans of food.

It took an entire day to make the 250-mile journey. They traveled eastward through Kennewick, and Pasco then northward on winding two-lane roads through the wheat country towns of Connell, Lind and Ritzville, past Sprague Lake where they saw the first stands of timber in the distance. From there they passed Cheney and crested the big hill, which led them down to the big city of Spokane. What a sight it was to see this huge city spreading out in the valley below! With infrequent stops for food and gas, this leg of the journey took them almost six hours.

From Spokane they continued northward on Division Street past the outskirts of town where Highway 2 divided into a "Y". Taking the right arm of the road they travelled east to Newport, Washington, crossed the Pend Oreille River (from the original French "pend d'oreille" - bend of the river, or "ear lobe"-shaped) which flows north-west out of lake Pend Oreille) and drove about ten more miles to Priest River, Idaho. The trip from Priest River north to Elkins Resort on Priest Lake, a distance of less than fifty miles, often took travelers up to three hours to complete. The route was over a narrow, two-lane graveled, pot-holed road that was rutty and washboard-rough from all the logging truck traffic that used it every day. The travelers were met frequently by towering logging trucks that came barreling southward, churning up huge dust clouds behind them. They learned to hastily crank up the windows and pull over as far as they could before they were enveloped in the boiling storm from the trucks. Lloyd had to turn the window wipers on to clear the windshield so he could see out.

Late in the afternoon they reached Nordman, a "town" that consisted of one building in which there was a grocery store, post office, bar, and restaurant. Again taking the right "arm" of the "Y" at Nordman they drove about three more miles to a small sign that read "Elkins." Turning down another dusty road they found Elkins Resort nestled in an abundant evergreen and birch forest at the edge of a twenty-five mile long pristine lake. The road passed several log cabins on a bluff overlooking the lake and ended at a large log building in a clearing near the shore. A small, wiry man in lumberjack attire (boots, jeans, plaid shirt, and suspenders) ambled up from a boat dock toward the building as Lloyd approached. This man who checked them in was Ike Elkins, the owner. He couldn't find a key to cabin #9 and said to "...pay it no mind. No one locks the door anyway." The tired family retraced their way back down the road and found their cabin, number nine, which sat beside a wide path with a panoramic view of the lake.

Mildred was exhausted and Grandmother Smith could barely get out of the car. The girls poured out and down the slope to the beach. The baby had slept on and off during the entire trip, lulled to sleep in his collapsed buggy by the rocking motion of the car. When he squalled, the little girls gave him a rattle or a bottle. His cloth diapers got changed only when Lloyd stopped for food and gas. He and the buggy bed were sopping wet on their arrival. Remembering this trip happily throughout her life, Mildred always laughed at how Tommy had actually dripped when they lifted him out of his buggy. He didn't seem to mind. He just wanted another bottle!

The small log cabin was one of about thirty that Ike was in the process of completing near the shore of Reeder Bay. It had a beautiful view across the lake to high Selkirk Mountains on the east. The view was enhanced by the lake's most famous peaks, Chimney Rock and Mt. Roothaan, of which the latter was nick-named 'Twin Peaks' and sometimes 'Twin Sisters'. The cabin had one bedroom framed by a low partition in which there was a double bed and a chest of drawers. The living room was a reverse "L"-shape and had another double bed in the foot of the "L". The kitchen area was at the top of the "L". A large cast iron wood cook stove was against the outside wall opposite the bedroom wall. A table and a few chairs were placed against the

bedroom wall on the kitchen side. Out back, in a small partitioned
shed, were sections for wood, an ice box for chunks of ice where perishable food could be kept, and an outhouse. On the windowed front
porch that extended all along the front of the cabin was a bunk bed,
also made by Elkins who had cut down four inch diameter young
birch trees for the frame and scavenged springs from vacant Civilian
Conservation Corps camps in the area. The two little girls slept on
these bunk beds and loved the adventure of it, while the adults and
baby slept inside. In future years, Mildred either scrounged around
the resort for a piece of flat plywood, which she put in her bed for
support, or brought one from home. The mattresses sagged from the
first time they used them and Mildred complained about them every
single time the family came to Elkins for the next fifteen years.

Both Mildred and Cecilia were excellent cooks and easily put the
wood stove to work. The cabin was so close to the lake that Mildred
could listen to the girls' shouts of glee from the beach without having to go up and down the steep path to check on them. On the
first day, and the rest of the week thereafter, the sun shone brilliant-
ly. Wonderful weather. Mildred didn't even consider that her fair-
skinned daughters would sun burn as quickly as they did, but the
truth became very apparent after just a few hours. They were blistered and sore for many days and had to wear their father's t-shirts
over their swimsuits for the rest of the week. The girls rarely needed
to wear shoes that week and often brought sand into the cabin for
which they were roundly scolded. They soon discovered that they had
also brought sand into their beds and when they climbed beneath the
sheets each night with their hot, sunburned legs and shoulders, the
sand, sunburns, and cold sheets were not a good combination!

With the cabin, which they had rented for $35 for the week, came
a big green wooden rowboat with their cabin number on it. One day
Mildred suggested they use the rowboat to go on a picnic, but Lloyd
decided to splurge and rent a motor for a couple of dollars for the
day. Leaving the baby at the cabin with Cecilia, the Smiths putted

out of Reeder Bay and headed north. Just past the narrows where Granite Creek enters the lake, they found a pleasant little beach with shallow warm waters. It was a perfect place for a picnic, splashing in the water for the girls, and a little snooze in the sun for the parents. Soon it was time to go home and they packed everything up and set out for Elkins. Unfortunately, just south of Granite Creek, the motor sputtered out and nothing Lloyd tried could make the thing work. There was nothing left but to row what seemed like several miles back to the resort. By the time the exhausted family reached the dock at Elkins, Lloyd's hands were blistered and his face and arms were badly sunburned. Mildred and the girls had each tried their hands at rowing, but it had quickly become apparent that they weren't very good at it.

Mildred had worried about the baby, too, because she had left only one prepared bottle for Cecilia to give him and they were long past the time for a second bottle. As they slowly moved down the lake stroke by stroke everyone knew what that little baby would do if he didn't get his bottle on time and wondered how well Grandma had braved the storm. When they got back to the cabin, the baby was asleep and Cecilia was sitting in a chair crocheting. She had diluted some evaporated milk and fed it to baby Tommy who didn't seem to care about the difference in taste so long as he got his fill.

At the end of the week when they returned home to the Yakima Valley, they arrived just as the bright orange sun was dropping behind the bare Rattlesnake Hills. Once again their trip had taken them through central Washington on a blisteringly hot day in which it was hard to determine if it was better to open the car windows and let the hot air blow on them or keep them shut and cook. This time little Tommy hadn't been so content to ride along quietly. He had demanded to sit up when he was awake, and fearing that he would topple out of his buggy, each person except Lloyd had to take a turn at holding him. Of course, each person ended up with a warm, wet lap!

Nearing Sunnyside, newly cut fields of alfalfa gave off heavy, sweet aromas. Hops were ready for harvesting and asparagus fronds had already gown tall and feathery in their fields. The Smiths were happy to be home, but they had fallen in love with Priest Lake and despite the arduous trip, hoped they would be able to go back again.

Elkins Resort 1943: Vergie Ellen, Lloyd, Cecilia Smith, Bobbie holding Tommy. In 2015 the number of this remodeled cabin is #21.

2 6

The War Grinds On

Doing without; health issues; a bomb

It WOULD BE THREE MORE years before the Smiths could return to Elkins for their summer vacation. Supplying the war effort had caused the nation's reserve of automobile tires and gasoline to become scarce for non-farmers, so the family could not travel far from home. Rationing important commodities became the rule for everyone. Because Mildred had cherished their first vacation so much, she located a modest little cabin to rent for a week at Nelson's Resort on Bumping Lake about 75 miles west of Sunnyside on Naches Pass in the lower Cascade Mountain Range. For the next two summers the family enjoyed the quaint cabin and the lovely setting there, but it didn't hold a candle to Elkins!

The little Smith girls were becoming independent, but Mildred was ever vigilant about them when they were outside playing. In 1942 when Vergie Ellen was five, Mildred had allowed her to walk the four blocks to the Liberty Theater to see a cowboy movie with the Whitenack family's seven year-old son Donald. The children were reminded to look both ways before they crossed the street, and so off they went holding hands. Only 100 yards from the house as they were crossing Edison Avenue a speeding drunk driver did not slow down before he hit both children in the middle of the crosswalk as the horrified parents watched. Donald's jaw and collarbone were broken. Vergie Ellen was badly bruised and dragged by her hair under the car until the man stopped, some fifty feet further. It was a frightening experience for the Smiths, and although both children recovered, it would be many years until they were allowed to walk to see a movie without an adult along.

As the war ground on, Sunnysiders became accustomed to the vagaries of supply and demand. Milk was delivered to the back door in glass bottles. A two- plus inch layer of rich cream rose to the top of each bottle and Mildred made good use of it just as Mrs. Steinke had done for her in Ewan. The news about the war was often bad. To distract them from bad news children were encouraged to look at popular newspaper comic strips: Joe Palooka, Batman, Mary Worth, Mickey Mouse, Donald Duck and Popeye. Mildred read these to her children. If Popeye chose to eat spinach to become strong, maybe the little girls would, too. But they were not cooperative in this matter. Comic books cost ten cents and featured the adventures of Superman or Red Ryder or Buck Rogers. The children made up games of cowboys and indians, whinnying and galloping all over the neighborhood pretending to be on their horses 'Tony' or 'Trigger' or 'Scout' chasing after 'bad guys', never dreaming it would someday not be 'politically correct' to pretend to capture indians. Sometimes they played 'war,' but this was also discouraged by many parents.

During the war years, the radio was a major source of news and entertainment. Edward R. Murrow opened his six o'clock news broadcasts with, "Hello America. This is London calling," and gave his listeners bits of information about what had recently been happening on both fronts of the war. He ended his reports with, "Good night and good luck," a rather ominous sign-off. After the news, the family could listen to "The Shadow", "Amos and Andy," "The Lone Ranger", "The Great Guildersleeve", or "Queen for a Day" on their Philco radio. Between Thanksgiving and Christmas "The Cinnamon Bear" series came on each afternoon at four-thirty, thrilling children with the adventures of Paddy O'Cinnamon, Santa's helper, as he traveled hither and yon trying to retrieve the Silver Star from the Crazy Quilt Dragon so it could be put it on top of the tree in time for Christmas. Television was another ten years away.

From the onset of the United State's entrance into World War II, Lloyd had developed a soaring sense of patriotism and tried to find a way to contribute to the war effort. One week after Japan attacked the U.S. Naval Fleet based in the Territory of Hawaii's Pearl Harbor he submitted a neatly typed application with cover letter in which he offered to join the Federal Bureau of Investigation:

Dec. 15th, 1941
Federal Bureau of Investigation
Washington, D.C.

To J. Edgar Hoover
My Dear Sir:

This is to offer my services, if such should be required during the present National situation. I present in brief form the following as my credentials and experience.

Education: Business Administration, Law (eligible to take the Washington State Bar Exam)
Experience: Post office clerk. Retail Merchandising clerk. Real Estate investments, including construction and remodeling (residence and income property)
Health: very good, do not wear glasses. Height 5'6", weight 140 lbs, Age 40
Family: Wife and two daughters aged six and three respectively. (Wife former High School teacher Latin, French, English, Music -operetta and piano -)

Birthplace: Lexington, Missouri. October 21st, 1901. Paternal Grandparents American. Maternal Grandparents, German and Irish.
Church Affiliation: Episcopal
Yours very truly.

His application form was returned to him without a response in the envelope from Hoover. By early January 1942 all adult men over the age of eighteen were required to register with the U.S. Government's Department of Selective Service so a pool for a draft of able-bodied soldiers could be established. At the age of forty, Lloyd submitted his card to Local Board No. 1, Yakima County, which was located in the Central Building in Sunnyside. To his dismay, he received his answer: III-A. His doctor, C.A. Hughes, MD, had discovered a mild heart murmur Lloyd had never known he had. Mildred was elated. But Lloyd tried again the next year on March 3, 1943. This time his answer was worse: he was 4-F. It was obvious he needed to hunker down on the home front.

Despite the rationing, most people figured out how to supplement their food supplies. A loaf of bread and a gallon of gasoline each cost about twenty cents. The government began issuing aluminum tokens worth one-third of a cent. To help out, many people were able to obtain eggs, milk, and meat from their farmer friends. Flour and sugar were more difficult to keep on hand. Condensed milk became a staple. And Spam, which is a shortened name for canned spiced ham. Fried Spam, ground Spam, Spam loaf, Spam sandwiches, Spam and eggs. To open a can of Spam one popped a specially made 'key' off the bottom of the can and inserted a tab near the top through a hole in the key. Then, by twisting the key around and around, the strip of tin attached to the tab pulled free from the lid allowing the lid to be removed. Inside that 12-ounce can was the protein part of dinner for five!

Because there was little other entertainment available for children, movies were very popular. Each movie was preceded by a short black and white film clip about the war fronts in Europe and the South Pacific and later about the devastation that had occurred there. It wasn't until the late forties that the two Smith sisters were permitted to walk by themselves to the Liberty Theater for the Sunday afternoon matinee where they could see a double feature for ten or fifteen cents and stay as long as they wanted. They had to be home before dark. They had to pass three or four taverns on the way, but those businesses, like most others including grocery stores and pharmacies, and even their favorite stores, the Holland Bakery run by former Dutch immigrant families and the Sugar Bowl where ice cream sodas and floats were served for about thirty-five cents each, were closed on "The Lord's Day."

Mildred and Lloyd were careful to keep adult information from the children, and most children were not privy to detailed news of the war, especially the news about the violence being reported in German internment camps and what the allied prisoners of war were experiencing in Asia. Neither worried much about the fact that Lloyd's grandfather had emigrated from Germany in the late 1800s, but there was frequent talk in the community reviling Germans in general. Many German families in the community began keeping to themselves or with their German friends more and more.

From Bobbie's Journal:

For many years I had a memory of one incident which was out of place in my mind until I learned some of the details about World War II later in my life. When I was about six years old my sister and I were spending a few days at my father's sister Pearl and her husband John Golob's farm out in the country. It was spring and the morning was cool and foggy. Vergie and I had finished breakfast, and got permission to go out to the barn to brush the two work horses Smokey and

Beauty who were finishing off their morning feed of hay and grain. While we were brushing those giant animals we heard a truck drive up and stop, then a man talking. We stepped to the barn door and watched as a man carrying a rifle got down from the bed of the truck. He then looked up into the truck where there were more men sitting on bench seats running the length of the truck bed on both sides, their backs braced against high side racks. He motioned for them to climb down. He lit a cigarette while he watched them climb down and assemble near him. It was all very casual. I was surprised to see that the "men" were really boys about high school age. Pointing to a shed across the lot from the barn, the man said, "Hup!" The others walked slowly over to the shed where they began picking up shovels and hoes. Carrying the tools they turned and walked out into the field in loosely formed double lines. Clearly a guard of some sort, the man carrying the rifle walked behind them. No one said a thing, at least that I could hear. Just at that time Aunt Pearl stepped out the back door of the house and hollered at us to get up to the house " Run! Right now!" and she would not let us play outside that entire day.

I found out later that this was a work party of young German soldiers who had been taken prisoner and sent to the U.S. to work in the fields to replace our farm sons who were fighting against them in Europe. Evidently they were being housed in a recently closed CCC camp south of town. As pieces of memories fell into place years later I realized I had witnessed an intimate vignette of the war. I could not have known then that my future husband's uncles, his German father's two brothers who had been reluctant Nazi soldiers, had been captured by the Allies and were in prisoner of war camps four thousand miles away in Germany and Russia at the same time I was watching these German teenage prisoners being marched into the field to weed beets for my American uncle.

2 7

When the War Ended

May and August 1945:VE and VJ Days
Schools; POWs; "Little Boy"; a death; a fire

IN THE EARLY 1940s SUNNYSIDE's elementary schools began to bulge at the seams. Like other Yakima Valley school districts, Sunnyside kept its operations budget to a minimum during the war. Mainline maintenance with only a few improvements to the district's buildings were made. Then classrooms became increasingly crowded; numbers of children attending school increased rapidly. By the time Roberta started first grade in 1944 (there were no kindergartens in Sunnyside), many church basements all over town had become overflow classrooms, often two classes per church. Each child was responsible for his or her own sack lunch or could walk home during the hour-long noon recess. Roberta's first grade classroom was held in a small church building on 9th street about two blocks midway between her home and Denny Blaine Elementary School to which the first graders walked for school activities and recesses. The church no longer had an active congregation, so two temporary rooms were fashioned by partitioning off the main meeting area with a plywood wall. A small opening on one end was used as a doorway between the two rooms, but the classroom in the back primarily used the rear entrance to come and go. A large black chalkboard was attached to each side of the plywood wall. Each room was equipped with a small stove. There were about twenty-plus children in each classroom who sat at old-fashioned desks on runners with ink well holes and lift-up lids.

Vergie Ellen attended Denny Blaine in one of its regular classrooms for her fourth grade year. As a precaution against fires or an air raid, the second floor of Denny Blaine had been equipped with a chute attached at the east end of the building through which the children could slide down to the ground in safety after they had climbed through a window to get to it. The country school, Wendell Philips, was also equipped with a slide attached under a second floor window. A buddy system was established at each school to ensure that everyone got out while the teachers took care of children with disabilities. How the children loved the fire drills! Each time there was a drill several boys would dash back into the building and try for another turn down the slide.

As the last two years of the war dragged on, most people tried to keep the day-to-day activities as normal as possible while worrying about a bombing raid from Japan. The curfews, nightly window blackouts and their abundant victory gardens were apparently successful and, except for not being happy about food and luxuries being rationed, most people were able to provide for their own needs.

Americans were shocked in the spring of 1945 when President Roosevelt died suddenly of a heart attack and his vice president, Harry S. Truman, virtually a small-town unknown, was sworn in. It was a huge blow to our military leaders, too. They feared the U.S. impetus might not be able to be maintained with a new leader at the helm just as they believed they could bring the war in Europe to a close within months. However, the U.S. government continued forward with only this slight hiccup. As Allied forces began to capture German cities and push toward Berlin, Hitler committed suicide in late April just before he would have been captured. The formal unconditional surrender of Germany was signed on May 7, 1945, in France, ratified in Berlin on May 8th, and was completed with the surrender of the Channel Islands by Germany on May 9th.

1945 was memorable for Mildred and Lloyd for another reason. Their seven year-old daughter Roberta had become noticeably fatigued and crabby during the winter. In mid-June Mildred finally took her to the doctor who diagnosed the child as having rheumatic fever. The best defense against the illness was the antibiotic penicillin, only recently approved for manufacture, but it was in short supply because 90 percent of the doses were being sent to the armed forces. Its use had dramatically reduced deaths from infection due to delay in getting the wounded from the front to medical stations. Because of this there was little available for citizens. The only alternative treatment for rheumatic fever was complete bed rest and aspirin. Thus, shortly after the end of her first grade year, Mildred and Lloyd moved Roberta's bed into their bedroom and after dinner that night Roberta was sent to bed for complete bed rest. For the duration of her daughter's illness Mildred fed, bathed, and changed bed linens, while Roberta was still in the bed. She remained there for nine months.

By the end of the summer, the United States warned Japan that it must surrender or suffer devastating destruction. Japan did not respond. On August 6th, 1945, while President Truman was meeting in Potsdam, Germany, with Stalin and Winston Churchill over how to partition Germany, he gave secret instructions to the U.S. Air Force to drop an atomic bomb, code-named "Little Boy" on Hiroshima, Japan.. While U.S. citizens slept unaware of these actions, the United States, braving probable repercussions from its allies, dropped an atomic bomb on the city, destroying 69% of it and initially killing 80,000 people. Hundreds of thousands later died of radiation poisoning. Stunned, Japan still refused to concede even though much of its aircraft and navy had now been destroyed. Americans hovered by their radios. Three days later, the U.S. dropped another atom bomb on Nagasaki. Tokyo would be next, they warned. U. S. citizens, some horrified, some elated, listened to their radios day and night hoping to hear that Japan would surrender. Finally on August 15th, Japan yielded. The surrender agreement was signed officially on September 2nd.

From Bobbie's journal:

"I still remember VJ (Victory in Japan) Day. It still plays like a movie in my head. It was a beautiful August day. I was half asleep in my bed listening to Queen for A Day on the radio. Mother was ironing in the kitchen. They announced in the middle of the show that Japan had surrendered. The live audience erupted with cheers and the announcer could barely be heard. Mother came and sat on my bed and listened with me. Within minutes the streets of Sunnyside filled with teen agers driving their cars up and down the streets honking their horns, waving and cheering out the windows. Church bells all over town began to peal. My bed was near a window and I had a good view of the street in front of our house. The neighborhood children rode their bikes around and around our block making motor noises with playing cards attached to their rear tire braces with clothes pins so that the spokes flapped the card loudly as each wheel whirled around the axle. I remember crying, not so much with the utter joy of it all, because I did understand why they were celebrating, but because I was not allowed to go outside and dance and cheer with the others. My mother, began to weep for joy and did not think to comfort me, and because she was crying I cried all the more. I was seven and confined to bed with rheumatic fever."

The end of the war did not change much for Roberta who remained completely bedfast until March 1946 without her feet touching the floor even once! She missed the second grade completely but did her lessons at home. Her teacher brought some workbooks and lessons to her twice a month and went over her lessons with her. That winter was a very, very long and lonesome time for the child.

The Smiths still had to use their ration books until the U.S. was able to reestablish its trade routes now that the shipping lanes were safe. It was almost another year before Mildred could buy bananas. When each of her children got their own banana to eat it was like getting a Christmas present. Bubblegum, which had been a rare treat, began to appear on the shelves in many varieties along with unrestricted supplies of sugar and flour. Our troops did not return home immediately for now they were put to work helping both Germany and Japan to reestablish their economies. In addition, the U.S. presence in the Philippines was necessary to help that country get back on its feet after being overrun by Japan. Gradually the coupons were phased out and the market began to function normally.

From Bobbie's Journal: *It was not until many years later that I learned that in the spring of 1942 most of the Japanese-Americans who lived in the valley had become victims of Executive Order 1099. They were given less than 48 hours notice to leave their homes and carry only what each could carry in one suitcase and assemble at the nearest train station. They were transported by train to fairground stables in the Portland area, where they were housed for two to three weeks. From there they were transported to Heart Mountain Wyoming Internment Facility. Years later one of those American citizens, Kara Kondo, who was interned briefly, became my friend whom I persuaded to speak to my Pacific Rim Literature classes about that experience. By that time ((late 1980s-1900s) she had traveled to Washington, D.C. to testify to the Senate investigation committee which later agreed to make reparations to families who had suffered that indignation. Another friend whose Japanese/Korean family was not interned joined the 442nd Division, fought and was wounded severely in Italy. Hiroshi Furukawa, one of my mother's high school students, became our family doctor in Sunnyside in the mid-1950s. Mother taught piano lessons to his three daughters.*

Mildred continued to teach piano lessons in their living room before and after school. From her bed in Mildred's and Lloyd's bedroom Roberta heard the same songs over and over again along with Mildred's admonishments: "Count!" or "Don't forget the sharp!" or "Not so fast!" or, "Let's do that again!" or "How much practicing did you do this week?" In March, Lloyd and Mildred drove Bobbie to Yakima for a consultation with another doctor who allowed her begin a gradual reintroduction to family life. She was exceptionally weak from having no physical exercise for nine months. By late spring she was allowed to sit on the porch in the sunshine for an hour; by summer she could play quietly in the yard where Mildred could keep an eye on her; by fall she was allowed to go back to school.

Roberta's third-grade classroom was in the basement of the Methodist Church. Her teacher was Mrs. Meyer. When the first of the 'baby boomers'* began to show up, Sunnyside schools completely ran out of classrooms. In 1947 the school district put a half-day schedule into place wherein elementary students attended school about three and a half hours either in the morning or afternoon. Those who wished to go for a full day were bused out into the country to Wendell Phillips, a small school southwest of town. Mildred did not want her children in half-day schools, so she was able to get Roberta into the busing program, but it was not possible for Vergie Ellen who was in the seventh grade at Lincoln School. Roberta loved riding out into the country on the bus, and she enjoyed the long recesses at Wendell Phillips. But by Christmas time, she had a relapse of rheumatic fever and the doctor pronounced either more bed rest or at the most, half-day school. Mildred had Roberta transferred to half-day school in town, but she missed her friends and did not care for her new teacher. Mildred was firm, but after much begging, Mildred agreed to let Roberta return to Wendell Phillips, but only if her daughter promised to do no running or hard play, and not tell the doctor!

The new Washington Elementary School was not finished in time for school to start in 1949, so part of her fifth grade was spent again at Wendell Phillips. In late winter students were able to move into the new school. Still overcrowding persisted. Roberta's sixth grade year was back at Wendell Philips. Then, finally, there were enough elementary classrooms in time for Tommy to start school in 1949. The school district then began building a new high school which was completed by the summer of 1954 so it would be ready for the bubble of students as they reached grades nine through twelve.

By the late forties Mildred's reputation as an excellent music teacher was firmly established in the greater Sunnyside community and she found she had to put potential students on a waiting list because to have as many as thirty students a week was not only a hardship on her, it was hard on her children whom she instructed to come home quietly from school or play and not disturb her while she taught. They had to wait with their school news until after the last student had left, and this also meant the girls had to help start supper by peeling potatoes and putting them on to boil.

In these years Mildred became a charter member of the Yakima Valley Music Teachers Association and made several good friends from within this group many of whom were also her piano teaching competitors. She became the main organist and choir director for Holy Trinity Episcopal Church, a position she loved and held for nearly thirty-five years. She was given the cross of service from the Diocese of Spokane for her many years of directing the choir and playing the organ. She also sang and played for funerals and weddings for which her fee was five dollars. She always put this money in the Holy Trinity's Sunday alms basin every time she earned it. Every March Millie entered her piano students in music adjudications sponsored by the Washington State Music Teachers Association held on the campus of Central Washington College (later Central Washington University) in Ellensburg, sixty miles to the north. Each year many of her students received 'excellent' adjudication scores.

In the meantime, Lloyd had become more and more discouraged with his job at the post office. There was little opportunity for advancement even after he had advanced to assistant postmaster. In addition, he began to have leg and back pains from standing on the concrete floor eight hours a day. His dream of becoming a lawyer began to haunt him again. Since he had had to quit school because he couldn't afford college expenses, and since he had accrued legal expertise having studied for the bar, he decided to put it into use and start his own insurance agency. He bought a building on Sixth street in the middle of the business district, quit his job one year shy of qualifying for a small pension with the U.S. Postal Service, studied for and passed the exams for insurance licenses, and opened the Lloyd F. Smith Agency.

In February 1947 Mildred drove to Walla Walla to visit her father. By this time Marian had passed away and Arthur had gotten a job as the supervisor of the trustee grocery store just outside the walls of the Washington State Prison, "The Pen." While she was there she attended a benefit for the Walla Walla High School Band sponsored by the Walla Walla Booster Club. It was a variety show put on by the inmates of the prison, produced by a "lifer," Bob Graves. The Master of Ceremonies was Eddie Sphect, and the orchestra leader was Bob Wyback, both of whom were "lifers." Permission to present the show for the general public was given by Mon C. Wallgren, governor, and Tom Smith, superintendent of the prison. Arthur was thrilled to attend with Millie.

Financially, Lloyd and Mildred struggled for the next ten years while Lloyd's business grew. Mildred's teaching money was a key factor in keeping food on the table during those times. Mildred's past experience in budgeting was well honed and effective. She could make three pork chops or a small pot roast sufficient to feed five people. No table scrap was ever thrown away and could often be seen somewhere in the next day's dinner or for Lloyd's lunch at mid-day. Lloyd added a realtor's license to his business and began buying and selling real estate. He purchased a lot on the corner of ninth and Edison, which had four wonderful hazel nut trees on it. He purchased the two-story Rodman house next door which had stood empty for

fifteen years, and later on he bought the Presbyterian Church property on the west side of their home. Thus, Mildred and Lloyd owned
the entire city block bordering Edison Avenue between Eighth Street
and Ninth Street.

The added property also meant added upkeep. The Smith children were now old enough to mow lawns with the family's push mow-
er in the summer and to shovel sidewalks in the winter. When you
have a whole block to do, it wasn't so much fun.

Lloyd had another apartment built at the back of the empty lot
property. This apartment was over a two-car garage and was larger
than the one behind their house. It looked across the narrow tree-
lined parkway on Ninth Street at the red brick high school that had
been completed in 1935. Mildred and the girls were now faced with
the task of cleaning up two apartments after renters left, some of
whom owed two or three months' rent. Mildred who had learned
the hard reality of having to face issues straight on had no problem
knocking on their doors and demanding the rent, but Lloyd could
never bring himself to confront anyone about it. Having been poor
during his childhood, he had great compassion for others when they
told him they were having financial difficulties. Accordingly, he was
reluctant to pressure them. Lloyd became accustomed to people ow-
ing him money.

It was Mildred who took action. The experiences Mildred had endured in her childhood only increased her expectations that people
should pay their way just as she had. Even though Mildred pressed
Lloyd to ask for a damage deposit or a month's rent in advance, Lloyd
could never bring himself to ask for either. Every time they discovered their renters had fled without paying their rent, Mildred gave
Lloyd the 'what for' and told him he could get a bucket and go clean
an apartment up himself or pay someone to do it. He always listened
to her calmly and then went on in his same way. When their apartments could not be rented in their unclean state, Mildred eventually
relented and saw to it that they were cleaned because the rent money

was paying the bank for their loans to build them. From her years of house cleaning she knew how the work should be done. Her girls learned about doing a job right the first time.

In 1947 the Smith family received the sad news that Lloyd's brother Victor was in Veteran's Hospital in Seattle and was gravely ill with hepatitis he apparently had contracted during one of his Merchant Marine voyages. He died before anyone could get there to see him. It was Lloyd's sad duty to go to Seattle to retrieve the body and bring it home on the train for a funeral and burial. While he was gone, the new apartment house on Ninth Street caught fire. The fire department, which was on the opposite side of the block on Eighth Street across from the Smith property could have driven out their doors, headed straight east down the alley for one block, and been at the fire in less than two minutes. But someone wrote down the wrong address and the truck went horn-blaringly westward out into the country in the opposite direction from the fire. When the firemen figured out that there was no fire where they had gone, they returned. By that time the smoke from the Smith fire could be seen from half of Sunnyside, but they hadn't noticed it when they drove back into the fire station. A neighbor ran across the street and told them to open their eyes because if they did they would be able to see the fire from the driveway and wouldn't need a blankety-blank address. The fire had burned for over forty-five minutes by the time the fire truck got there. Some of the firemen ran down the alley and beat the truck there!

Mildred and her children went out into their back yard and watched the building burn. Just as the firemen thought they had the blaze out, they were called to another fire. In the middle of the night simmering embers in the apartment burst into flame setting the place on fire again. By the time the firemen got this second fire out, the whole upstairs apartment was in ruins and had to be completely gutted before it could be restored. It turned out that Mildred had hired painters to refresh the empty apartment. Evidently a worker had left cleaning rags and paint supplies against one wall too near a heater. Even though the apartment was not a complete loss and the insurance Lloyd had taken out helped restore it, it was a blow to Lloyd.

Dad's office in Sunnyside

2 8

The Post War Years

Happy times; music and a dog; illness; an explosion

WITHIN A YEAR AFTER THE end of the war, life in Sunnyside began to return to normal. The economy grew stronger, the children were healthy, Lloyd's business was growing so quickly that he had to hire one, then another secretary. Vergie Ellen and then Roberta started piano lessons with their mother and a few years later both began taking violin lessons from Geraldine Colby. Roberta had become the ultimate tomboy, playing marbles, tearing the knees out of her play trousers, (no jeans then!) climbing trees, and playing softball with the boys on the school grounds. Vergie was more of an indoor girl. The sisters had outgrown the second-hand scooter Lloyd had bought for them and passed it on to their little brother. Lloyd bought a girl's bike for five dollars from the Benedetti family and Bobbie began riding the bike all over town, even out into the country a couple of times to try to beg a ride on one of the Golob's good cow penning horses. She didn't realize that these horses, especially their fabled 'Peanuts', were too hot for an untrained youngster to ride. Vergie had to complain to her mother to get any time in on the bike. There was no use calling their middle child 'Roberta' any more. She had become 'Bobbie' to everyone.

Within a few years of the end of the war, movies began arriving that glorified both battle arenas. At first the films were in black and white, but when color, then Technicolor technology was incorporated, children and adults flocked to the Liberty Theater on Sixth Street to watch in awe as the adventures filled the screen. National pride soared. The United States was the biggest, strongest, and best nation in the world! Western films were made by the dozens.

Then came musicals such as "South Pacific," "Oklahoma," "Seven Brides for Seven Brothers." Characters sang and danced their way through these stories, even the gang members in "West Side Story." Good almost always overpowered evil. Reality wasn't as important as the entertainment component.

The Community Concert series agreed to swing by Sunnyside with the warning that it would probably last more than a year. Mildred saw to it that their family attended. As it turned out the Lincoln Junior High School gym and bleachers filled to capacity for decades while Sunnysiders enjoyed such acts as the Von Trapp Family Singers and the Boston Pops. Attendees wore their Sunday best and hob-nobbed during intermission. By the end of each concert it was so warm in the gym that the youngsters had to struggle to stay awake.

It was in this milieu that the Smith girls reached their teens. About that time Leroy Darling was hired to be the Sunnyside High School music director. For three or four years Darling turned the modest Sunnyside High School music department band and choirs into the pride of Sunnyside. Its marching and concert bands put on amazing half time entertainment at football games, played exuberantly at basketball games, and provided the community with outstanding spring concerts. The high school choirs wowed audiences. Of course, one didn't play a violin in the band, so both Vergie Ellen and Bobbie took up band instruments: Vergie chose clarinet and Bobbie took up French horn after asking the junior high band director what instrument he needed in his band. "French horn," Roger Finch replied.

"What instrument do you play?" "French horn," Bobbie replied, not really knowing what one looked like, and then went home and told her parents that Mr. Finch had asked her to start French horn lessons. The girls kept on with their violin lessons, too, and were in a string quartet that included Wilma Vice and Adelaide Darling. They were often invited to play for social events.

Encouraged by Mildred, the girls enjoyed their experiences in the school music department, sometimes helping out in the orchestra with either their violins or band instruments, marching in parades and half times, rehearsing for and being in splendid spring concerts. They also sang in their church choir directed by their mother.

They especially enjoyed the marching band. Their dog Shorty, a gift from their uncle Crans, was not allowed in the house and often tagged along behind Vergie Ellen when she walked to the high school grounds to practice marching routines. But Shorty, who insisted on marching beside Vergie Ellen INSIDE the band ranks, couldn't seem to memorize the maneuvers and kept tripping up members as they turned this way and that. Vergie Ellen got into trouble more than once from the fiery-tempered Mr. Darling who demanded she leave her dog home. Shorty, however, a very clever black and white traveling salesman terrier cross, always figured out what he was missing after the girls snuck out of the yard. He was certain to catch up with the band when he'd hear the drums or the band playing as it marched up and down the streets of Sunnyside. Tying him up didn't work either as he howled mournfully and pulled and leaped against the rope. This drove Mildred wild and she'd turn him loose.

On one occasion, for another of Leroy Darling's innovative football half-time performances, the Smith family brought Shorty with them to the football game and kept him on a leash at the sidelines. When the band marched out on the field during halftime and closed with "How Much is that Doggie in the Window?" Tommy released Shorty and out he ran onto the field to find Vergie. The crowd loved it. Mr. Darling knew how to work the room! For years afterward, and after Mr. Darling's exit to California to a bigger venue, whenever Shorty heard the band playing, (Tom later played the trumpet in it), he'd trot off after the sound, often using the middle of the street as his own.

The Smith children had a fondness for animals. Vergie Ellen brought home free banty chicks she'd gotten at a carnival. Lloyd had to build a pen by the back door. There followed many generations of chickens that even laid eggs, the queen of whom was "Cheeper." On one chilly Sunday afternoon as the two girls walked to the Liberty Theater to go to a show Vergie spied an injured pigeon and insisted they bring it home. The saga of "PeeWee" followed. Mildred allowed the girls to keep the pigeon in a box in the basement, then in the chicken pen. PeeWee had developed a permanent limp from his broken leg, though he was well enough by spring to fly off. There were, of course, several generations of gold fish, and one very special dog, "Lucky."

Even Lucky's start in life was shadowy. Renters had moved into the Rodman house (The house next door was always called the Rodman house even after Lloyd bought it.) They had a registered female golden cocker spaniel that they intended to use for show and breeding purposes. Mildred warned them about Shorty, the town roue who could smell a female in heat from a mile away. Sure enough, one day when they let their dog out to squat, Shorty nailed her. If they could have caught him they surely would have beaten him to death, because, of the seven pups in her litter, four were dressed in their traveling salesman tuxedos. The Smith girls were thrilled with all the puppies and asked to have one. The neighbors told them they would have to pay five dollars for one. When Mildred found this out she was miffed, but told the girls they would have to raise the money by themselves, thinking, of course, that would never happen. Vergie Ellen raised the majority of the funds and Bobbie kicked in her dollar and a quarter. Before Mildred could blink, they now had two dogs PLUS a flock of chickens!

The girls named the pup "Lucky" because he had a little strip of white on his chest in the shape of a seven. Shorty tried to ignore the happy-go-lucky wiggling pup, which tried every trick it could think of to get him to play. Shorty snarled and snapped at him, but Lucky just seemed to think it was part of the game. The Smiths took both dogs with them on two or three trips to Priest Lake and the dogs would growl at each other over which one got the favorite spot behind the wood stove. As it turned out, Lucky was anything but. He was run over and killed on April Fool's Day when he was four.

Every spring, Shorty, who eventually became arthritic and half-deaf, remained hormonal. Often he'd sense romance in the air and leave the yard to find a lady. He'd miss dinnertime, and come back with a new set of body parts chewed to shreds despite his advancing age. Until the last years of his life he would tackle any dog of any size (including German shepherds) and hang on until he was a bloody mess. He'd drag himself home and sleep under the porch for four or five days and then emerge triumphantly, albeit half dead. It never occurred to any of the Smiths to have him neutered.

As Shorty continued to age and avoided getting run over or killed by larger dogs during his spring forays, Mildred began feel sorry for the old guy. She had never allowed him in the house, but began to have pity on him and let him sleep by the kitchen radiator on cold days and nights on his own rug where his old bones and stiff joints gladly soaked up the heat. During the day, he wouldn't consider sleeping in the sun on the front or back porch in safety. He preferred a warm sunny spot on the asphalt in the middle of Edison Avenue, one of the main streets in town. For several years cars drove around the "dead" dog that never moved

Shorty lived to be seventeen. After both girls had graduated from high school and had left for college, Tom was given the sad duty of hauling the dog in the red wagon to Drs. Mulqueeny's and Stevens' Vet Clinic to have him put down. Shorty could no longer get up on his feet by himself and groaned in protest at his aching body's refusal to function. Mildred told Tom it was his job to take care of this. The old dog didn't even protest and lay wrapped in his blanket as Tom pulled him the seven or eight blocks to the clinic. Apparently the dog sensed he was close to the end. When they laid Shorty on the table, he looked over at Tom with his cataract-filled eyes and sighed. He was done. Doc Stevens said later that he just showed Shorty the needle and he died. After Tom brought him home, they buried him in the back yard in one corner of Mildred's victory garden.

Mildred and Lloyd allowed their children a lot of freedom as they grew up and the Smith children enjoyed roaming all over Sunnyside. The forties and fifties were creative years when children made their own entertainment. Sledding in the park in the winter was a favorite pastime. They donned their bulky snowsuits and dragged their sleds across town to the park and trudged up the hill with them. They didn't even think to ask their mother to drive them there. Down the hill they slid, starting by the edge of the Sunnyside Canal at Harrison Avenue and plunging down the slope as far as they could go: sitting up, lying down, double, triple, sometimes standing up. After several hours when they were wet, cold to their core and their fingers and toes were numb, they had to drag their sleds home again. By this time they often had developed huge raw areas on the inside of their thighs where their damp snow pants had rubbed. Hand lotion applied there stung like crazy for a few days. As teens they would hear of a frozen pond in some farmer's pasture, or a section in the bottom of an empty canal, drag an old tire along to burn, douse it with kerosene, and skate until it got dark. Home they'd go smelling like burned rubber and get a scolding from Mildred for the pungent odor that had to be washed out of their clothes and hair.

On Sunday afternoons it was always a treat for the Smiths to take a drive out in the country to visit friends or relatives. Those were pleasant occasions and often the only times all the Smith cousins (six boys and two girls) interacted. Mildred or Lloyd would not call ahead, just drop in, as was usual for many families in those years. The Smith clan rarely planned family get-togethers ahead of time. Mildred enjoyed inviting Lloyd's mother Cecilia for Sunday dinner, especially if Mildred found out none of Lloyd's sisters had asked her. Mildred had become very fond of her mother in-law and saw to it that the Smith kids dropped in on their grandmother regularly. Mildred also discovered that Lloyd's three sisters and their families often got together without including them. This hurt Mildred's as well as Lloyd's feelings. Perhaps it was a Catholic thing, but Lloyd's sisters had always seemed cool to Mildred. When the older cousins (Dick and Don Golob) left home, the Smith girls took over mowing Cecilia's lawn and running errands for her. She always had a decanter of homemade root beer sitting on her dining room buffet as a treat.

In the forties and fifties fireworks could be purchased at the variety store. Kids could buy big clumps of lady fingers and larger firecrackers. One favorite activity was to light a firecracker, plop a tin can over the top of it and watch it blow up into the air. Lady fingers, which were attached on one long wick, provided a wonderful long series of pop-pop-pop-pop as the package flipped and twisted while all two dozen crackers went off in rapid succession. Of course, there were punks to light them and sparklers to hold and race around or swing in lazy-eight circles. There were no warnings. If you got burned, it was your fault.

Tom, however, had a certain fascination for firecrackers by the age of seven. One of Mildred's nieces, Florence's daughter Jean and her husband Jack Amorde and their three sons, Michael, Scott and Pat, drove up from Oregon to visit the Smith family over a Fourth of July weekend. After having a large dinner, the Smiths decided to go for a ride to show the relatives around Sunnyside and the surrounding countryside. There wasn't enough room for everyone to go in one car, so Michael, age nine, and Tom, who was seven,, were left home and told to behave themselves. A couple of hours later, the family returned and Mildred went into the kitchen to prepare a light supper. Her feet stuck to the floor. She mopped up the spot wondering what she had spilled. Then she went over to the stove, more feet sticking, and saw that there were a couple of chunks of watermelon and some juice spilled on the counter top. She wiped up that, too. Then she began to look around. There were more pink chunks stuck to the cupboard doors, on the window and even on the ceiling. There were chunks of watermelon all over the kitchen! Tom and Michael were called in and, after a little prodding, they admitted that they had stuck a firecracker in a chunk of watermelon, set it on the kitchen table, and lit it.

Mildred told Tom that he would be cleaning up her kitchen until the mess was all gone. For the next week, long after the Amordes had left, Mildred found a spot in the kitchen for Tom to scrub daily.

@ 1949: Mildred's choir at Holy Trinity: L-R: Billy Flower, Mildred, Vergie Smith, Patty Flower, Bob Munson, Mary Lee Flower, Charles Flower, Sarah Margaret Flower, Bobbie Smith, Rev Slocum.

2 9

The Priest Lake Years

Huckleberries, a boy goes missing, hijinks

EACH SUMMER THE SMITH KIDS looked forward to their annual trip to Priest Lake, Idaho, especially Mildred who came to depend upon this annual respite in her busy life. Christmas and the annual trips to Elkins became the lynchpins around which each year cycled. After a few years the family was able to stay at the lake for two weeks, and one year they stayed a month. For the longer periods Lloyd spent only the first and last weekends with the family, then drove home to work. When Lloyd was there Mildred could use the car to go huckleberry-ing. She'd gather up the children and off they'd go with the promise that as soon as their sand buckets were filled they'd come back so the children could get back in the lake.

Huckleberrying was the big adventure of each vacation for Mildred. The kids weren't so thrilled because they knew Mildred usually kept her promise and made them stay in the woods until all the containers were full. Her favorite spots were up Lamb Creek where bushes had appeared about ten years after a large area had been logged. Off they would go with a picnic lunch, water and mosquito repellent. The dogs went tearing around the woods chasing squirrels to their hearts' content. If the pickings were poor after a hard winter or a dry spring, Mildred would finally relent and head back to Elkins, but not until they had enough for at least one or two pies. In a good year Mildred was able to make jam right there in the cabin on the wood stove. She made huckleberry pies, huckleberry pancakes and spooned huckleberries on their dishes of ice cream, on which Mildred would splurge once-a-vacation and buy at the store.

During the times when Lloyd had driven home in the car, Mildred and the children had neither reason nor way to go anywhere else. Mildred loved the quiet of the cabin where she could read a magazine in peace or take a nap. The kids spent their days in the water and on the beach except when an occasional August thunderstorm would roll in. When a front moved through rapidly and the weather changed, the lake churned up. It was great fun for the kids to run out on the swimming dock, throw an inner tube in, jump in after it, climb aboard and ride the high waves into the beach. If they could hear thunder, even if they couldn't see lightning, the rule was they had to come out of the water. That often meant reading comic books, playing card games or assembling puzzles at the kitchen table or down at the lodge. Sometimes the electricity would go off for an hour, sometimes for a couple of days.

The Smith kids roamed all over Elkin's Resort, exploring the cool, big ice house with chunks of ice layered in sawdust for the "creek" cabins not yet electrified. Each year they walked over the footbridge across Reeder Creek to Andy's grave where a distraught owner had buried his deaf and aged dog. Andy had gone to sleep in the shade of the man's car while the owner went into the store to pay his bill; the man then ran over the dog as he left. The children thought this was the saddest story they had ever heard and always left a few sprigs of wildflowers in the circle of stones for Andy, whom they'd never met.

On a few occasions the children walked the beach trail north past a dozen or more cabins on leased land all the way up to Grandview Resort and then home again. Mildred always required the children to tell her before they left on one of these traipses through the woods, but she rarely told them they couldn't go, nor did she worry about who or what they might meet. On days they were really bored, they dogged the heels of some of the resort workers, Tommy always asking, "Why are you doing that?" or "Why are you going there?" or "When do you eat lunch?" or "Do you like chopping wood?" When no one was looking, the kids tried their hand at chopping wood because there was always an axe left by the pile in the wood shed. They never cut off a toe or finger, but there were some very close calls that sent them scampering back to the cabin where, of course, they never told Mildred what they'd been up to. A favorite adventure was to get to ride to the dump with "the hired guy" and watch black bears pawing through the heaps of garbage. Sometimes they'd ask for permission to go, and sometimes they went without their mother's knowledge.

The girls were always required to look after their brother, to whom everyone was a friend and who frequently made himself a part of others' activities whether he knew them or not. He loved to go down to the boat dock about six o'clock and watch fishermen tie up and show off their catches. "Boy, I'd sure like to go out fishing like that someday," he'd say to anyone who might listen. But no one got the hint. Eventually Lloyd rigged up a fishing pole for him and bought him a jar of fish eggs. The few fish he caught off the boat docks were squaw fish and not edible, but you'd think he'd won a derby! The family ooohed and awed over the ugly things and had to display them in a bucket of water or in the frig for at least a day. Mildred soon learned to bury the fish far from the cabin because the dogs kept digging up the carcasses and rolling in them. The dogs were allowed to come in the cabin (they were roamers, chased squirrels, and Shorty was a lothario wherever he was), to keep them out of trouble. Cougars, bears and coyotes were known to cruise through the cabin areas during the night. Sometimes there would be a skunk and no one wanted to drag a smelly and reluctant dog to the lake with a bar of soap. Cleaning them after they'd rolled on a dead fish was bad enough.

One evening Tommy was still down at the boat dock when it was time for supper. Mildred sent Bobbie down there to tell her brother to come home, but he didn't want to and told her he wasn't going to. Lacking complete diplomacy and switching into the 'You have to do what I tell you" big-sister-mode, she then told him, "If you don't you are going to be in big trouble, buddy-boy!" "Am not!" he replied and pushed her (fully clothed) off the dock into the water, then ran. When Bobbie sloshed in the cabin door, she was fuming, but Mildred thought it was funny and had a good laugh. She turned to Vergie and told her to go get her brother and tell him to get home or he'd get no supper. But Vergie who was not going to risk getting shoved in the drink, only went close enough to yell at him. And he shook his head resolutely, "No!" After she reported back, Mildred had to put the supper aside and go retrieve her son. She armed herself with a wooden spoon. When they returned, he came in the door grinning as usual and got his supper after all.

On another occasion, Tommy, the true social animal in the family, begged and begged to have a marshmallow roast on the beach like many of the other vacationers did in the evenings. Mildred told him, "No," then "No" again, and finally "When I say 'no' Tommy, I. MEAN. NO!" Shortly afterward at dusk one evening, Mildred noticed that Tommy was nowhere to be seen. She stood on the cabin porch and called for him: no response. She sent the girls looking: no brother to be found. Then she went to the lodge and the store and the docks: no Tommy Smith. By this time it was after nine o'clock and nearly dark. When Mildred asked Ike Elkins, the resort owner, if he'd seen the boy, Ike became alarmed that the five year-old had not turned up. He got a flashlight and started looking around the resort, too: by Reeder Creek, the ice house, the creek cabins, and the wood barn. By this time Mildred was thoroughly alarmed. She and the girls started walking up the beach stopping at each campfire and asking, "Have you seen a little boy? His name is Tommy." At the first fire, no one had seen him. But at the second and the third and the fourth the answer was, "Yes, he was here a little while ago. He ate a few marshmallows, then said he had to go." Mildred was half running up the beach by then shouting "Tommy!!! Tommy Smith, if you are there you better get right over here!" Slowly a shadowy short figure holding a long stick with a marshmallow dripping off the end emerged from a group of people around a beach fire. Everybody stopped talking as the frantic mother reached out and grabbed her son. "What on earth were you thinking?" she shouted at him. " We thought you were lost!" "It's OK, Mommy," he said grinning and calmly patting her arm, "I ollays knew where I was."

One summer when they arrived at their favorite cabin, #17, they were surprised to see that the cabin next to them had burned down. It had once joined onto theirs as a sort of duplex, but had been separated and moved northward about fifty feet. Its replacement, a modern cabin, was being built. Then when they walked into their cabin the family was stunned to discover that there was a refrigerator and an electric stove in their cabin. The wood stove was gone. The next year a toilet and shower had been installed in a little room at the end of the front porch. Next was a full set of lights that didn't stutter out each night when the generator was shut down. The next year or so, they discovered that the front porch had been enclosed and combined with the interior of the cabin, and the interior "L" had been partitioned to make a second bedroom. Luxury! Who needed a shower? The Smiths had the lake! The little shed behind the cabin that had housed the ice box and the wood supply for the wood stove disappeared. Lloyd shook his head because each time a new feature was added, the rent went up. He was really unhappy when the rent went up to $95 a week!

The beds stayed the same, however. The old CCC camp bunk bed springs just kept sagging as the children grew in size and weight. Whoever slept on the bottom bunk couldn't sit up suddenly in the middle of the night without getting her hair tangled in the springs of the upper bunk. That was usually Vergie who disliked the climb to the top layer. Every year Mildred complained bitterly to Ike or Sue Elkins about the saggy mattresses and how her back ached each morning, and then she fussed at Ike's son Al Elkins after he had taken over running the resort, for all the good it did. Mildred solved the problem by stowing her own piece of plywood in the trunk of the car before they left Sunnyside. If she forgot, Mildred combed the resort and pestered the help until they found her a board to shore up the mattress. Soon, even Sue Elkins' hand-stitched heavy-as-heck crazy quilts disappeared, and the dishes and pots and pans were scrambled to the point that the family might have only enough cracked or chipped plates to serve four, not five people. If a nearby cabin emptied while the Smiths were staying on, Mildred would often send one of her children over to it after it had been cleaned to swipe a pot, plate, glass, frying pan lid, an extra fork, or mixing spoon, before the new renters arrived. If, in the next week the new folks next door commented to Mildred about how sparse their cooking utensils were, Mildred would often reply, "Yes, ours, too." For food, if the Smith boxes that Mildred carefully packed at home ran low, the Elkins store carried bread, milk, eggs, bacon, frozen hamburger, some canned goods, breakfast cereal, pancake mix, syrup, and, best of all, popsicles.

Over the years the same families came at the same time, so each summer became a time to greet familiar faces and remark how their children had grown and who had done what. Two such families were the Dieters and the Brookses. Ike Dieter was the boxing coach at WSC (Washington State College, later Washington State University). He was very well-known, but the Smiths didn't know it at the time. Ike Dieter and Ike Elkins had become buddies over the years. Dieter had first come to Elkins Resort when it was a fishing camp shortly after Ike Elkins had bought it in 1932. It was such fun to listen to the two Ikes shoot the bull.

Just a few years older than the Smith girls, Muff Dieter (later Edwards) had become a good friend of the Elkins' youngest daughter, Joni. The preteen Smith girls watched the teenagers sun bathing on the swimming dock and idolized them from afar. Twenty years later by happenstance the Dieters, the Edwardses, Mildred, and Bobbie's family met up again in the Reeder Bay Camp Ground in the 1970s and reconnected. After Ike Dieter retired, he decided he wanted to learn to play the banjo. His son in-law Ron Edwards took it up, too. But Ike was half deaf and couldn't carry a tune in a bucket. So when Ike started strumming, and mumbling the words, Ron would play and sing out heartily so everyone sitting around the fire knew what song it was and could join in.

The Brooks family was from Goldendale. Alva, an attorney, was seldom seen during their month at Elkins. It was rumored that he was a "B & B man" (book and bottle). Muriel, his wife, took one dip a day in the lake, and played bridge every afternoon at the lodge. Their adult children, Jim Brooks and his wife Mybrit and their children, came a few times, but their daughter Jerrine from Seattle came with her two sons every summer and stayed at least a month. Mildred often cut Jerrine's boys' hair in exchange for a boat ride in the Brooks' classic Chris-Craft boat. On several occasions Jerrine took Mildred and her children up to the head of the lake to Mosquito Bay at a place called Shipman Point where they could run off a beautiful sandy beach and jump right into the lake where there was a drop off. It was in this same area that Nell Shipman had made her silent movies in the early 1900s and the kids enjoyed poking around the remains of the animal cages used in her movies. Among them were "Light on Lookout" and "The Grubstake," The lodge used in the movies had burned down. Nearby was the wreck of the "Tyee II," a supply boat that had run aground after an attempt had been made to scuttle it. The kids crawled all over the Tyee, the bones of which can still be seen on the shore more than sixty years later.

Jerrine had a marvelous way of telling a story, usually about one of her faux pas, which would leave Mildred laughing so hard she had to dab her eyes. Once at her home in Seattle Jerrine tripped over her dog and broke her leg. She came to the lake on crutches sporting a very heavy plaster cast on one leg. When she came out of her cabin one evening, she spotted a black bear that had wandered over to the outdoor eating area of the resort near the bar and had begun licking up the remains of a Hawaiian barbecue left on the tables. Jerrine turned around quickly, went into her cabin to get her camera and when she returned to the cabin porch, she came face to face with the bear, which had followed her. Later she maintained that both bear and woman did a shrieking duet and fled in opposite directions. It took her until the next day to find her camera in a nearby bush where she had flung it.

Jerrine loved to play jokes on everyone she knew at the resort, including short-sheeting her sons' beds. One night she managed to take down a heavy elk head trophy from the lodge's main room and took it by cabin windows where her friends were enjoying a quiet evening of cards. The Smiths were one of those lucky ones and came pouring out onto their screened porch to see the beast, but they couldn't see anything in the dim light. They did hear, however, Jerine's well-known cackle fading into the woods.

Many years later, her boys grown and gone and the Brooks' power boat sold, Jerrine accepted an invitation to go for an early morning waterski tow behind a friend's boat. She was fully clothed and didn't want to have to hike back to her cabin and change into her swim suit. She thought, "Why not?" and told her friends she'd to go for a spin in her street clothes. She didn't realize that once they got wet her polyester pants and sweat shirt would weigh her skinny body down so much that she couldn't get her rear up out of the water so she could stand up on the skis. She made the whole loop behind the boat in a squatting position. Later she said of her adventure, "Best damn enema I ever had!"

The Smith family often returned home from their summer vacations at the lake with something notable: sometimes monumental sunburns, a new story of Jerrine's, a new adventure, or huckleberries, but it was always something unique. One year the children caught the measles from a family they had been playing with all week. The other children broke out with them on their last day at the lake. Two weeks later the Smith kids began breaking out with the measles. In a different summer, another family's children began to feel sick right after they arrived for their vacation. Over the next two weeks, one by one, all five of those children came down with the mumps. It was too late for the Smith kids. When they got back home to Sunnyside, one by one they came down with the mumps, too. It took six weeks for the mumps to run their course. By that time summer was almost over and school was about ready to start. Throughout those years Mildred and Lloyd gave their children a precious gift: unique and happy childhood memories at "the lake."

THE SMITHS AT ELKINS: BOBBIE HOLDING "SHORTY", MILDRED, LLOYD, VERGIE, TOM

Things Begin to Change

Patriotism; a hot summer; polio; hammers and nails

IN THE MID-FIFTIES, TEN YEARS after the end of the Second World War, patriotism still ran high and life was good in Sunnyside. Dwight David "Ike" Eisenhower, the U.S. Army five-star general who directed the Allies to victory in Europe and who had virtually no political experience, was talked into running for president. He was immensely popular and was easily elected by a grateful nation. The bobby sox era eased to a close as country and rhythm and blues rose in popularity with their twangy vocals and themes of the common man's troubles. Elvis Presley, a hip-gyrating newcomer to country/western/R & B, sometimes called "rockabilly" music, may have failed an audition to Arthur Godfrey's Talent Scouts, but he began getting record deals, which led to a spot on Ed Sullivan's "Toast of the Town," a black-and-white television variety show in 1956. He sang the ballad "Love Me Tender." The rest is history.

"I Love Lucy" was the most-watched sitcom. Crooner Pat Boone topped the record charts with his version of "Ain't That a Shame." The black-and-white movie "The Blackboard Jungle" startled audiences with its daring social statement about teachers and students in New York City schools, while musical extravaganzas such as "South Pacific", "Seven Brides for Seven Brothers", and "Oklahoma" became smash hits for both Broadway and film audiences.

With new schools built to accommodate the "baby boomer" generation of children born during the forties came new teaching techniques to modernize the way children were taught. Didn't work. Lots of confusion, and Sunnyside High School students rebelled by staging a walkout in the middle of the day at the high school. The Korean Conflict had ground to a standoff when the DMZ (Demilitarized Zone) at the 38th Parallel was established and our boys began to come home from Asia. Albert Einstein, the famed recipient of the 1921 Nobel Prize for physics, died in 1955, and a child who would one day design software for personal computers, become an entrepreneur and use his wealth to support scientific research and health services aimed at eradicating poliomyelitis throughout the world was born to Mr. and Mrs. Bill Gates senior in Seattle. In 1955 with life so abundant, no one in 'small town U.S.A.' was expecting an epidemic.

The summer of 1955 had been a warm one, a veritable drawn-out "dog days of summer," with weeks of hot, dry, breezeless days and airless nights. For relief, restless Sunnyside teens could fill a car with their friends and go to the Starlight Drive In for one dollar per car. Sometimes there would be two features showing and at least one cartoon. That would be good for nearly five hours of entertainment. For the younger set, running through yard sprinklers or a daily trip to the swimming pool was a must. Kids could get a season ticket to the pool for five dollars, or pay by the swim depending on their age: twenty-five cents for twelve and under; fifty cents for teens; seventy-five cents for adults. Mildred and Lloyd's children earned their money for season passes by mowing lawns for a dollar each. (Lloyd did not believe in allowances.) The two Smith girls also babysat for seventy-five cents an hour, and in 1955 Bobbie got jobs picking asparagus and cherries, and as an unpaid lifeguard for the summer to work off her season pass. Oh, the sunburns!

When the country kids could persuade their parents to drive them into town, they, too, would join their friends at the pool, which was the main attraction in the Sunnyside Park located between Fourth Street, Harrison Drive, and Edison Avenues. The pool dressing room facilities were very basic: concrete floors that became slippery ("no running allowed!!") as each day progressed, three-sided dressing areas with canvas curtains on sliders, a toilet, two or three shower heads. The dressing room always smelled of bleach and chlorine. At the front desk swimmers collected a wire basket with a number on it as they entered the facility, put their street clothes in the baskets and gave them to the attendants after first attaching a safety pin with the basket number on it onto their swim suits.

Those not in the pool happily played in the park on the swings, monkey bars, and slide. It was great fun to climb to the top of the six-foot-tall slide and jump onto the metal for a swift flight down to the ground. Kids learned very quickly to keep a piece of clothing under their upper legs if the sun had been shining on the metal because on some days you could fry an egg on it. When the children got too sweaty and hot, they would run over to the public water fountain for a cool sip of water. The concrete fountain had a continuous bubbler in the center and it was not uncommon for adults and children alike to slurp up a cool, refreshing drink of water by putting their lips and mouths close to, and sometimes touching, the cool rounded surface where the water came out.

On many outlying farms bolder, older country kids might sneak off and take a dip in a favorite spot in the many miles of irrigation canals that brought water to the fields. Canal swimming was forbidden by authorities and by most parents because the canals had dangerous under currents that often could not be detected from the canal banks, and occasionally sucked an unaware swimmer underwater into a gate where they might be caught and drowned. But kids jumped in anyway for the thrill of it as well as for the flow's coolness. If there was a canal nearby, some field workers might jump in when they finished hoeing or harvesting a long row and resume working the next row soaking wet, but certainly refreshed for a while. Canals were also a good place to "pee" surreptitiously. No one worried about what other substances could be found in the water, but it was common knowledge that you just don't drink irrigation water.

A great number of children were accustomed to going barefooted throughout the summer, (except for church on Sunday mornings) until school began. Flip-flops had not been invented, and tennis shoes were not yet the rage. Leather shoes were too confining. They were for school, anyway. There was always at least one bandaged toe or knee among the groups of children playing here and there across town. In many sunny places sidewalks were too hot to walk on with bare feet and the asphalt tar in the pavement became so soft in places you could dig up a wad of it to roll in your fingers.

By day's end everyone looked forward to the relief of summer evenings when all the doors and windows would be thrown open to entice the air to move, if only a little. If you had a fan, that helped, too. Few people had air conditioners, but air conditioning of a sort could be found downtown at Killingstad's Hardware store under their ceiling fans, which turned steadily overhead just inside the front door. There were lots of lookers and few real buyers many afternoons, those who wanted to stand under the fan for a minute or two and be glad to see a friend so they could stay there under the moving air and chat rather than shop.

By August, farmers had begun to harvest their crops. The sweet smell of cut alfalfa and mint hay baking in the hot sun was a reminder that summer was nearly over. Asparagus season had ended in late June followed by the cherry crop; then peaches and apricots were harvested and the first blush of pears was beginning to show on the trees. Once the nights began to cool off in mid- to late August, early apple harvest would follow and grape harvest would begin once there were enough cold nights to set the sugar in them, then back to the later apple crops. After July had morphed into August, vacation trips were ending, and preparations for school began.

The Smiths, tanned and rested, returned home from their annual two-week-long trip to Elkins Resort. Mildred had picked huckleberries, made several batches of jam and frozen two or three pies. Her garden had produced well in her absence, so now she had some heavy weeding to catch up on. She canned tomatoes, corn, green beans, and occasionally peaches if she could get them free. Lloyd's real estate and insurance business was doing well and his involvement in city affairs, now as Sunnyside's mayor, kept him busy, too. Vergie Ellen was in business school in Spokane; Roberta was looking forward to her senior year of high school; and Tom who would enter junior high school that fall was relishing his last days of freedom.

Shortly after returning home from Idaho, Roberta, who had resumed life guarding at the pool, came down suddenly with an apparent case of the flu. She developed a nasty headache and was very ill for about ten days. Only cold compresses and aspirin could take the edge off her headache and she could not stand to be in a room with the bright sunlight coming in the windows. If she moved her head or got up from a lying position to a standing position, it felt like a boulder was crashing around inside her brain. She had some nausea and she ached from head to toe, but neither Mildred or Lloyd considered taking her to a doctor because her temperature wasn't alarming: 100 in the morning and 101 or 102 in the afternoon, but no worse. She could not even stand to watch the family's new black-and-white television set, and spent many hours a day sleeping upstairs in her hot and airless bedroom with cold towels on her forehead. Gradually she began to feel better. The more she began to walk around, eat normally, and interact with the family the better she felt each day. But the illness had taken the starch out of her and she had no desire to do anything but stay inside or in the yard for the next couple of weeks. She dragged herself to cheer leading practices, then came home and went to sleep. The bright sun continued to make her wince.

The two valley newspapers, the Yakima Morning Herald and the Yakima Daily Republic, had reported that a rash of polio cases had occurred in other parts of the United States and Europe, and reminded readers that a member of the traveling troupe of "Oklahoma" had died in Italy from polio in July. Along with the news that President Sigmund Rhee of South Korea had renewed attacks on truce talks, Senator Joseph McCarthy was accusing prominent people of secretly being 'Red,' and that Thomas Mann had died, it was noted that the East coast was experiencing a rising number of polio deaths in young children. Moreover, the Yakima Valley Medical Society was still not completely convinced that the Salk Polio Vaccine was safe and had requested that Yakima County postpone continuing the vaccination program for elementary school children. The Yakima Valley shipment of 10,701 doses received in May 1955 had been shipped over to the west side of Washington, where it was needed as second shots for school children there. Yakima County Health District was promised that it would receive another shipment once physicians approved its use. Ironically, on the same page was a syndicated column exhorting parents "...to sign papers to allow their children to be inoculated through the schools or sign up at their doctor's offices." Still there was little information about the symptoms of the disease or how to prevent it. In the meantime a local insurance business, the Lombard-Horsely Agency, advertised a polio insurance policy that would provide "...up to $5,000 for treatment of each person..."

In late August, a couple of weeks before school was to start, Sunnyside High School's football turnout began on the football field at Lincoln Junior High School. Practices were held in the late afternoons when the heat was still blistering. The boys perspired heavily and a few became nauseous and weak from dehydration. Jim Mallery, Sunnyside School District Superintendent Dr. Kenneth Mallery's middle son, was a big kid in all respects: robust and strong physically, and huge in personality. The family was new to Sunnyside, but Jim and his younger brother Peter had become rapidly popular among their new peers. Their older brother John was already away in college.

Word began to spread that several children in the community had become ill with something that was not acting like a 'normal' flu. Mickey Reeves, a town kid, was one of them. Within days, names of other sick children were added to the list. Then Julie Reeves, Mickey's four year-old sister, became ill. The word "polio" began to be openly voiced with alarm. The news that eighteen year-old Jim Mallery had gone home sick from practice still had not connected the dots for anyone. Like the Smiths, who took care of their own ailments, many families did not go to the doctor without very good reason: a broken bone, a cut that had to be stitched, etc. But a few days later, when Jim's brother Peter became ill, Dr. and Mrs. Mallery became alarmed. After several days Peter seemed to get better, while Jim did not. The severity of Jim's illness increased daily and he became too sick to get dressed and go to the doctor.

Dr. Hiroshi Furukawa made a house call to the Mallerys and decided Jim needed to be hospitalized. Could it possibly be polio? When the results of Jim's spinal tap test came back as positive, he was immediately transferred to St. Elizabeth Hospital in Yakima forty miles away where a polio ward had been established. Jim's illness escalated rapidly, paralyzing him from foot to chest. An iron lung was hastily located and made available to him, but while his caregivers tried to get him stabilized and while he was trying to get someone to tell him how long he'd be in the hospital, his face turned gray, he rolled his head to one side and stopped breathing. It was September 7, 1955.

Mildred was asked to play the organ for Jim Mallery's funeral. It was held in the biggest church in Sunnyside on a blisteringly hot, cloudless September day. The church was filled by Jim's stunned classmates, family, friends, high school faculty, and community members. Jim's brother Peter who had been hospitalized briefly and had come home briefly had been returned to the polio ward in Yakima the morning of the funeral. It seemed unreal that such a healthy and physically powerful teenager could have been taken down so easily by this silent attacker, and now his brother was ill, too..

It turned out that the worst outbreak of polio in the history of the United States had already occurred in 1952, but for some reason the fear of polio was more prevalent in urban areas than in rural communities like Sunnyside. (If you couldn't see it, it couldn't get you.) In the early fifties an increase of polio cases had occurred primarily in urban areas when summer was at its hottest. The two greatest urban fears of the American public in the fifties were atomic war and polio.

Dr. Jonas Salk had been researching a polio vaccine for seven years. In early 1955 the news broke that a polio vaccine had been perfected and would be tested on "Polio Pioneers." School districts across the nation were invited to sign up to participate. Sunnyside was one district selected for the test for grades six and under. Nearly two million school children across the United States participated in the vaccine trial, which was declared a success on April 12, 1955, but the vaccine did not get distributed in time to save the life of older children, in particular, Jim Mallery. Tommy Smith received the vaccine as a sixth grader.

Polio is a fickle disease. Mickey Reeves never recovered the use of either of his legs and used a wheelchair for the remainder of his life. His younger sister Julie recovered completely. Oldest brother Jim Reeves remembers his mother sitting at the kitchen table with her head in her hands sobbing.

He wrote, "I try to recall those terrible last months of 1955, but for the most part I draw a blank. Only snippets of events do I recall. My mom frantically taking [younger brother] Bobby in for Gamma Globulin shots...Looking in thru the hospital windows for a glimpse of Mick...Jim Mallery's funeral...Football season being cancelled...my Mom crying..."

Years later when Mildred reflected on that summer and the polio epidemic she said,

"I had no idea that Roberta might have contracted a slight case of polio that time she was so sick. I thought she had the flu. We all did. It did not dawn on me to be overly concerned about her since her fever was not very high. I did not know about the other sick children at the time. Maybe she got it, maybe not. But I shudder to think that I didn't pay more attention to her at the time. When I was growing up there was no one who worried about me and I didn't know I should be worried about my own children. I had just learned to tough it out. They did, too".

What is notable is that in 1955 public trust of bureaucracy was still high in the United States despite growing apprehension over the presence of U.S. troops in Korea. Most parents waited patiently for the vaccine to be approved for use in school children by the Yakima Valley Medical Society, then most gladly gave permission for their children to be given this vaccine, which had had no lengthy trial periods. In today's society, that would never happen because of tighter FDA regulations as well as greater public awareness. A few years later the oral vaccine developed by Albert Sabin was marketed and became the preferred method of polio vaccine particularly because it was easier to administer to small children and became a routine preventive measure along with the chicken pox, diphtheria, whooping cough, tetanus, and measles vaccines. Prior to 1955, the standard protocol for becoming resistant to any of these diseases had been to come down with a case of each as a child, and trust that immunity would last for the rest of the person's life. However, when it was determined that at least 1% of persons receiving Sabin's oral vaccine would still come down with polio, a combination of the vaccines was developed. Roberta's illness in August 1955 was never diagnosed.

Just as mysteriously, Peter Mallery's polio appeared to slow its progression, unlike the way it had galloped through his older brother. However, as he began to recover, it became clear that Peter had lost the use of his legs and would need to use crutches for the remainder of his life.

In the spring of 1956 Bobbie graduated from high school. She chose to go to the University of Washington to pursue a degree in education, and to follow her boyfriend John Sahr there instead of going to Washington State University where she had a music scholarship. Fortunately, she also had another scholarship she could apply to any state school, and that helped ease the financial burden for Mildred and Lloyd.

Now there was just one little chick in the nest. The first thing Mildred did was to buy a second-hand dishwasher because Tommy was far harder to corral for dish duty than the girls had been. A couple of years later, she threatened Lloyd more than once that he would come home one day and find that she had taken a sledge hammer to one living room wall to open it up to include their current bedroom which she would use as a piano alcove. Next, she told him she would hire a man to pull her ugly plywood cupboards off the kitchen walls and install a real countertop, not pressed wood, put new linoleum down, and get rid of the radiator. Realizing he was horn-swaggled before he said one word, he agreed to a remodel. Mildred hired carpenters and had them add a two-story addition onto the back of the house. Finally, she had a beautiful new kitchen with birch cupboards, a built-in dishwasher, a large dining/family room, and had another bedroom built over the new kitchen and moved the front door. She paid for it with her piano money, and grinned the whole time.

The Smith home after it had been moved across town to 4ᵗʰ Street. It was rotated 90 degrees on the lot from its original orientation on Edison Avenue. The new two-story addition is on the right, and the new front entrance was moved from the left (near the yard light) to the center.

3 1

More Changes

Graduation, a wedding, a move, a death

IN JUNE 1960, BOBBIE GRADUATED from the University of Washington with a B.A. in Education. She interviewed for and got a job teaching Latin and English at Bothell High School north of Seattle. She and John Sahr, her long-time boyfriend from Sunnyside Junior High School days, had become engaged the summer before and had set June 19th for their wedding at Holy Trinity Episcopal Church.

Lloyd and Mildred drove over to Seattle for their daughter's graduation, which was held in Hec Edmundson Pavilion on the UW campus. It was a huge affair and Mildred could not help but remember her own small graduation thirty years prior, to which no one in her family had come. John and Bobbie found an apartment just off Roosevelt Way in the "U" district. During finals week the two had moved most of her things there, and John's parents had brought his things and some furniture the previous week. After just two days at home, the Smith family--Lloyd, Mildred, Bobbie, and Tom--drove back over to Seattle to attend the wedding of Bobbie's cousin Phil McKibben, Lloyd's sister Angela's son. Then back to Sunnyside where the next week was filled with last-minute details of the upcoming wedding, which mother and daughter organized.

Russ and Mary Milby, Mildred's uncle and his wife, drove from Breckenridge, Missouri, to attend their grand niece's wedding. Bobbie had visited them in the summer of 1959 while on her way home from her sorority's international convention in French Lick, Indiana. After a side trip to New York City she had also visited Nina Rose, (Mildred's cousin) and her husband Duncan in Baltimore with whom she stayed for a few days. A big thrill for Roberta was taking the train into Washington, D.C. from Baltimore to meet Washington Democratic Senator Henry M. Jackson for lunch in the Senate Dining Room. This had been arranged by Lloyd who was an active Democrat and admired the senator. She also visited the offices of Warren Magnuson, the other Democratic senator, and Catherine May, the Republican representative from the Yakima Valley who was also very popular with her constituents. Roberta next travelled to Lexington, Missouri, to visit Elizabeth (Aunt Lizzie) Smith and her daughter Alberta. Aunt Lizzie Smith was the widow of Pearl Smith, one of Turner Smith's brothers. Next she took the train to Breckenridge, Missouri, to visit Russ and Mary Milby. Russ Milby was Arthur's brother.

So it was very pleasing to have the Missouri Milbys come for the wedding. The rehearsal dinner was held at the Sahrs' on Friday night. On Saturday Vergie Ellen and her husband arrived from California unexpectedly, having been able to get a few days off from work. There wasn't time to make another bridesmaid's dress, so Vergie became the coffee-pourer at the reception. The morning of the wedding found Bobbie and Mildred out in the country at the Sunnyside Nursery choosing long-stemmed blue stock for the standing floral arrangements. Bobbie had finished her bridesmaids' "bow" hats the night before, and now had to complete the finishing touches in the church.

It had been a beautiful day, sunny with a slight breeze until the early afternoon when the earlier breeze grew into fitful gusts and the air began to cool. As 4 p.m. approached, enormous gray clouds blew in and stacked one upon another. Mildred didn't mind because the church, which had no air conditioning, would remain comfortable for the seventy-five or more guests. It was Father's Day. The guests had gathered in the little church. Cecilia Smith and her daughters Pearl Golob and Louise Mercille took their places in the second row. Jim Sahr escorted John's parents, John and Elsie Sahr, to their seats. Tom escorted his mother Mildred to her seat in the front row. Then John and his groomsmen came in the side door and assembled in front of the altar with the Reverend George Ames. Peggy Gathman sang "Ave Maria." The organist broke into Lohengrin's March. The bridesmaids began walking down the aisle. Just as Bobbie and her father walked from the parish hall and up the steps to the church door a monstrous gust of wind caught the train of her wedding gown and flipped it over her head and settled like a blanket, crushing her veil and mussing her hair. A great flurry of activity ensued while the errant wedding dress was flipped back where it belonged, the hair patted down and the veil repositioned. No one thought to check to see if the small crown of stephanotis holding the veil was still centered on the bride's head. It wasn't.

It wasn't until several weeks later when the photographer finally got the proofs to the Smiths that Bobbie discovered her wedding veil and crown had been askew throughout the whole ceremony and no one had said a thing! In addition, the photographer had decided to use a new wide-angle lens and a new brand of color film. The end result: The wedding party looked short and fat and the color quickly began to fade on all the photos.

But a disaster it was not. The reception afterward went as planned with the bride and groom enjoying the celebration with their friends and relatives after having had a nearly ten-year courtship. Mildred, however, was exhausted. She had taught piano into early June and finished off the year with two spring recitals because she had so many students. This had meant extra lessons for some and two long dress rehearsals. Then followed two trips to Seattle, and the wedding in the next week, plus entertaining company. This had been the first wedding since her own in 1934 in which she had been involved from beginning to end. Vergie had gotten married in California the previous June with little notice. Now with the Milbys arriving and Vergie and her husband arriving, plus a bridesmaid staying at the house, Mildred had been under the gun for several months. It took her well into the summer to recover. There was no Priest Lake for them that year, but Lloyd and Mildred did manage to take a long weekend off and drove to a Washington beach where Bobbie and John met them. Tom, Bobbie and John went clamming. Mildred and John enjoyed seeing who could eat the most clams.

The next few years were full for Mildred. Beginning the spring of 1961 Lloyd began to experience some health problems and had to undergo surgery to have a section of his bowel removed. He was a reluctant patient. Tom graduated from high school that May and went off to the University of Washington in the fall. In June, Vergie's son, Kenneth Lloyd was born. Mildred took the bus to California and spent ten days with her first grandchild and Vergie. Cecilia Smith died August 6, 1961, at the age of 91. She had had a long, hard life that had included breast cancer when she was in her 70s, but she had always been kind to Mildred, who was deeply saddened by her death. Lloyd, only recently recovered from his surgery, wept at his mother's funeral. In October, Bobbie and John's son John David was born in Seattle where John was in his senior year of dental school. Because Mildred had a full roster of piano students, she and Lloyd could only spend a weekend in Seattle with Bobbie and John and their first child.

During the early 1960s Ellen Milby's health began to deteriorate. Fred had died suddenly of a heart attack in 1958. He had confided to Mildred that he was worried about Ellen's mental state and Mildred had agreed to look after her. For a few years Ellen was able to manage on her own, but soon was having trouble with her neighbors, or so she thought. One day Mildred received a phone call from a neighbor of Ellen's who told Mildred that if she didn't do something about

Ellen, the police were going to step in. Apparently Ellen had become paranoid about where her garbage cans sat and who was stepping on whose property. Mildred made a quick trip to Milton and discovered that, indeed, Ellen was not managing her affairs or her personal care well. She returned home, discussed the situation with Lloyd, and they agreed Ellen should be moved to Sunnyside where Mildred could look after her more closely. Knowing it would not work to have Ellen in their home because of so many stairs and all the students who came and went, Mildred reserved a room at a local nursing home, contacted the family lawyer, James Salvini, and moved Ellen to Sunnyside. After a rough couple of weeks, Ellen began to settle in, and with Mr. Salvini's advice Mildred went to court and had herself appointed as Ellen's legal guardian in both Oregon and Washington. She moved Ellen's money to a bank in Sunnyside, invested some of it, and made several more trips to Milton to clear the house and get it ready to rent. (Mildred was to inherit the house and all its contents.) Then she wrote Harold, Florence and Crans long letters explaining why she had taken this action thinking they would be glad to have her be responsible for the care of this very cranky relative whom neither her older brother and sister had ever liked.

But they were not glad at all. After a few angry phone calls, Harold and Florence decided to sue Mildred, accusing her of usurping their rights as heirs and trying to abscond with the assets of Ellen's estate. They also implied that Lloyd had put her up to this. Believing completely in this conspiracy theory, Florence and Harold were furious. Mildred was stunned; Lloyd was embarrassed. When two hearing dates were set, Mildred and her lawyer drove to Pendleton to attend them. Each ended with a ruling supporting Mildred's actions, which she stated were aimed at preserving what resources Ellen had so that she would be supported by her own finances until her death. Harold was incensed to have lost his opportunity to receive his inheritance before it was used up, and shouted at Mildred that he would take her "to the highest court in the land." Then he fired his lawyer.

In early 1962 before Lloyd had recovered completely from his surgery the previous spring, Vergie called to say she had been abandoned by her husband and had no means of support for herself and her baby. Mildred and Lloyd sent money via the Episcopal church in San Rafael for Vergie to buy a bus ticket to come home to stay with them. The total time without children Mildred and Lloyd had spent together during their marriage was the first eleven months before Vergie Ellen had been born plus the six months after Tom left for college in the fall of 1961.

John Sahr finished dental school in June 1962, and because he and Bobbie were absolutely broke (they had $33 and some odd cents to their name), he joined the Army and borrowed money so he could to get to boot camp. Bobbie, pregnant with baby number two, came home and stayed on the farm with John's parents while John drove to San Antonio, Texas, for his basic training in the blazing heat of summer. Then he borrowed money again to buy a plane ticket from Yakima to Boston for Bobbie and the baby. For the next two years, John was stationed at Fort Devens, Massachusetts, where their daughter Kathryn Ann was born in February 1963.

Lloyd had struggled with his health during this time and came down twice with pneumonia. Then he got a staph infection in his nose that threatened to get in his blood stream and become deadly. When Mildred finally got Lloyd to go to the doctor, Dr. Furukawa injected him with a huge dose of penicillin to hit the infection hard. While it did halt the progress of the infection, Lloyd had an allergic reaction to the drug and broke out in a rash that covered most of his body and itched like fury for days. He was more miserable from the rash than the infection and the experience did not improve his opinion about going to the doctor.

Vergie began working at Lloyd's office to help out and was invaluable in keeping it open and functioning during Lloyd's absences. Mildred took care of Kenneth and taught piano lessons as well. Each person in the household was responsible for keeping on top of his or her job. It wasn't too long until Mildred began to show the wear and tear on her while trying to juggle her responsibilities and she began having a series of hard colds. But baby Kenny thrived. He loved his Gamma and his Mommy, and he insisted on calling Lloyd "Daddy."

During this time, Tom came home from the UW where it seemed he had not been ready for the rigors of the academic aspects of college life. A quarter or two at Yakima Valley Junior College was helpful and soon he enrolled at Western Washington University in Bellingham where he began a major in political science and held a job at a radio station. During the summer he met a pretty young woman, Mary Ellen Englehard from Spokane, and the two were soon engaged.

Shortly after the Sahrs' second child Kathryn was born in February 1963, Mildred flew out to stay for two weeks with them. Exhausted by her heavy teaching schedule and never having stamina for travelling, Mildred was ill most of the time she was there. She remained worried about how things were going at home with Lloyd, the business, and with Vergie Ellen having to run the household as well as work and take care of Kenneth.

After two years in the army, the Sahrs returned to the Valley in 1964. They selected Yakima as home and soon John started his dental practice. Yakima was only a 45-minute drive to Sunnyside and they enjoyed visiting Lloyd and Mildred as well as Vergie Ellen and Kenneth. The Sahrs' third child, a daughter, Elizabeth, was born in Yakima in September 1964.

Mildred continued teaching piano, playing the organ at church, directing the choir, attending meetings of PEO, a women's philanthropic organization, the Washington State Music Teachers, playing the piano for Kiwanians at their luncheon meetings every Thursday, and every August attending Sea Fair on Lake Washington in Seattle where she and Lloyd hobnobbed with the other mayors from throughout the state.

By the end of spring 1965, Mildred's reserve hit bottom. She realized that she was not going to be able to continue caring for four year-old Kenny, teach piano, cook and clean, and take care of her other responsibilities. She still was doing all the music at church, and she was active in PEO where she had held an office nearly every year. She and Vergie found a day care facility for Kenneth that spring, and although it was costly, it was good for everybody concerned. Florence and Harold were planning to sue her for the second time, but Crans called Mildred to say he believed her version and wanted nothing to do with the suit.

Tom and Mary Ellen were married in mid-August 1965 in Spokane. To the delight of the extended Smith clan, Mary Ellen was Roman Catholic and the wedding was at Sacred Heart Catholic Church on Spokane's South Hill. It was a lovely wedding, but Mildred and Lloyd were both exhausted and were glad to get back home to Sunnyside. Tom's grades had been very good and he had surprised his parents with the announcement that he was going to apply to Gonzaga Law School in Spokane. Both Mildred and Lloyd were exceedingly pleased. Maybe their son would be able to achieve Lloyd's own unfulfilled dream of becoming a lawyer.

Only a few months later in mid-December 1965, Lloyd suffered a severe heart attack. An evening phone call to Dr. Furukawa set Millie in motion. She drove Lloyd to the hospital rather than waiting for an ambulance. Lloyd remained in the hospital for over a week and gradually seemed to be regaining his strength as Christmas approached. The plan had been for Bobbie to drive from Yakima on Wednesday, December 22nd, to visit Lloyd in the hospital while Mildred watched her children. But during the night and early morning of the 21st and 22nd, a moist cold front moved through the Valley and covered the roads between Yakima and Sunnyside with a sheet of black ice. Both radio and TV alerts warned people to stay off the roads.

When Bobbie called Mildred at 10 a.m. with the news that the roads were still bad and that she was apprehensive about striking out on the two-lane curvy, ice-covered roads with her three children, Mildred said, "Please stay home. I just don't want to have to worry about you, too." Relieved, Bobbie did. She and John and the children would arrive as planned on Saturday to spend Christmas day with Mildred, Vergie and Kenneth. The plan was for each family member to visit Lloyd for short intervals during the day. Lloyd expected to be released on the 26th. But it was not to be.

At 5 a.m., December 24, 1965, Mildred called to tell Bobbie that Lloyd had died at three-thirty that morning from a massive heart attack.

Aftermath

Unexpected turns in the road
Sunnyside 1965 - 1968

MILDRED STRUGGLED EMOTIONALLY, FINANCIALLY AND physically for the
first year after Lloyd's death. Although exhausted after the funeral, two weeks later she decided to resume teaching her piano students. She and Vergie had to keep up the routine because
both Kenneth and keeping the office open required it, but they
struggled. Besides diverting her attention from her grief, teaching also gave Mildred some needed income because Lloyd's will
had left Mildred in a bind. He had followed his bank friend's advice and put his half of their assets into an irrevocable living trust,
which was to be managed by the Old National Bank of Spokane.
However, because Lloyd had purchased so many pieces of property during the course of his real estate transactions, there was little
disposable cash in the bank. To complicate matters, the manager
of the trust also did not release any assets to Mildred while he was
sorting out the properties, the rentals and the business. All the
rent receipts and the income from the Lloyd F. Smith Agency went
into the bank to apply to the real estate mortgages. Mildred saw
no income from it for over six months. If she had not been teaching, and had she not built up a small savings account of her own,

she would have had no way to pay for her utilities, buy gas for the car, or even buy groceries.

Finally, she confronted a bank official, who, after a tongue lashing from her, did manage to make some funds available for her. It had become apparent to Mildred right away that many of the small houses Lloyd had bought were not in good condition and had dubious value either as rentals or as potential sales. Mildred authorized the bank to clean some of them up and get them sold, but this took time and the bank dragged its feet. It took nearly a year for the estate to go through probate, and it took some leaning on the bank by Jim Salvini, her lawyer, to get it done.

In the meantime, Vergie ran the office and got temporarily certified to keep both the real estate and the insurance businesses going. There was enough income to pay its bills and provide Vergie with a small salary, but Mildred got nothing. As soon as she got a true picture of the financial situation, Mildred, who had no intention of keeping the business, put it up for sale. Lloyd also had purchased another building in the downtown area with a good, steady renter that Mildred intended to keep, along with the building the agency was in.

1966 was hard on Mildred. Lonely for her husband, upset over the mess in the estate, having an active five year-old's needs to think about and Vergie and the office to worry about, she found great solace in her students. Their parents were wonderful to her as were her PEO sisters and the parishioners at Holy Trinity. That she didn't hear much from Lloyd's family was a sorrow for her. Vergie, in the meantime, enjoyed her work at the office and hoped Mildred would change her mind about selling the business. Mildred discovered that the business had slipped a little during the two years prior to Lloyd's death, probably due to his declining stamina, and within a year after his death it was noticeably in decline.

Mildred recalled the previous four or five years when Lloyd had had a series of health issues. She had become worried about him and had made doctor's appointments for him with Dr. Furukawa whose office was on the floor above Lloyd's office. Repeatedly she had received a call from Marion Furukawa, Dr. Furukawa's wife and nurse, that Lloyd had failed to appear for an appointment. Frustrated, Mildred would make another appointment, called Lloyd's office and had the secretary block out the time, and told Mrs. Furukawa, "You just go down there and take Lloyd by the arm and tell him he has to go with you!" This worked a couple of times. A few months after his death, one day when Mildred was rummaging around in the bathroom's medicine cupboard, she discovered a pile of prescriptions that Lloyd never had filled dating back three or four years.

By the end of 1966 Mildred had received a low offer to buy what was left of Lloyd's business and she knew she needed to accept it. Vergie began looking for work in Yakima while Mildred considered the offer. Mildred turned again to Jim Salvini for advice and he said he thought she should sell. She also tried to force the bank to liquidate at least some of the small rental houses that had become empty and give her half of the proceeds while the other half went into the trust. But they were slow to act. Mildred took the lead and hired a crew to clean up, repair, and paint several of them, after which the bank got interested and then put on the market. Then the trust office in the Sunnyside branch of the Old National Bank of Spokane closed and consolidated with the home office in Spokane. Now she had to deal with someone she did not know who was two hundred miles away! By early spring of 1967, Mildred had agreed to sell the business, Vergie and Kenny had moved to Yakima so Vergie would be near her new job, and Mildred was near exhaustion in an empty, quiet house.

A month or so later, one June afternoon while Mildred was finishing up a post card she intended to dash over to the post office and mail before it closed at five, her doorbell rang. At the front door was a gentleman whom she did not recognize. They spoke for a few minutes about how he had known Lloyd and done some business with him, and was sorry for her loss. Mildred was friendly, but cool because she wanted him to leave so she could get the postcard mailed. Clearly he wasn't ready to leave, so she sighed and asked him to come in. After some idle talk and while Mildred, thought to herself, "When is this guy going to leave?" he mentioned that he had lost his wife Angie in a car accident the summer of 1966 in which he and two of his daughters were also injured. By the time he left, Mildred had decided he had a pleasant personality and agreed to go to dinner with him in a few days. She was amazed at herself, but she needed diversion.

In July, the Sahrs planned a two-week trip to Priest Lake and Bobbie insisted that Mildred come with them. They had purchased a small camping trailer, which they used for one week, then rented a cabin at Elkins for the second week. Mildred was reluctant, but finally agreed to come along. It had been eight years since she had been to the lake and a lot had changed in her life during that time. Most of all, she needed a change of scenery and a chance to breathe the clean, fresh mountain air.

Once there, the family quickly established a routine of late breakfasts, off to the beach about 10, lunch at 12:30 to 1, back to the beach for the afternoon. Mildred enjoyed watching the Sahr children's antics in the water, which reminded her of her own children in the very same place only twenty years prior. She loved the quiet of the trailer, then of the cabin after lunch when she took a nap. Of course, everyone had to go look for a board for her to put between the mattress and the springs once they moved into the cabin. She insisted that the mattresses had not been changed since they had first come there in 1943!

Bobbie noticed that Mildred had been acting somewhat subdued for the first few days, but she attributed that to how tired her mother was, and the new experience of being in such close quarters with their family. On the second or third morning, on one of those gloriously beautiful days as they settled in on their beach towels under the red- and white-striped beach umbrella, Mildred announced, "I have something to tell you." Then she giggled. Bobbie immediately went into a "high alert" mode. She said, "What's that?" and Mildred giggled again.

Mildred then told Bobbie the story about writing the postcard and having the doorbell ring. Giggle. She described how she had made the man stand on the porch because she didn't know him while he told her he had known Lloyd, and that, because it didn't seem as if he would go away until she let him in, she invited him in. Giggle. They talked for a while, he about his family and their auto accident and she about her children, Lloyd's unexpected death, etc. Then she had looked at her watch and realized she had missed the mail and became a little miffed. She thought to herself, 'Why won't this man just leave?' Giggle. Then he had asked her out to dinner and, because she was totally unprepared to be asked and had no reason not to, she had accepted. So unlike her. Giggle.

All of a sudden the light dawned. Bobbie realized she was now the adult and Mildred had become the teenager. So, let's get the details: Where did you go? Where does he live? What do you know about him?

His name was Chester Karl Schlien, Chett, for short. He was a farmer from Mabton, a little town southeast of Sunnyside. His wife, Angie, had been a highly respected elementary school teacher in Mabton before her death. She had also had breast cancer. Their three daughters, Carolyn, Nayda, and Marlys, had all been excellent students through high school, and were working toward professions: Carolyn had graduated from WSU in vocational business and was to begin teaching in Camas that September; Nayda was at WSU pursuing a degree in elementary education, and Marlys had gone to business school and had a well-paying job at Battelle NW in Richland. The death of their mother had been a blow to the girls who were now concerned about their father's depression and lack of appetite. Each of his daughters took turns coming home on weekends to Mabton to be with Chett and to cook up a week's menu for him.

A year after Angie's death, and spurred on by his daughters, he acknowledged that he needed to get out of the house, to go out with friends, or visit neighbors. He finally had gotten the courage to ask a woman out. Because he didn't want the rumors to fly in Mabton, he thought of Lloyd Smith's widow in Sunnyside. He didn't know her, but he had liked and respected Lloyd. Maybe she'd like some company, too.

On their first date, they had gone to dinner at Hill's Cafe out on Highway 410, which skirts the north side of Sunnyside. They had both had a very enjoyable time. Giggle. Mildred was not used to being escorted by such a gentleman. Giggle. Lloyd had figured if a woman was strong enough to go out for dinner, she could open her own doors and take her own seat. Chett, however, rushed to open Mildred's car door, open the cafe door, and hold her chair while she sat down. Giggle. *And,* he had asked her for another date! Giggle.

On their second date, they had gone to the Safari Room, just a few blocks from Mildred's house on Edison Avenue in downtown Sunnyside. They had walked from Mildred's to the cafe and back. Chett had taken hold of her elbow when they crossed the street. Giggle. He asked if he could call on her again. Giggle.

In the meantime, Nayda had come home for the weekend and found her father much less depressed. There was still food in the freezer that he hadn't eaten that had been fixed by Marlys the weekend before. "Dad, are you eating? There's food in here." "I went out a couple of times," he replied. "Well, good for you! Did you go with anyone?" "Just a friend," he said, clearly not planning to tell her which one. Before she left, she fixed him a casserole, and put it in the freezer. When she got back to her apartment, she immediately called her sisters and reported the good news.

Mildred was concerned about the expense of going out to eat so often. She had to watch her finances very closely and didn't know what Chett's circumstances were, so when he called again, she suggested she make the meal and they would eat at her house. All she had on hand was a pot roast, so she fixed that with potatoes and carrots, and cooked up a peach pie she had frozen the previous summer. Giggle. Little did she know how Chett loved pot roast and home-cooked meals! She was definitely surprised when he got up from the table to help clean up the kitchen! Had Lloyd ever done that? Giggle. She had sent leftovers home with him. Giggle.

What a revelation! Mildred had a *life*! Bobbie was thunderstruck and yet very happy for her mother. She was even more impressed with the giddiness Mildred was displaying. It had been a long time since Mildred had been this light of heart. Bobbie definitely was going to have to meet this man. And now that the secret was out to Mildred's family and while Mildred was on this trip, Chett planned to tell his girls that he was dating. Giggle.

a Wedding, a Life

Sunnyside - 1967-1972

By Thanksgiving 1967 it was evident that Chett and Millie were an item. It wasn't long until Chett popped the question and Millie accepted. Mildred had resumed her teaching schedule when school started, but now Chett was a frequent dinner guest and the two of them conspired about how to get their two families together to meet each other. Bobbie met each of Chett's daughters one by one, and Vergie had met two of them, but Tom had not met anyone. He was now very busy in Spokane, a newly licensed attorney working for the State Prosecutor's Office. Mary Ellen was busy with their two infant sons, Eric and Michael, born in August 1966 and August 1967.

Initially, Chett's daughters were mildly pleased for their father, but Nayda was concerned by Chett's increased interest in Mildred and felt that he was being unkind to their mother's memory by "taking up" with a woman so soon after Angie's death. All the girls had worried about Chett's deep depression following the accident, but to take just one woman out, then date her regularly was rushing it, Nayda thought. Neither family had known the other and all three of Chett's daughters preferred that Chett take his time with the relationship. Both sets of adult children wanted to check each other out, but all six were spread all over the state and it was difficult to get together at any one time. It wasn't until Nayda talked to a Mabton neighbor about her concerns about Chett's and Mildred's relationship that she saw it in a new light. The neighbor told her that it was precisely *because* Chett and Angie had had such a good marriage that Chett might want to try again. That helped. Mildred had met Chett's girls one by one, and they seemed to like her. She told them up front that after her own experience with a stepmother, she never wanted to be one herself. She and Chett drove to Yakima for him to meet Vergie, Kenneth, and Bobbie and her family.

In the meantime, Harold and Florence's second attempt to sue Mildred over the estate of Ellen Milby finally was resolved in early fall. At a hearing in Pendleton a different judge again sided with Mildred and suggested that she should have taken some recompense from the estate for all her work. Plus, she had paid Mr. Salvini out of her own pocket. But he did side with Harold and Florence on one issue: Fred and Ellen's rings. Mildred had removed them from the house and put them in a safe deposit box in Sunnyside for safekeeping. Fred's large diamond and Ellen's wedding ring were notable, plus another ruby ring of Ellen's. The judge ruled that since Mildred had removed the rings from the house before Ellen's death that they were not among the contents of the house, and therefore not directly inherited by Mildred. He suggested they be divided among the heirs. Mr. Salvini suggested that the furniture had been removed also so the house could be rented, but it was Ellen's intent that all the furnishings would go to Mildred, and she had acted responsibly by putting the rings and the furniture in a safe place. The judge did not yield. Harold and Florence took the rings and they were never seen again. Mildred's life could move forward once again, but by the time she returned to Sunnyside, she was greatly saddened and was not on speaking terms with her brother and sister.

On Thanksgiving Day 1967 at Mildred's insistence, the two families gathered at Mildred's for Thanksgiving dinner. Mildred and Chett could each talk about their late spouses with respect and love in front of their families. There were many questions asked as the Smith "side" tried to get to know the Schlien "side" and vice versa. When the adult children compared their growing up years, which had been only a few miles from each other, each of them had different reference points to their previous lives: different friends, different relatives, different churches, different experiences, different home town, different schools. None of them had crossed paths. For Chett, the hardest part was getting used to the turmoil that Mildred's six grandchildren brought to the gathering. Kenneth and John were six, Kathy was four and a half, Betsy was three and a half, Eric was one, and Michael was three months old. Later Chett admitted to Mildred he wasn't sure he was ready to be a grandfather, but a grandfather of six all of a sudden was a lot to absorb.

The highlight of that first Thanksgiving dinner with the Schlien and Smith families had to be when Tom stood up and proposed a toast to the engaged parents. It was a rousing wish for good health and great happiness for years to come. He raised his glass of wine and drained it. The others cheered and took sips from their glasses. Then someone else made a toast to the joining of the two families. The group shouted, "Hear! Hear!" and sipped their wine while Tom drained his second full glass of wine in less than two minutes. Following the third toast, someone suggested that they'd better stop toasting and start eating before Tom fell off his chair.

Now that their intent to get married was announced, and their adult children had given their approval, Mildred and Chett set a date for the next February after Mildred turned sixty and was eligible to receive Social Security. Chett's birthday was the next month when he could begin to draw his Social Security, too. On February 10th, 1968, wearing a new lime green dress, Mildred and Chett were married in a small ceremony at St. Michael's Episcopal Church in Yakima. The Rev. Riley Johnson officiated. Mildred didn't get a long walk down the aisle or a bridal gown, but she did get the sanctuary this time! Each of Chett's and Mildred's oldest children were their witnesses: Carolyn for Mildred and Tom for Chett, while the remaining four offspring "stood up" for them. A small reception was held following the ceremony at Bobbie and John's home at 1212 South 21st Avenue in Yakima. Mildred had had made a chicken casserole herself and it cooked while the ceremony was being held. Chett's sister and brother in-law Florence and Al Ivey attended as did Mildred's long-time friends Maynard and Aileen Shearer, eighteen people in all. There was a lovely wedding cake and Tom toasted the couple again, this time with champagne. In honor of aunt Ellen, Bobbie remembered to light the candles on the table. After a weeklong honeymoon on the coast of Oregon, Mr. and Mrs. Chester Karl Schlien returned to Sunnyside and Mildred's new life began. But first they must settle their finances.

The Bride and Groom toast each other
February 10, 1968

Chett and Mildred realized that the worst thing they could do to their adult children at this point in their lives would be to merge their separate estates. To do so, they felt, would be to deny the parts their deceased spouses had played toward their current financial stability and might cause petty jealousies or hurt feelings to develop between their two sets of adult children. So Millie and Chett made new wills, which included some critical financial decisions: (1) They would keep their pre-marriage finances completely separate and not co-mingle any of their assets; (2) Mildred's children would not inherit from Chett, and Chett's children would not inherit from Millie. They even went so far as to have a grocery purse into which each put a twenty-dollar bill at the same time, and from that wallet alone bought all their groceries. When the money got low, each would put another twenty in. They shared a small checking account from which their other usual bills were paid. Each month they deposited money from their separate pre-marriage funds.

It was a sweetheart deal from the beginning because none of the offspring had any opportunity to be jealous or doubt the integrity of their stepparent. Thus, as Mildred sold her houses and buildings, Chett and his daughters had no access to the proceeds, and likewise when Chett sold his Mabton home, his ranch, and other farmland near Royal City, Mildred and her family were, as Mildred liked to say, "out of the picture." This decision was made without their offspring's input and when revealed, was completely acceptable to all. It made for a solid foundation on which the two families could forge their new family status without having any financial issues between them.

Chett, happily freed from the rigors and responsibilities of farming and the impact farming had on his arthritis, began to yearn for the open road. He and Millie purchased a used Airstream trailer and went on many short trips throughout Washington. Hooked on traveling, and after experiencing another bout of arthritis the next winter, he convinced Millie that she should stop teaching piano so they could go south for the winter in their little Airstream. Millie had to admit the teaching was wearing on her, even though she had reduced the number of students she taught each day. Chett didn't like to see her work so hard, and he didn't like being in competition for her time. Finally, in April 1969, Mildred held her last student recital in the Washington Elementary School Auditorium. From her students and their parents she received a large bouquet of roses. A few days later down the road they went.

In the meantime, Chett's daughters had begun to build their own lives. Mildred became "mother of the bride" three more times: Marlys and Kirk Williams were married at Holy Trinity Episcopal Church June 21, 1969; Carolyn and Walt Quantrille were married in the Sunnyside Methodist Church on August 2, 1969, and Nayda and Greg Littlefield were married in Moses Lake on June 10th, 1972, at Mt. Olive Lutheran Church where Kathy and Betsy Sahr, now nine and almost eight, were candle lighters, and Johnny Sahr and Kenneth Rosson, both nearly eleven, pulled the long rope to ring the church bell after the service.

In the first two years of their marriage Chett lost his mother Marie Schlien, and Mildred lost her aunt Ellen. Both women had been in the Sunnyside Nursing Home at the same time and for the first year or so Marie had been able enough to look in on Ellen who was falling further and further into the shadows of senility. The two women passed away within a few months of each other. For two winters, Chett and Millie travelled to Arizona where Chett luxuriated in the warm, dry climate. Golf became his passion. No longer having to worry about Ellen or Marie, Millie and Chett bought a larger trailer then they bought a double wide mobile home on Sam Snead Avenue in Apache Wells Park in Mesa, Arizona. Never dreaming she would ever be a golfer, Millie bought a set of golf clubs and began to learn the game. Millie also affiliated with the PEO chapter there and joined St. Mark's Episcopal Church in Mesa. The couple realized they liked this life: nine months in the sun during the fall, and winter, then up to the cooler, more moderate climate of Washington for the spring and summer to visit their six children and growing number of grandchildren. Life was good.

MILDRED'S LAST STUDENT RECITAL WITH FLOWERS FROM HER STUDENTS

1975: Millie & Chett in front of their home.
Apache Wells, 2522 Snead Drive, Mesa, Arizona

34

The Arizona Years

Mesa Arizona - 1972-1987

IN THE NEXT FEW YEARS Chett became the grandfather of six: Karl and Kraig Williams, Angie and Lori Quantrille, and Bryce and Kayla Littlefield arrived to round out the next Schlien generation. Mildred's family began to realize that Chett's coming into their mother's life probably gave her an extra ten to fifteen years of happiness. Mildred sold the family home in Sunnyside and had her grand piano shipped to their new address in Mesa. She loved having it handy whenever she wanted to play and playing it helped keep her arthritic fingers more flexible. They enjoyed all the perks of a warm climate and senior citizen activities. One Christmas morning Mildred wrote to Bobbie in snowy Selah,

"...I'm sitting on our patio in my shorts and it's 72 degrees out. I'm thinking of you and your family and what excitement must be going on at your home, but I am so content here that I can't imagine being anywhere else..."

Mildred enjoyed her PEO group, and both Mildred and Chett joined golfing groups. They went square dancing and attended potluck dinners. Mildred carved out a tiny plot of hard desert in their yard and buried garbage faithfully there for years until she had created a rich little area in which she grew abundant tomatoes, roses and petunias. They had new friends for dinner and afterward played cards or were themselves the guests at others' homes. Mildred bought a bike and rode out into the desert that bordered their Apache Wells development. They took jaunts out into the countryside visiting other interesting communities and scenic locations. They marveled at cotton fields, orange and grapefruit groves, and nut farms. They even took a couple of long road trips on their way to or from their summers in Washington, even going as far as the east coast one time and traveling to visit Moriarty, New Mexico, where Mildred had been born.

As 1980 rolled around, Millie began to have a growing apprehension that all was not well with Chett. He had become increasingly forgetful and his driving became so erratic that Millie made sure she went with him on every errand so that she could be his co-pilot. He had trouble playing golf, forgot when he was supposed to meet his buddies on which course, and fumbled with his tools. He had begun awakening during the night and wandering throughout the house, sometimes unlocking doors, or turning on light switches or stove burners. He forgot words when he was trying to say something, but of course, Millie thought, we all do that. Millie researched supplements for the elderly and they both began taking them.

When his girls and their families came to see them in Arizona, Chett seemed to brighten up and they thought Millie was noticing something that wasn't there. At first, she agreed with them, because she, too, had noticed she had less energy, had lost her interest in playing golf, sometimes forgot words, and forgot where she put things, walked into another room and couldn't remember why she'd gone there. Maybe this was just a part of the aging process.

The two of them had attended many meetings that are popular around areas where senior citizens retire: heart health, new miracle vitamin therapy, new this, new that, etc., and had tried out some new ideas that made their children cringe when they told them what they were doing: chelation therapy and coffee enemas among the more outrageous. Mildred continued their regimen of food supplements, bought a book about prescription medications that she used as her reference bible, and began to eliminate certain foods from her own diet. She bought a yogurt-making machine and began making her own yogurt. Some days Chett's behavior was just fine; other days she became alarmed. The more she read, the more convinced she was that something was wrong with them both. For herself, she was convinced she had developed Burghers Disease and COPD which are caused from having inhaled cigarette smoke over a long period of time. Since she had grown up with her father's heavy smoking and then Lloyd's smoking during their marriage, she was convinced she had breathed in secondhand smoke for forty-five years and was now ill from it. However, her doctors did not agree and suggested she might be a little depressed, something that frequently occurs in the elderly. This suggestion made her furious.

Chett, on the other hand, in his farming years had used insecticides and pesticides on his crops year after year. He had never worn a mask and sometimes had not used gloves when he handled the containers. Perhaps these substances had entered his system and were now causing him some harm. Yet, Chett's girls still did not see the change in his behavior in the same light as Mildred did until Chett's driving became a concern for everyone.

By 1982 Mildred was now a constant copilot in the passenger seat giving Chett complete instructions about what lane to be in, how fast to go, when to brake, where to turn, and where to park. One of their friends thought she was nagging him and should back off, but if she didn't give him instructions, he made mistake after mistake and nearly caused several accidents. Bobbie's children refused to ride with them if he was driving, and Bobbie shared her concern with her mother that Chett's poor driving was endangering her life. By 1985 Millie herself was becoming afraid to drive with him, and the trip north in the summer pulling the trailer was very scary for her. When Chett's girls tried to talk their dad out of making the long drive north every summer, he wouldn't listen to them. When Millie's kids tried to do the same, they got the same result.

One summer a few years earlier, they had decided to stay in Arizona for the summer, but Millie who suffered mightily from the heat stated later that that experience nearly killed her. Chett enjoyed the heat, and refused to install an air conditioning system in their mobile home. All they had was a swamp cooler which, on the hottest of days, merely moved the warm air around a little. At night while Chett snored happily away in their bedroom with the temperature above 90 at night for days on end, Mildred paced the floor and couldn't sleep.

The winter of 1986-1987 was very difficult for both Chett and Millie. Chett's confusion increased and his speech faculty lessened. Mildred did not remind him when his driver's license needed renewing, and when he discovered his license had expired (he got a ticket) he was adamant about going to go take the test, but he refused to study the booklet. When he went to the DMV to take the test, he had to use a machine and did not understand how to use it. He failed. He was given another chance to come back in a few weeks, but eventually he forgot. However, he still wanted to drive. Finally, after he got another ticket, he agreed to let Millie do the driving.

Millie was running out of steam and made the decision that the winter of 1986-1987 would be their last winter in Arizona. They were both nearly seventy-nine. Chett had begun to need Millie help him with his personal hygiene. Millie knew she needed to get Chett home to be nearer his girls so they could share what quality time he had left. On February 25, 1987, she wrote Bobbie:

"I'll hold out as long as I can, but I know I'll need help and free time away. 24 hours is already rough. Not having all the household worries & work & errands; meals and housework provided would be a big help and give me some time for myself. A change will be hard for both of us but I'm afraid we've reached the deciding point."

She had begun to worry about their finances looking ahead into the future at the possibility that Chett would sometime have to go into a nursing home. He did not have long term care insurance and didn't know if he was too old to qualify for any. She worried about how long Chett's finances would last, remembering that her aunt Ellen had been in a nursing home for six years. Then she admitted that she, herself, was having medical issues, especially with the pain in her legs at night, her heart skipping beats, and her fatigue. She had discussed her concerns with Chett's daughters, and in Bobbie's letter went on to say,

"Nayda and Marlys have sent brochures of their new retirement apts both sound nice. "I'm ready to make the move especially for Chett to be near one of his daughters. I know I'll need help (soon)."

Marlys and Bobbie suggested they fly down to Phoenix and take a long Memorial Day Weekend to help Millie and Chett move home, pulling their trailer with Chett's Buick, and driving the little Subaru SUV Millie had bought several years earlier. Millie insisted they would all four sleep in the trailer each night while on the road to save money. Millie didn't want to wait until after schools were out because the heat was already affecting her. The plan was put into action.

Marlys and Bobbie arrived on a Thursday afternoon at the Phoenix Airport, but there was no Chett or Millie to met them. Leaving Marlys to watch for their parents where they had deplaned, Bobbie went down to the baggage area to see if they were there. What she saw shocked her. Millie was leaning against a pillar weeping. She looked frail and appeared to be ready to keel over. When Bobbie hugged her and got her to sit down, she asked her mother where Chett was. Mildred replied, "I don't know" and began to weep again. It seemed that Chett had left his favorite baseball cap with the caption "World's Best Grandpa" in the car, and had turned around to go get it just as the two of them reached the airport baggage area.

Mildred tried to persuade Chett to stay with her because he had been getting lost so often lately, but he pulled away from her and said he was going to go get it. Since they had barely gotten there on time to meet the plane, Mildred didn't know what to do, so she watched Chett walk toward the parking lot with a sinking heart. She knew she was too weak to take his arm and force him to stay with her, so she decided to try to find an airport security person to help and paused to look around. That's when Bobbie found her leaning against the pillar weeping, with no security personnel in sight.

Leaving her mother, Bobbie ran up the escalator to find Marlys and let her know what was going on. Just after the three women gathered and Marlys was leaving to find Chett or a security person, he appeared down the long hallway with a big grin on his face. He had come from a completely different direction than where the car was parked, and sure enough, he was wearing his ball cap. He had found the car, but had gotten turned around on his way back and had had the sense to ask " baggage?" from someone who told him which way to go.

After they got home, Mildred took each daughter aside and told them that she was not ready for the trip home because Chett had been following her around for the last couple of weeks going through boxes and unpacking suitcases after she had filled them. The worst incident had happened that morning. Chett had decided to go outside and move his golf cart, but he had gotten the forward gear mixed up with the reverse gear and had pressed his foot hard on the accelerator and, when the cart started going in reverse, he was so surprised that he didn't remember to take his foot off and brake. By the time he got stopped, he had taken out two of the neighbor's awning supports and one of theirs. The neighbors had already left for the summer, and Mildred was flummoxed. Frustrated, she had gotten angry with him, and then felt guilty because he was oblivious to the extent of the damage and she had hurt his feelings.

The girls got on the phone quickly and called a mobile home sales business that said they could send someone out first thing in the morning. Then they started trying to help Mildred finish what she needed to get done. Bobbie helped pack while Marlys diverted Chett into the living room with pictures and stories about her boys and Kirk. Mildred was a wreck and so tired she was afraid to sleep and afraid she wouldn't sleep. She asked Bobbie and Marlys to listen for Chett in case he got up in the night and started wandering. The plan was to leave by noon the next day and try to drive two hundred and fifty miles.

The next morning while the women finished loading the Subaru and the trailer, Marlys noticed she couldn't get the interior trailer light to come on. Upon investigating, she discovered that the battery was dead. A few days prior, with Mildred's help, Chett had managed to get the trailer hitched up to the car, so Marlys suggested she start the car and see if they could get the battery charged that way. But the car battery was dead, too. Apparently, when no one was look- ing, Chett had gone out to the trailer and turned all the lights on in both the trailer and left the car door open. Before bedtime, Marlys had noticed the light and had gone outside and shut the door and locked the car. Overnight the juice in both batteries had drained away. Exasperated at yet another problem to fix, Millie asked Chett angrily, "Chett, did you go out and turn those lights on?" "Yes," he replied. Millie said, "But why, Chett? Why did you do that?" He, knowing something was wrong but not realizing what, was crestfallen to see Mildred so angry. He replied, "Because it was dark out and you needed to see."

Chett's sweet disposition had been the reason he was trying to help. Picking up things and moving them, or turning on lights and switches was his way of trying to help. The more tired Millie got, the sharper her tongue and the shorter her temper got. Chett, while try- ing to help out, had only made things more difficult.

Once again, the girls got on the phone. They found someone to drive out immediately to the house to charge the two batteries. That was a seventy-five dollar house call. Then Millie wanted to quibble over repair costs with the man who came out to assess the damage to the neighbor's house and theirs from the golf cart attack. Bobbie told her, "Mom, at this point, you need to agree to whatever it's going to cost because we absolutely HAVE to get on the road in order to get up to Washington by Monday afternoon. Bobbie, an English teacher, had to be back in her classroom at Selah High School on Tuesday morning, and Marlys, the business manager of her husband's dental practice, also had to be back to get her boys off to school and herself to the office on Tuesday morning. This was not going to be an easy trip even with all things in order.

3 5

Moving Home

May 1987

AFTER A LATE BREAKFAST AND hastily cleaned up kitchen, they pulled away from Apache Wells about 12:30. Bobbie and Millie were in the lead in the Subaru with Marlys and Chett in the Buick pulling the trailer. They got to the end of the block when Marlys honked, stopped and got out of the car. Bobbie got out and met her in the street. "The Buick is out of gas," she said with her eyes as big as dollars. "It's on empty." Pause of disbelief. "OK, I guess we find a gas station," Bobbie replied looking up at the blue Arizona sky. "Mom will know where the nearest one is."

But Millie did not want to go to the nearest one, because it was more expensive. So she directed Bobbie to drive in the opposite direction of the way they needed to go to get out of town so they could gas up both cars at their favorite gas station. This took another half an hour. Finally, the caravan drove west, then north out of Mesa and over to Highway 10, which led to the route they were going to take. Half an hour after that at 1:30, Millie said, "You need to pull over at that exit and stop in that town." "Why?" Bobbie asked. "Because we haven't had lunch and I need to feed Chett." (translated "It's past noon and noon is when we eat.") Finally, parked in a shady spot Millie remembered from a previous trip, Bobbie said,

"I'll help you make some sandwiches and we can eat going down the road."

That was not to be. Mildred never ate "going down the road." Mildred ate at her trailer table and never hurried through her meal. Mildred also never hurried in the sandwich-making process. Each slice of bread was buttered just so. Each slice had just this much mayonnaise and that much mustard and the proper piece of hand-washed and patted dry lettuce, two slices of turkey, and cut in half properly, put on a plate, with a couple of pieces of carrots on the side. Milk for everyone. "No thanks for milk," Marlys said. "I'll just work on my Pepsi." "Oh, no," Millie said, "You shouldn't drink that." Marlys had milk.

After they ate, of course the utensils had to be washed and put away. Still Millie would not agree to get back in the car so they could go. Her food wouldn't digest properly if she didn't take a little rest. "Chett needs his nap," she said. "Don't rush us!"

So Bobbie and Marlys went outside and had a parley. Obviously, they had not taken into account the need for Millie and Chett to keep to their usual routine while on the road, so this was going to mean careful planning each day to assure that they would cover enough miles to get them home by Monday evening.

Finally, they got on the road again. At 4:30, Millie said she was exhausted and had enough traveling for one day. She knew of a good KOA campground in the next town and wanted to pull in there. Another mid-road consultation: both Marlys and Bobbie were aghast. However, Bobbie also could tell Mildred's exhaustion was real. When they pulled into the KOA Campground, they found a shady spot where Marlys could back the trailer in without having to unhook the car. Marlys and Bobbie sauntered over to the restrooms after they had gotten the trailer set up while Mildred and Chett relaxed for a few minutes.

Both young women were incredulous. Actually, they were frantic. "Do you know how far we got today?" Bobbie asked with her arms outstretched, palms upward, "Fifty!....FIFTY MILES!" Marlys rolled her eyes and answered, " FIFTY. Not Two hundred and fifty. FIFTY!" "OK. We need a plan," Bobbie said. "Now we know how they do lunch, so we've got to plan for that." So the sisters hatched the plan for the next few days: up early, cup of coffee, piece of toast, go down the road and after fifty miles, take a break and eat breakfast. After breakfast, drive a hundred more miles, take another break for lunch. Plan an hour and a half for lunch and rest. After lunch, drive a hundred and fifty to two hundred miles, about four or so hours, and stop for the day. That should give the folks enough breaks, and get the caravan home on time.

After a small meal of more leftovers from Mesa, they made up the trailer for sleeping. The bed the sisters shared each night on this journey was a revelation to both Marlys and Bobbie. It was slightly wider than a twin and not so wide as a full. The first night Bobbie rolled right off her edge onto the floor which Mildred thought was hilarious. In fact, they all did, but it didn't make sleeping any easier to know that they could scarcely move without waking the other one up. Happily the floor was only about 14 inches lower than the mattress, and Bobbie discovered that if she slept on her back with her outside foot on the floor, she wouldn't roll off. It read like the trite beginning of a bad novel: "It was a hot, breathless Arizona night. The old man snored like a lumberjack trying to start his chain saw. The two people in the narrow bed slept fitfully on the lumpy mattress..."

In the morning Mildred made it clear right away that an early departure was not "in the picture." They were absolutely not going to go anywhere without having first eaten breakfast. Furthermore, Mildred believed in a good, hearty breakfast of oatmeal, yogurt, toast, eggs, coffee, and juice to start the day. In addition, she didn't like to hurry her old fashioned oatmeal. It needed its full fifteen minutes to cook. Furthermore, in order to eat their meal, the bed where Bobbie and Marlys had spent the night ("slept" being fictional here) had to be folded up, the bedding put away, and the tabletop brought back out because that's where they all must sit to eat. (Marlys and Bobbie had offered to eat outside sitting in the lawn chairs. Didn't happen.) After their meal, they had to clean and stow before they could hit the road.

By the time they got underway Saturday morning it was nearly 10 a.m. They stopped for lunch after they had gone a little over a hundred miles. By late afternoon about 5:30, they had traveled another hundred and fifty miles. After two days on the road, they were now one-third of the way home and had only two more days to get there. The sisters became seriously worried when Mildred began to complain in earnest. Why are we rushing so? Why do we have to be in Richland by Monday? Why can't you girls take a couple more days off of work and not hurry us? It isn't fair to us because we are so tired from getting ready to go and all the trouble and the heat. What Millie had forgotten was that the daughters had serious job responsibilities and both truly needed to be back at their jobs by the next Tuesday.

For Bobbie, her students were in the last two weeks of school; her seniors were almost ready to graduate and had final exams and projects to submit and be scored. The timing was tight and she had already taken a day and a half off to fly to Phoenix the previous week. Bobbie and John also had pastures they irrigated with hand lines, a field of alfalfa nearly ready to mow, and horses to feed. When she was not there to do her share, her husband, a dentist, had to do chores both evening and night. Marlys was the business manager of her husband's dental practice. The end of the month meant salaries and bills had to be paid, insurance claims sent in, schedules filled in, supplies ordered, and general order kept. In addition, Marlys and Kirk's two boys were still at home and had busy school and sports schedules. The sisters had chosen the long weekend over Memorial Day because Mildred had insisted she could not wait until June after school was out to move because of the heat in Arizona. The other four siblings could not get away from their jobs, either.

As Marlys and Bobbie met in the restroom for a planning session on their second night on the road, they agreed that they were going to have to be firm with Mildred about needing to get to Marlys and Kirk's home in Richland, Washington, by early Monday evening because Bobbie still had another eighty-plus miles to drive from there to her home in Selah. By this time they were tired and frustrated, but knew they could not push Mildred too hard.

Afterward, Mildred was indignant about the trip home. She believed the daughters had been grossly unfair to her and Chett to force them to "rush" home. She kept this opinion for the rest of her life (twenty more years), occasionally reminding her two errant daughters how unfair they had been to force her and Chett to "hurry". Nevertheless, she did her part each day and despite Memorial Weekend traffic and breaks in the day for rest stops, the weary travelers arrived in Richland about 6 p.m. on Monday evening. The sun was bright in the west when they rolled in. All four travelers were exhausted and glad to not have to face another day on the road. Mildred was utterly exhausted even though she had dozed off and on in the car, as had Chett. She was in a daze. Chett was tired, but cheerful and helpful. He and Marlys as well as Bobbie and Mildred had had wonderful conversations in the cars reliving happy times of their growing up years while they rolled northward. Bobbie, who had been drinking colas and coffee all afternoon was both wired and spent. She knew she had to get home within two hours or she'd be in trouble. After briefly helping to get the folks set up and hugging everyone all around, she drove Millie's Subaru home to Selah. Driving into the setting sun, and dealing with the holiday traffic took the full two hours to get to the Sahrs' little acreage in the Selah countryside. She walked in the door, said hello to John and went to bed.

Over the next few weeks with her typical enthusiasm and cheerful disposition, Marlys helped the folks settle in in their trailer, then found a retirement apartment complex for them to move into. It was another move and another beginning.

Kennewick and Yakima

Respite, another move, a farewell

1987-1990

MILDRED AND CHETT MOVED INTO a two-bedroom apartment at the Royal Columbian in Kennewick, Washington, a month or so after they arrived in Richland. The Royal Columbian was a retirement apartment complex that had recently been built on the south side of town in a developing area. The Royal Columbian had an assisted-living wing, which meant if Chett needed to be in assisted care, he could still be near their apartment.

The Tri-Cities area of Richland, Kennewick, and Pasco had experienced a boom in the 1950s through the 1980s due largely to the U.S. government's Hanford "Reservation" just north of Richland. In 1940, Kennewick and Pasco were two medium-sized, agriculture-based towns on opposite shores of the Columbia River near the junction of the Snake and Yakima Rivers. The small town of neighboring Richland began to develop during World War II during the secret Hanford Project. The plutonium used in the atom bombs dropped on Nagasaki and Hiroshima in August 1945 was manufactured there. Richland rose rapidly to support the Hanford area and a new infrastructure was formed in short order, with housing, schools, police, fire protection and government, to support the thousands of families who poured in for war time, then post-war jobs.

With Marlys's help, Mildred found medical providers for both her and Chett and began the process of settling in. Their ground-floor apartment was ideally situated because it "felt" like their own little cottage with outside and inside entrances. They could walk outside to sit in their lawn chairs on their private little patio whenever they wanted, and did not have to negotiate stairs or crowds of people to do so. Furthermore, all of their meals were prepared for them if they so desired.

By the end of summer a buyer had been found for their Apache Wells home. Bobbie and Millie flew down to Phoenix, rented a car, and for the next week, packed, sorted, held a patio sale and re-sorted what didn't sell into boxes which they delivered to needy organizations in the area. It was very hot and very muggy, often punctuated by brief electrical storms. By the end of each day both women were wrung out. A moving company was hired to move the pieces Mildred and Chett could use in their apartment, and her precious grand piano, which would not fit into the apartment, was sent to Bobbie's house in Selah. Both were relieved to get back on the plane and fly home.

After returning home, Mildred received a phone call from the Mesa realtor asking her to buy a new toilet for the second bathroom in the home that, upon inspection, appeared to be cracked. Mildred was indignant. "It wasn't cracked when I left it," she asserted. But the realtor persisted, saying that the buyers would not sign off until a new toilet was installed. "Then you'll have to foot the bill out of your commission!" Mildred retorted. And that's exactly what happened. When the final papers came, there was no line item for the new fixture.

As they settled in their new two-bedroom apartment, Mildred was grateful to have their meals provided, but still chose to make their breakfasts, and sometimes their lunches. She immediately found fault with the quality of institutional food, and preferred to cook in her apartment for breakfast and lunch most days, even when she

didn't feel well. The Royal Columbian's meals were served in a dining room buffet-style, which Mildred disliked intensely because it was
difficult for Chett to manage his own tray and he had trouble choosing which foods to eat. Marlys filled in wherever and whenever she
could and became Mildred's right arm. She saw to it that Mildred
had frequent breaks from the care and supervision of Chett, and began driving them to doctors' appointments. She took them for rides
and brought them to her house for dinner on weekends. Marlys also
began to manage Chett's finances completely and realized that in
recent years Chett had made some less than great investment decisions. Nayda and Carolyn made frequent trips to Kennewick to see
their father. It became clearer to them that their father was definitely
in decline.

Mildred joined a local chapter of PEO and enjoyed making new
friends there, as well as with the congregation of All Saints Episcopal
Church in Richland. Bobbie drove to Kennewick to visit about once
a month and began to listen to Mildred's concerns about her own investments, half of which the bank still controlled from Lloyd's Trust.
Mildred realized that the returns she had been receiving from her
own investments in her part of the estate had outpaced those managed by the bank. After hearing her concerns for a year or more,
Bobbie looked at the monthly statements and this raised a flag of
concern for her, too. The bank, in the meantime, had closed the
Spokane trust department and had relocated all the trust accounts
in their trust office in Portland, Oregon. Mildred continued to feel
betrayed by the bank's handling of the trust Lloyd had established
and she believed he would not have wanted it to be invested by people
who had not known him nor had met Mildred personally. Because
the trust was, as Mildred said, "small potatoes," she believed it had
become a low priority in the bank's larger portfolio. Mildred and
Bobbie decided to watch what the bank did closely for the next several months, and in the meantime Bobbie would chart the investments
and show the reports to her and John's financial advisor.

In 1988, Mildred was again showing the wear and tear of constant supervision and began to fret about Chett's decline. Encouraged by both the Schlien and the Smith children to get additional help, Mildred did seek out the services of the Royal Columbian. This helped, but concerned that Chett might go outside unobserved and get lost, Mildred opted to change apartments and move to a smaller one on the third floor. In this apartment, Mildred had trouble sleeping because of Chett's loud snoring. On her eightieth birthday, which all the families celebrated in the little family living room area on the main floor, Mildred expressed her worry that she wasn't doing all she should for Chett. Tom's remark to her was, "So, Mom, what other seventy-nine year old do you know who has held a twenty-four-hour-a-day, seven-days-a-week job for several years?" She agreed she needed to get more help.

Shortly after Chett's eightieth birthday in March, Mildred chose an apartment in the assisted care wing of the complex and moved Chett there. She knew he would be confused, and it broke her heart. She began spending eight to ten hours a day in his apartment helping him out. She took him to all his meals and ate with him in the dining room in the assisted care wing, which was essentially a nursing home. Aides came in and out during the day to bathe, help him dress, and undress for bedtime. Mildred was able to slip away for a nap in the afternoon while Chett took one in his room. She slept better at night. It was just enough to keep her going.

By this time Chett had almost lost his ability to speak. At first, the two of them would laugh about his saying, "button" when he meant "bread," or "car" when he meant "spoon." While his speech difficulty increased, Chett's balance and ability to walk also began to be compromised. It was all Mildred could do to guide him to the dining room, or out to the lobby for a little exercise. She had to begin feeding him with a spoon when he could not remember how to pick up his own utensils. Chett realized something was wrong one day. Out of the blue he said to her, "This is not fair to you." That was the last complete sentence he ever spoke. Mildred's reply was, "It's what we do for the people we love."

In the midst of all the hard parts of this period in Chett's life, came a little ray of sunshine. A woman, "Mary," also resided in the assisted-care wing. She took a fancy to Chett and began to come up to him and want to hug him. At first Mildred was offended and complained to the aides about her. Their response was that she was really harmless and was a really good person. One day, Mildred found Mary in Chett's apartment, and that upset her. Again, she complained. Evidently the staff paid more attention to where Mary and Chett were. Mildred never found Mary in the apartment again, but she began finding Chett and Mary sitting on the sofa in the living room area of the care wing. They were often holding hands and grinning, both contented and very pleased with themselves. Mildred tried a new approach.

"So who is your friend, Chett?" He looked surprised and then looked at Mary. He grinned. Mary, who also had lost her speech ability, smiled happily. "Is it Mary?" Mildred asked. Chett and Mary continued to grin, and Mary reached over and patted Chett's knee. "Hello, Mary," Mildred said, and Chett looked at Mildred with a far away look in his eye. At that moment, Mildred realized that Chett had probably forgotten who she was other than someone he knew.

She sat on the sofa with them for a few minutes, then decided to get up and leave to see if Chett responded in any way to that. So when she said, "Bye, Chett. Bye, Mary," neither of the other two reacted except for Mary who kept a strong hold on Chett's hand as they watched her walk away. Then Mildred walked to the door and pressed the code to exit. She looked back and saw that Chett and Mary were still sitting happily on the sofa. Later, when Mildred called Marlys, and then Bobbie, she told them wistfully that Chett "had a girlfriend." Mildred hated to admit it, but Chett's having a friend whose company he could enjoy meant that she could have a couple more hours in the day for herself. It was sad to feel relief about it, but she did.

As the end of 1989 approached, the staff told Mildred that Chett would soon need complete, fully assisted nursing care, which the Royal Columbian did not offer. She would need to look for a facility for him quickly as he had reached the limit of their care abilities. Marlys and Mildred looked in the Tri- City area, but Marlys was not happy with what she found. Then they decided they should look in Yakima, where there were far more nursing homes to choose from.

At this point, Bobbie got into the search. Her husband John's father, John W. Sahr, had recently been admitted to Good Samaritan Nursing Home on 40th Avenue, and John's mother, Elsie, had moved into an apartment adjoining the nursing home to be near her husband. Marlys and Mildred drove to Yakima to look at the facility and agreed that it would be much more acceptable than anything they had seen previously. So in December, Chett was moved to Yakima. Shortly thereafter Mildred found an apartment in nearby Orchard Park Retirement Apartment complex, about four blocks away. Bobbie took over from Marlys as the contact person for both parents.

In addition to his dementia, Chett's body was beginning to break down. He developed an infection in his left heel that refused to heal. A dermatologist was called who referred them to a surgeon who performed a debridement of the infection site there in the nursing home. Every day Mildred drove over from her apartment in mid-morning, tended to her husband, fed him his lunch, nodded off in the chair beside his bed, fed him his supper most days, checked his infection site, then went home. Bobbie came after work one or two times a week and on weekends. Chett's girls came almost every weekend. In the meantime, John's father continued to lose ground so Bobbie's visits were divided between the two fathers.

Christmas was somber with both fathers in failing health. In mid-January 1990, John W. Sahr passed away. Shortly thereafter, Chett slipped into a light coma and became more and more unresponsive. Mildred continued her bedside care. Sometimes Chett did not move for hours on end. In the next bed was a man ("Bill") who often spent long hours unattended. Mildred soon began to run interference for both men. "Bill needs his Depends changed," she'd say to an aide when the smell in the room became overpowering. Or she'd say, "Bill needs to get into his wheelchair," to the nurse. Then a few hours later she'd find an attendant and say, "Bill has been sitting in his chair for over two hours. He's falling asleep. He needs to go back to bed." Bill also had a penchant for fresh air. Many times when entering the room, one's first view of the room would be Bill naked as a jaybird lying in his bed. Sometimes Mildred would catch him taking his hospital gown off and say to him, "Bill, let's pull the sheet up. You're flashing everyone in the hallway," or "You're making all of us blush." He'd just smile as if to say, "Caught you looking!"

In February, Chett was moved to another room. By coincidence it was the same room and the same bed in which John W. Sahr had died a few months previously. By mid-March it became difficult to give him any nourishment or water. He slipped deeper and deeper into a coma. In mid-April Mildred called Chett's girls. "He's not going to last much longer," she reported. They came and stayed for several days over a weekend. Still their dad lingered. Finally, on a Monday and Tuesday, one by one, they reluctantly left to return to their jobs. On Thursday, April 19, 1990, Bobbie drove to Yakima after school to sit with Mildred by Chett's bedside. While Mildred fussed over his infected heel and Bobbie swabbed his mouth with a wet foam sponge, Chett opened his eyes, pursed his mouth as to say, "Oh!" and was gone.

3 7

Yakima

1990-1997

CHETT WAS LAID TO REST beside his first wife, Angie Schlien, the mother of his three daughters, Carolyn, Nayda, and Marlys. Chett and Millie had discussed the "where" of burial at great length when they made their wills shortly after their marriage in 1968. Both were completely united in their belief that each should be buried beside their first spouse, their first partner and other parent of their children. For Chett, this meant his body would lie in tiny Mabton Cemetery, just north of the town of Mabton where he and Angie had raised their girls. Surviving him were his eldest daughter: Carolyn Quantrille and her two daughters, Angie Marie and Lori Kay; his middle daughter and her husband, Nayda and Greg Littlefield, and their two children, Bryce and Kayla; his youngest daughter Marlys, her husband Kirk Williams and their two sons, Karl and Kraig. Mildred's family also mourned Chett, who had been like a father to them for twenty-two years: Bobbie and John Sahr and their three children, John D. and his wife Eliza, Kathryn and her husband Nick and their two daughters, Laura and Erin, and Elizabeth and her husband Michael and their daughter Ellen; Tom Smith, his wife Mary Ellen, and their two sons Eric and Michael; and Vergie Ellen Lougheed and her son Kenneth Rosson. Also surviving Chett was his sister Florence Ivey,

276

her husband Al, and their son Donald and several cousins. Buried with Chett was his "Best Grandpa in the World" baseball cap.

Of their twenty-two years of marriage, Mildred realized that the last half of it had been consumed with Chett's progressing Alzheimer's condition. At eighty-two she was once again a widow and exhausted to the core. In late April Mildred, Bobbie and Tom traveled to Milwaukie, Oregon, to visit Vergie Ellen's husband Joe Lougheed, who was dying of colon cancer. They returned for his funeral in May. Then in early September, Lloyd's sister Louise passed away in Sunnyside having suffered from breast cancer and colon cancer for several years. Mildred and Bobbie visited Louise in a Sunnyside Nursing Home shortly before her death. Mildred had always felt a closeness to Louise, who had been kind to the Smiths on many occasions. It was a hard year for Mildred and her extended family.

With her usual efficiency, Marlys got to work in sorting out Chett's financial affairs. The three sisters conferred at every step of the way. Mildred turned everything over to "the girls" and Marlys was efficient in closing the estate and dealing with Chett's remaining properties. She sold the trailer and the Buick. Mildred had already replaced her car, the Subaru SUV, with an Oldsmobile Cutlass. Chett's girls kept in close touch with Mildred and treated her as if she were their own mother, calling and writing her, and coming to visit. They continued this attention for seventeen more years.

When Carolyn and then Nayda were diagnosed with breast cancer, the family was devastated, then rallied. Nothing could compare to the devotion of the sisters who lost days and days of work to support whichever one of them was seeing a doctor or receiving a treatment. Marlys and Kirk, and Nayda and Greg took Carolyn to Mexico and Spain on trips they had planned for themselves. Carolyn signed up for additional trips on her own. Nothing was going to keep her down.

Like her mother Angie, Carolyn, the first sister to be diagnosed with breast cancer, had a mastectomy in 1984. Nayda followed suit a few years later. Both went through extensive chemo treatments and Nayda also had radiation treatments. Finally, after thirteen years and many rounds of treatment, Carolyn succumbed on June 19, 2003. She is buried next to her parents in the Mabton Cemetery.

For Mildred, the ups and downs in her life settled into a routine wherein she could focus on herself as well as keep in closer touch with her six adult "children". She affiliated with a PEO Chapter in Yakima and became a member of St. Timothy's Episcopal Church just a few blocks from her apartment. She even sang in the choir for a few months, but evening practices became too tiring. Both affiliations became enamored of this alert, feisty, petite lady. She began studying nutrition with a vengeance, but only through selected sources she picked herself, so all her information was exceptionally biased. When she read something that agreed with her own perception, she became convinced that she was correct and those who didn't agree with her were in error, including doctors and cooks. She made it her job to try to educate the cooks at Orchard Park about the menus the nutritionists had chosen for the residents as well as the way the food was prepared. She harangued the managers with complaints and was not shy about discussing these issues with her tablemates at meals. Many of her opinions about food were based on her early years when refrigeration was not widely used. To her way of thinking, all vegetables should be cooked through and through, in other words limp, or as Bobbie used to describe them, "completely dead." Meat should never be served with any part of it showing pink. Most of the meat served at the Smith home in the early years had been, while tasty, dry. Mildred wanted her food cooked that way, but didn't get her preferences very often. She did make some good points about nutrition, but she voiced her opinions so persistently that she resembled a dog shaking a rug until it flew apart.

Mildred enjoyed coming out to the Sahrs' house in the country where she could get a meal cooked to her own liking. But gradually, she began eliminating more and more foods from her diet to which, she decided, she had developed an allergy, rather than digestive issues. She dropped everything from the nightshade family, including potatoes, tomatoes, peppers and onions. She began to eat more bread and heaps of green salad (sans tomatoes and green peppers) with her meals because she complained that that was the only way she could get filled up by the meals served in the dining room. She eliminated red meat. Next, she developed a problem with flatulence, so she quit eating green salad.

Bobbie began buying Mildred liquid food supplements to get additional vitamins, minerals, and calories in her. Mildred had specific taste preferences and limited the flavors she would drink. Then, instead of drinking the whole carton down, Millie would sip the contents little by little, often taking two days to drink one container. At Mildred's request, Bobbie began taking Mildred to health food stores where Mildred bought a complete set of tissue salts, which she had read were all that a person needed for aches and pains caused by the imbalance of one's body chemistry. She studied her tissue salts "how to" book until it was in shreds. When Bobbie ordered a new one for her, she rejected it because it had a new format.

After her arrival in Yakima, Mildred had difficulty finding a medical doctor to take her as a new patient. Finally an osteopathic physician agreed to take her as a new Medicare patient, but Mildred didn't especially like him, (because he didn't agree with her opinions about medicines and nutrition) and she complained about him after every appointment. When Bobbie started going to her appointments with her to listen to what was discussed, she discovered that at some time during an appointment Mildred would always challenge the doctor if he wanted to prescribe something to treat her complaints because he, as she informed him, didn't know anything about nutrition or holistic medicine and if he did, he should advise her about natural solutions instead of drugs. Mildred consulted her drug "bible" reference she had bought in Arizona, and sure enough, there would always be a description in the "possible side effects" list of reasons why she should

not take what any doctor ordered for her. Then at her next appointment she would roundly scold him for prescribing something "that
was clearly" not good for anyone, especially the elderly. She read
every word on the information sheet she got with each prescription.
If there was a side effect, she was certain to experience it even before
she had enough in her system to have made a difference. In her
mind, if, after taking a new medicine she didn't have a good night's
sleep, it was caused by the new prescription. If she got a headache,
or became momentarily dizzy, it was the medicine. If she had indiges-
tion or flatulence, it was the new medicine. She may have been right
in many of those instances, but she preferred to teach the doctor, not
listen to him. When her doctor countered that he was merely trying
to address her complaints, she, of course, continued to have them.
She complained that he was treating the symptom and was not interested in finding out the cause. She did not believe that the aging
process was a factor in her complaints.

By this time, her arthritis pain was now a daily and nightly issue
with her. Already a light sleeper for years, the pain in her back, toes,
ankles, hips, wrists, and/or fingers became her Armageddon during
the long night hours. She began taking the maximum amount of
Tylenol each day to lessen the pain, and, while it eased her discomfort, it never completely erased it. Her doctor eventually referred her
to a "pain" specialist who prescribed Tylenol 3 on top of the maximum amount she was already taking on her own, but then she began
having digestive problems.

Bobbie began looking for substances other than Tylenol that
might ease Mildred's pain but would not cause her mother to have a
tender stomach. By chance she was watching TV one day and saw a
special health report on a new substance, glucosamine, which seemed
to be effective in reducing the pain in joints affected with arthritis
without having any adverse side effects. With only limited trials, the
FDA and AMA were not ready to approve this substance until more
clinical trials were completed, but it seemed promising. One could

purchase it in health food stores. Bobbie consulted her daughter in-law, an MD at the University of Washington Hospital in Internal Medicine who had read the early reports. While there didn't seem to be any side effects, Eliza was not ready to send her patients to the health food store to try it out. Health food stores were notorious for charging high prices for supplements that may or may not have had FDA or any other approval.

Still hopeful it would help, Bobbie got Mildred a supply of glucosamine. After about a month Mildred realized she was not experiencing the stabbing pain she used to have, and was sleeping through the night better. She was able to back off Tylenol 3 completely, and took the over-the-counter strength at regular intervals. For Mildred, this was a blessing. For Bobbie, it meant Mildred might be less angry with her doctors and less focused on her pain every time she and Bobbie had a conversation. Mildred quit going to the "pain" doctor altogether.

For eleven years each July from 1988 to 1998 Bobbie took Mildred on a four or five-day road trip to Roseburg, Oregon, to visit her sister Florence Groshong near Florence's birthday. The old wounds from the problems with Aunt Ellen's estate had softened with time and they were now speaking to each other. Neither of the two sisters ever mentioned the painful experience they had had when Florence and Harold had sued Millie over the estate of aunt Ellen Milby. Evidently bygones were bygones. Mildred, however, would have liked more closure than the outcomes of the hearings, but she had no intention of initiating that conversation. What was right was right. As a matter of principle, Mildred believed Florence should be the one to open that door. That never happened. On some of those visits, Harold and Arah drove to Roseburg from Coos Bay, Oregon, and in 1991 Mildred and Bobbie drove to Coos Bay to celebrate Harold's 90th birthday. Harold also never mentioned their legal battles nor his threat to Mildred to "take her to the highest court in the land." It was as if it had never happened. Mildred decided she would never get an apology from either sibling and let go of that hope.

The visits were delightful and it was just as well that the painful experience was never touched upon. On several occasions, Bobbie and Millie stopped by Milwaukie, Oregon, stayed the night, then picked up Vergie Ellen for the remainder of the trip to Roseburg. John Sahr always commented on how much Mildred and her daughters could talk. "It's the Fisher genes," Mildred would laugh. Evidently none of Martha Albertson Fisher's children or her husband David could 'best' grandmother Fisher in that department. All Martha's daughters had the same genetic make up. Mildred would say, "I do remember, even when I was just little, how my mother, when she got angry or upset about something could skin someone alive with her tongue. Mother didn't stop until the object of her verbal assault was reduced to a pile of potato peelings."

In 1992 Mildred began a writing campaign in which she scolded various people about the way they did business. On December 5, 1992, Mildred wrote the Presiding Bishop of the Episcopal Church in New York City in response to his annual Bishop's Fund Appeal. Indignant that the Bishop's Fund had insulted her intelligence by asking for donations even while they (in her opinion) mismanaged their business, she enclosed a check for ten dollars with the instruction that it was to be used "to feed the hungry only" and not for administration purposes.

Sometimes the topics of Mildred's indignation and Vergie's information from a late night show were discussed in the car on their road trips and the dialogue would get heated. When Vergie joined Mildred and Bobbie in Milwaukie, even Bobbie got shut out of the dialogue and was content to drive while listening to mother and sister banter.

It was also in 1992 at age 84 that Mildred began to write a journal of sorts in a spiral notebook. It began...

"A start toward my recall of the events of my life...which may explain to my family how I became who I am."

She never completely finished her narration, but at 97, still reading for pleasure and complaining about her dimming eyesight, she did write a letter to the Spokane Valley Library thanking them for bringing "84, Charing Cross Road" by Helen Hanff to her apartment complex for her to read. She included in her letter a book report about the book and why it was good for the elderly. Also in her journal was a book review of "Anna Karenina" and several itemized lists of programs of classical music she listened to on public radio.

In that ten-year period, the Milby cousins enjoyed the get-togethers, too. Ron Milby, Harold's son, rarely saw the rest of the family, so when he showed up, it was fun to catch up. Ron had a happy disposition and was fun to be around. Florence's daughter, Connie Hunnicutt, lived in Roseburg, too, and was the family's key caregiver for her mother. She and her husband Wally were gracious hosts and pleased to see her mother's pleasure in the short visits. Florence celebrated her 90th birthday in 1993 with a big hoopla at the country club in Roseburg. All three of her daughters were there. It had been many years since Vergie and Bobbie had seen their other Groshong cousins: Louise Hancock of Modesto, California, came with her son John. Jean Amorde of Rocklin, California, and Connie Hunnicutt and her husband Wally of Roseburg and their sons Greg and Steve and their families also attended. Harold, now 94, was very frail. His wife Arah and their son Ron and his wife Winnie attended. It would be the Milby siblings' last gathering.

In 1996, after struggling with their health and having to be in assisted care, Arah and then Harold passed away within a month or so of each other. A double funeral was held in Milton for Harold and Arah. Arah's ashes were buried with Harold in his casket in the Milby plot in Milton. Florence had become very frail and was obviously shaken by her brother's death. At the graveside for the final commitment, she sat in a wheelchair wrapped in a blanket, grieving.

As Florence declined in health, she no longer could stay by herself in the retirement apartment complex where she had been living. As her eyesight dimmed from macular degeneration, she became angry, stubborn and difficult. Her violent outbursts were hardest on her daughter Connie for whom visiting her mother became emotionally upsetting. Gentle Wally stepped forward and filled in. Six months before Florence's death, Bobbie and Millie drove to Roseburg, again for Florence's birthday. Just as Mildred was about to leave, Florence became irritated at the nurse's aide who brought Florence some juice and a couple of cookies. Something about the cookies irritated Florence who shouted at the nurse, then threw the plate of cookies at her. That was the last time Mildred saw her sister. A small funeral was held in Roseburg in early January 1997, at St. George's Episcopal Church in Roseburg. Florence's ashes were inurned in the Church's columbarium. Neither Mildred nor any of her family could attend because of severe road conditions between Yakima and Portland. Mildred was now the last surviving member of her immediate family.

Harold, Mildred, Florence
Harold's 90th birthday
1991 Coos Bay, OR

3 8

Yakima to Spokane

1998 - 2003

In August 1998 Mildred had a heart attack. Bobbie and John were at their Idaho cabin awaiting the arrival from Seattle of John D. and Eliza Sahr and their newborn baby, John Isaac. At home in Yakima Mildred who had not been feeling well all day, had tried to get in to see her doctor, but the schedule was full and the nurse was adamant that it would be two days until they could squeeze her in. Feeling worse as the day progressed, she called again. This time the nurse was very curt, but again she did not ask for Mildred's specific symptoms. Finally, at about three that afternoon when she was supposed to be having a massage in the health room in the Orchard Park Retirement complex she asked if the masseur would take her to the doctor, which he did. The nurse was indignant when Mildred showed up without an appointment. She let her sit for forty-five minutes in a wheelchair in the waiting room while the doctor saw his other patients. When the doctor happened to walk behind the front desk and saw Mildred sitting there with her head drooping over her chest, he asked the nurse what Mildred Schlien was doing there. "She says she's sick!" the nurse replied. "I told her we did not have room in our schedule to see her." He sighed and responded, "Well she's here, so let's see her now." When he listened to her heart he had the nurse call an ambulance.

"Mildred," he said, "You're having a heart attack, but we'll take care of you." She replied, "O.K. Finally!"

The E.R., staff consulted with a cardiologist at his private heart clinic. Because of her age and because she appeared to be so frail, the cardiologist and E.R. personnel agreed to do nothing extraordinary except watch her closely. After all, a ninety-year-old was probably not a good candidate for any extensive procedures. However, when the cardiologist arrived at the E.R. he found a "perky little lady," who gave him the full run-down of what had been going on. Surprised that Mildred was so alert and well-spoken, he decided that she was, indeed, capable of going forward with the normal procedures for heart attack patients. However, this meant having to transport her to the heart center at another hospital. So back in an ambulance she went and off to the other hospital. By this time Bobbie had been called in Idaho and was on her way to Yakima with her son John D. It was a five-hour drive.

When they arrived at 11 p.m. they found Mildred propped up in her bed, resting and able to tell them everything that had happened. The next day she had an angiogram and then had a stent placed in an artery. A few months later the stent failed, so she had another go at it in January. Eventually she had a pacemaker placed and largely did fine with it.

Bobbie had resigned from her teaching position in 1995. Not only was Mildred, then 87, needing more of her time, but so was John's mother, Elsie, who was 96. Within a few years it had became apparent to Bobbie and John Sahr that they were struggling to keep their acreage up even with John's sister Pat who now lived with them and did her one-third of the work. Each had an ailing, elderly mother. They knew they would soon need to move to a smaller place, but where? They knew that there was nothing holding them to the Yakima Valley since none of their children had returned there after college. Two had settled in the Seattle area where they had established their professional careers and were raising their families. Their youngest daughter had married a New Yorker and was living near Albany, NY. The Sahrs also knew that they could not move away as long as John's mother Elsie Sahr was still living. In fragile health since her husband died in 1990, it would be too hard on her to move her from where she lived comfortably in a group home in Yakima. Elsie celebrated her 100th birthday in 1999 complete with a Sahr family weekend reunion in August of that year held at the Sahrs' and a big birthday celebration on her October 1st birthday at Among Friends, where she lived. At 91, Mildred was one of the more lively guests. In December 2001 Elsie slipped away at the age of 102, having lived in three different centuries.

In the meantime, Mildred kept up her writing campaign. Besides scathing notes to the managers and kitchen staff, she scolded the Herald-Republic in Yakima about their poor use of grammar and was mentioned in Editor Sarah Jenkins' column:

"Mildred Schlien of Yakima, an ... eagle-eyed Word Police Officer, objects to the misuse of another simple word...Mildred reports that she often finds the word "only" misplaced. And its placement - like the space between in and to - definitely can change the meaning of a sentence." (Herald-Republic February 17, 2002)

A year or so following Elsie's death, Bobbie and John knew their responsibilities with the acreage, horses and Millie were taking a huge toll on them. They needed to downsize. It would be hard to leave the place where they had raised their children, and where they had nearly a three-hundred-degree view over the Naches Valley to the Cascade Mountains on the west and the Selah Valley to the east. Their choices were two: the greater Seattle area where two of their families lived, or Spokane where Bobbie's brother Tom lived and was only a two-hour drive to their cabin at Priest Lake.

The time came for Bobbie to approach Mildred, now 95. "Mom, John and I are going to downsize and we are either going to move to the greater Seattle area or Spokane. You are coming with us and you don't have a choice." Mildred looked up at Bobbie, rose up to her full height of four feet ten inches and without a pause replied, "Well, I'm glad that you want me to come with you, but I'm not going to Seattle!" Surprised, Bobbie said, "Well, why not?" Mildred immediately ticked off the reasons by counting her fingers for each point: "There are too many people; too many cars; too many trees, and too much rain. You'll have to leave me here!" So Bobbie responded, "What do you care? I will be doing most of your driving." Her terse response: "I don't care. Leave me here. I'm NOT moving to Seattle!" So Bobbie went home and told John, "I guess we had better think harder about moving to Spokane." And he said, "Fine by me. I can't see us living near Seattle, either."

In March 2003, with a sale pending on their rural Selah acreage, Bobbie drove to Spokane where she and Tom looked at possible retirement apartments for Millie. They chose a newly built retirement complex, Harbor Crest on Spokane's South Hill, which, like the Royal Columbian in Kennewick, had a similar assisted living component. In mid-April when their house sale went through, the Sahrs moved to their cabin on Priest Lake and hired a contractor to begin building a home for them in Spokane Valley. Pat moved back to her home in Hoodsport, and in May. Tom, Bobbie and John moved Mildred to her new Spokane apartment.

Once more, Mildred was on the move. This time it was a return to Spokane where seventy-odd years earlier she had experienced her first opportunity to be truly happy. Even though Mildred had fond memories of her college years in Spokane, and even though she was thrilled to be living near her son and his family, the move was very hard on her. At ninety-five, she had to leave her Yakima friends of thirteen years and adjust to yet a new apartment, a new routine, new friends, and (train) new cooks and doctors...again. Almost immediately Bobbie began the quest to find a health care provider for Mildred, but none of the ones who were recommended wanted to take on a ninety-five year-old woman who was on Medicare.

Within a few weeks, in true Millie fashion, she solved the problem with a full frontal assault. One evening while Bobbie and John were at their cabin in Idaho, Mildred thought she was having a heart attack and called Tom to take her to the hospital. It was a perfect way to find a cardiologist and an internist!

Spokane 2003 - 2007

Her way

The last few years of Mildred's life were fraught with difficulties amid the joys of being near family. Her failing health, her suspicion of collusion between her medical providers and pharmaceutical companies, and her focus on trying to force the management and cooks of Harbor Crest to change their ways according to her mandates were a constant source of irritation to her and a concern to her family. She was adamant about not being given additional prescribed medicines even after arriving at her doctor's appointment with a laundry list of complaints. She was even more adamant about having the right to and the knowledge of self-medicating herself with numerous supplements and health food store products, and she tried to get her physicians to listen to her information (her "research" usually from only one source) about the benefits of tissue salts or why this or that pill should never be prescribed for an elderly person because of its side effects. Of the many appointments Bobbie attended with her over the years there wasn't one in which the doctor didn't eventually look at his watch. Later Millie would snort, "All they think about is money!"

Few people could really refute Millie's logic because she was such a sharp-witted, vigorous (except for her arthritis) 95+-year-old with whom you did not want to get into an argument. Once she had decided something or had taken a stand on a particular topic, it was carved in stone forever. She loved to remind people (primarily Bobbie and Tom) that her cardiologist (after a frustrating appointment during which she refused most of his advice) after trotting her down the hallway to check her oxygen level which turned out to be at 95 percent, once had told her, sighing, "Mildred, whatever it is that you are doing, keep doing it!"

Even though Bobbie and Tom tried to distract her, conversations would always come around to the incompetence of everyone from the cooks at Harbor Crest to President George H.W. Bush. Tom would change over to his attorney tactics while trying to get her to reason through some of her obsessions, but she would catch on to his tone of voice and tell him to quit acting like she was in a courtroom!

One highlight for Millie was when several paintings of Carolyn's were hung in her honor in a meeting room of Spokane Falls Community College. Carolyn had been a highly regarded professor there. She had completed most of her paintings during the years she fought cancer. They were her therapy.

L-R: Marlys, Lori, Millie, Bobbie, Tom, Nayda

For the last couple of years of Millie's life, Bobbie brought meals from her own kitchen five or six days a week and took her mother out for lunch or dinner at least once a week. Mildred liked to go to a buffet-style restaurant on the corner of Pines and Sprague in Spokane Valley because she liked the way they cooked their turkey (moist and well done) and she could always get one or two vegetables cooked the way she liked them (completely limp, but hot). It was also a way to get her out of her apartment for a while.

On other occasions, when the family met at different restaurants for a special celebration, Millie usually complained about the noise or the draft, or the food, or the dim light, and would usually try to get in a conversation with the wait person about what she couldn't eat on their (inadequate) menu, and did the waiter know how the cook prepared the food, why did the fish always have to be battered because she couldn't eat the starch, she didn't want the vegetable (because it would be raw) that came with her meal so could they provide her with an alternate vegetable (no peas or potatoes because they were too starchy, etc.) and be sure to bring her meal to her while the food was still hot. Mother's Day at Anthony's, a birthday at the Spaghetti Factory, and dinner at Luigi's after The Lion King matinee were memorable in that regard. Mary Ellen, Nayda and Marlys tried their best to accommodate Millie's requests, too, but all of the girls held their collective breaths waiting to see whether Millie would or could go along with the place, the food choices, the lighting, the temperature or the volume. When someone suggested she might as well just accept the entree and side dishes as shown on the menu and not to complain, she would huff up and declare, "I'm just telling it like it is!"

With these requirements in mind, the restaurant was always chosen by someone who had eaten there and was certain there would be something on the menu that Millie could or might choose. In their homes, the families always cooked what Millie was currently eating (it often changed). Millie was always grateful to be asked and usually she gladly accepted. Many of her friends at Harbor Crest were amazed at how many visitors Millie had and how attentive her family was. Millie was familiar with many of her friends' particular problems and was not shy about giving them advice from her "research." A lesson learned from Millie for all who knew her was how many seemingly minor (to them) difficulties the elderly face every single day which they must deal with and which affect their ability to feel well and/or be self-sustaining. It was humbling.

By mid-2006 it had become apparent that Millie needed to be in a fully assisted care facility, but she resisted that message. Harbor Crest had a few extra services, but they were in a transitional period and lacked consistency. Millie was prone to countermanding their instructions, often refusing help in her apartment (she wouldn't let some housekeepers in the door) then complained about the cost of living in such a place. She believed if she didn't use the services, she shouldn't have to pay for them.

She kept a journal of absolutely everything that went on each day, using three lines of tiny writing in each line space of a spiral notebook: when she took her meds, when she took Tylenol for her arthritis, who visited her, who stayed for lunch, how long she napped, etc. She entered notations in the middle of the night when she couldn't sleep. Often when she got her bill, she discovered she had been billed for a guest lunch on a particular day when she didn't have a guest, so she'd check her journal for proof. Likewise, she went to them to have her bill adjusted when she had had a guest and management hadn't recorded it.

Because she was still so alert (she passed her internist's subtle check of her mental capacity with flying colors), her doctors had an on-going struggle to make her feel better despite her refusal to follow their directions. Frequently, one would ask her if she felt depressed or anxious. (She knew if she admitted she was, they would write a prescription for an antidepressant.) She would reply, "Of course I'm depressed! I'm sleep-deprived. My arthritis keeps me awake at night so I'm tired all the time. Old people get tired." They were usually charmed by this feisty little woman even though she frustrated them. At each appointment each doctor knew they would be getting another lecture about how little doctors know about basic nutrition, and how they were over-influenced by pharmaceutical companies.

Once she complained of having a spider bite on her ankle. Her doctor asked to see it and she stood up, took two steps to the examination couch, climbed up, turned around, sat down and hoisted one ankle up and set it on the opposite thigh before either Bobbie of her doctor could assist her. He laughed and said, "She's more nimble than I am!" "Thirty years of doing yoga will do that for you," she replied. When the doctor looked at the bite on her ankle, he said, "Well you've been scratching at it, but I don't think it's a spider bite." She replied in a huff, "Well, then you've never seen a spider bite!" End of discussion.

Over one long winter, in addition to demanding that Tom raise her bed on one side because her apartment floor was sinking, she began to complain about having bedbugs in her apartment. Management finally had her rugs shampooed and she refused to go back into her apartment until late that evening because of the fumes from the cleaning substances. Bobbie washed her bedding and turned her mattress: no bugs. Tom flipped cushions and vacuumed her hide-a-bed couch: no bugs. One day she found some kind of bug in her davenport and put it in a jar for proof. It was never identified, but it *was* a bug.

August 2005. Mildred's last visit to Priest Lake. View south over Reeder Bay from the Walczak's deck

Next she told Tom he needed to raise her bed even more on one side because she was afraid she would fall out of bed due to the sinking floor. To please her, he raised the bed twice as high as he previously had raised it (about three inches), which *increased* the likelihood of her falling out, but she was much happier having her way and Tom had learned not to argue with her logic.

In November 2006, at the suggestion of the Sahrs' daughter in-law Eliza, Bobbie mentioned to Millie that they might want to consider contacting a hospice for their services. At an appointment with her doctor for treating a sore on Millie's lower back near her buttocks that would not heal, he agreed to this plan and also filled out a POLST form (Physician Orders for Life-Sustaining Treatment) to be placed on her refrigerator door) in clear view for any emergency personnel who might be called to assist her in her apartment. Mildred was agreeable. After coordinating this with the management at Harbor Crest, a hospice nurse came to Mildred's apartment to dress her "wound." A few hours later Mildred called Bobbie to tell her that the hospice nurse couldn't have been a real nurse because she didn't even know how to put a bandage on a wound because "It felt like she taped a book to my backside." Mildred removed it herself. The nurse was not happy to be called back to redress the sore or face a lecture from Millie.

Bobbie's Journal,
Spokane: April 3, 2006

Tom visits mom for a couple hours Sunday aft. He notices bandaids on two of her fingers. She says she has a fungus on her fingers and she has been digging it out and her fingers are sore. On her ring finger, left hand, she has scraped away at the edge of the nail exposing some of the nail bed. She has in effect removed about one-fourth of the nail. Tom calls it "self mutilation" which I'm not certain is appropriate in this instance. Nevertheless, she is becoming more and more focused on it and even told me the other day she "worked on it" for a couple of hours in the middle of the night recently.

Her eyesight is poor (one cataract in one eye and the other eye has blurry vision after an attempt at a lens implant and laser correction several years ago)...but, of course, she is unwilling to accept that her poor eyesight is the result of aging. It's the doctor's fault. Millie believes he is an incompetent doctor; again her belief that young doctors don't know enough to treat her appropriately.

We agree that we will continue to monitor these particular issues, as we monitor her other issues : starch in her food; spiders biting her legs during the night ; her apartment floor sinking; drafty windows, etc.

By Christmas 2006 several more sores had erupted on Millie's legs, indications that her skin was breaking down as well as her body's ability to heal itself. Mildred also did not feel well and began to skip meals. Bobbie would arrive to find that even the food she had brought for Millie's previous night's dinner had not been eaten and Millie admitted she had not gone to the dining room and had not eaten the meals that were brought to her in her room because they were cold when they arrived. She refused to use her microwave. She needed more care than she was getting in her isolated apartment.

After a search of the greater Spokane area, an adult group home for women was found in Spokane Valley. One bright factor was that it was much closer to Bobbie's home in Spokane Valley than the apartment on Spokane's South Hill, a twenty-five minute drive each way. It was bright and cheerful and seemed to be the perfect answer for Millie who vociferously wanted to avoid going to a nursing home. Millie moved in in late December, but lasted only three weeks, during which time she actually did fall out of bed and criticized nearly everything the management and staff tried to do for her, especially regarding the food.

Mildred was not at all subtle about her complaints. When Bobbie tried to coax Mildred to allow some time to get used to the protocol, Mildred flew into a rage and reduced Bobbie to tears exclaiming that Bobbie "had not grown up after all (she was 67 at the time) and didn't know what she was talking about." This happened twice. Bobbie phoned the hospice counselor for help, cowering in Millie's bathroom in tears after one confrontation with her mother after which her mother wheeled happily to the lunch table. The hospice case worker reminded Bobbie that this was the aging process at work and was not the real Millie. "Easy for you to say," Bobbie muttered. "You're not the daughter. Your mother did not just chase you down the hallway as fast as her oxygen-laden walker would allow her, shouting that she was surprised that you'd never grown up!" and yelling "Come back here! Don't you walk away from me!" Fearing another confrontation, Bobbie wrote a note to her mother and left it on her bed:

January 13, 2007

Dear Mother,

I don't know what it is like to feel as ill as you do, to have a heart which day by day is wearing out, to suffer from arthritic pain, or to not be able to eat many different foods.

I don't know what it feels like to lose control of all the things I have always managed on my own.

What I do know is that I love you deeply, and I am happy to be by your side as you make this journey.

Love, Bobbie

Mildred never mentioned having received the note. Meanwhile, the owner of the group home told Bobbie and Tom that Mildred was not adjusting well at all and perhaps a move would be advisable. On January 19th, Millie called Tom telling him she felt abandoned and "Bobbie is angry with me." Tom: "How do you know?" Millie: "Her face tells me." I tell Tom, "That was fear! She was chasing me down the hallway yelling, "Come back here!" and I wouldn't."

A few days later a hospice counselor called Bobbie to tell her that there was hope. A woman who was associated with hospice operated a one-client-at-a-time hospice care in her own home, and this room was now available. Did we want to consider it? Bobbie took a couple of friends and her brother over to Kim's place for a look. It was a nondescript ranchette on a quiet little street in Spokane Valley. Yes, this would do. It was their only option left except a nursing home. Bobbie made the arrangements to move Millie on a Thursday. On Wednesday Bobbie had surgery on one foot to remove a suspicious mole. On Thursday morning, when Bobbie and John arrived at the group home where Millie had been living, the management there was so glad to be getting rid of her they had her things packed and piled by the front door. Millie's comment to the other ladies as she left was that she had left her phone number and if any of them needed her help (for their poor meals) they could call her at that number and she would call the police to protect them.

Bobbie told Mildred that they were going to look at a new place for her to live in, but she had not been completely truthful. Mildred did not know she was going to be left there. Mildred thought she was going to go back to her apartment at Harbor Crest, but that management had told Tom in early January that Mildred needed more care than they were licensed to give and that she could no longer live there either. Mildred was bright and cheerful in the car, happy to be away from the group home. By the time they arrived at Kim's, Bobbie was nauseous from pain medication from her foot surgery, and extremely apprehensive about how Mildred would react because she had not been completely truthful to her mother.

The hospice nurse Paula was there because everyone involved with this move knew it was going to be difficult. While Paula and Kim distracted Mildred in the living room, Bobbie and John started carrying in Mildred's things. Mildred caught sight of them as they were just about finished and cried out, "What are you doing?" Paula told her, "Mildred, we're going to try out having you live at Kim's for a while." It was then that Mildred realized she was being moved without her knowledge and the whole trauma of her abandonment experience at fourteen years old came flooding over her again. She began to cry and shout and accuse. "How could you do this to me? Why does my family always abandon me?" While Kim tried to soothe Millie as well as keep her from rushing over to Bobbie who stood rooted to the floor in absolute shame and devastation, Paula came over and said to Bobbie, "When you get all of Mildred's things in her room, go home and do not come back for three days. She will be fine and we will move her in. Remember, this is the disease talking, not the mother you know."

Bobbie sobbed for the entire ride home and threw up as soon as she got in the house. She slept for a few hours, then paced the floor for the rest of the day and night, sleeping little and agonizing over every step the family had taken to try to make the best decisions they could about Millie's care. She talked to Tom and they wept together over the phone. The next day they met at a café, held hands across the table and wept together again. Over the phone Marlys and Nayda wept, too.

On Sunday, Tom and Mary Ellen Smith, friends Gwen and JB Skierka, and Bobbie and John Sahr met at Millie's Harbor Crest apartment which they now planned to empty by January 30th. They removed items to use in Millie's room at Kim's: pictures off her walls, her dresser, her favorite chair, and Gwen brought a lovely area rug from her own home. When they arrived at Kim's, dreading what they'd find, they found a happy, pleasant Millie who stunned them all by announcing that Kim knew how to cook just the way she liked! Kim told Bobbie in an aside, "I'm no dummy. Paula told me what was important to Millie, and I just won her over by cooking her oatmeal to the glue stage and serving her vegetables and meat hot and well-done!"

Paula and Kim told Bobbie later that the previous Thursday had been a hard one, that Millie had had a fairly severe emotional breakdown, but that the experience had been somewhat cathartic for her, also. Millie eventually told the two women about her experiences of canning peaches, her beating, and banishment to Laurelwood, and going to four high schools. Retelling those stories helped Kim and Paula understand Millie as well as lead her away from those traumas to what had later been the joys of her life. In addition they tried to help her understand her family's desire for her to be in a loving, caring environment where she alone was the focus of the care. By Sunday, thanks to Paula's gentle guidance, Kim's cheerful demeanor, good cooking, and the kindly presence of Kim's husband and his mother who also lived with them, Millie had become a member of the household. Most of all, she was grateful to not be in a nursing home. Millie had accepted this and was reconciled to it. She was sleeping well and eating well. Kim had even encouraged Millie to sit in the kitchen and chat while she prepared the meals, often asking Millie's advice about how to cook this or that. Furthermore, she was happy to sit with Millie who talked to her about tissue salts, nutrition, and amyloidosis as well as her opinions about the problems caused in medicine by pharmaceutical companies. Clever woman indeed!

4 0

The Final Stanza

A birthday celebration and a parting

FOR TWO WEEKS LIFE AT Kim's was good for Mildred, all things considered. Bobbie no longer had to bring meals to her mother every day,
but sometimes she'd bring something that she knew Mildred would
enjoy and that Kim could heat up: a piece of salmon, some asparagus,
fresh fruit or a slice of pie. Bobbie also did not need to spend long
hours with Mildred each day, which was helpful because she and Tom
and Mary Ellen began to pack up Mildred's apartment to go into storage. Bobbie was finally able to tell Millie that they had cleared out
her apartment. Mildred accepted the reality that it was too expensive
to rent an empty apartment while Millie was living at Kim's, and that
she would not get the quality of care she was getting anywhere else.
She was grateful to learn that her most precious personal things had
been moved to the Sahrs' basement storage room, and that her furniture was in a rented storage unit. In particular, every day Millie could
look at aunt Ellen's "dog" picture, painted by Millie's mother Effie in
1909 which was hanging on Millie's wall near her bed.

Marlys and Nayda made the long drive to see Mildred each weekend from their homes in Richland and Moses Lake. Their visits were
uplifting to Mildred who loved hearing about their families and what
they had been doing. They fussed over her and made her laugh and

asked about her life there. All four sisters and Tom were planning a 99th birthday party at the Sahrs' for Mildred on Saturday, February 3rd, (the day after her actual birthday) and sent out thirty or more invitations. Mildred, however, did not cooperate with this plan. She didn't want a birthday party and adamantly refused to go to it. She didn't "..want to be this old!" Plus, with her bent back and shrinking size, was the old dilemma, "What would I wear?"

Even with her good care at Kim's, Mildred's leg sores would not heal. Two older sores continued to be infected and deepened almost to the bone. Her internist dropped by the house, checked and re-dressed the wounds, and gave her a little hug to boot. Gwen Skierka came regularly to "do" Millie's hair and insisted that Millie attend the birthday party that was being held for her. Mildred told Bobbie to cancel the party. But Bobbie only cancelled the out-of-town folks. Her daughter Betsy had already purchased her ticket from Albany, New York, and was coming. Vergie Ellen, Ken and Theo Rosson were coming from Portland. Millie's nephew Dick Golob and his wife Barb drove from their home in Sunnyside to visit her mid-week when they learned the party was probably going to be cancelled. About three days before the planned party day, Mildred relented and finally agreed to go to Bobbie's: "Might as well have some cake and ice cream."

February 3, 2007, much like the day on which she was born, the weather was cold and crisp. Snow covered the ground and was piled along the streets and walks. Nayda and Marlys picked Millie up in Marlys' Cadillac and positioned her in the heated back seat. On the drive over, Mildred asked Marlys to turn off the seat heater because, she said, "I'm warm all the way up to my belly button." The fellows carried her in the house and placed her gently in the big reclining chair surrounding her with pillows and propping her sore legs up. There she held court for two hours, alert, greeting each and every one by name, and literally saying her goodbyes. There were no tears on anyone's part, except in the kitchen where

Millie couldn't see. She was the queen, attended by all in her court. It was a wonderful afternoon. She mentioned all the birthday parties she had never had when she was growing up and that it was good of her family to do this for her. She also told Bobbie that she did not want another birthday. Bobbie said, "C'mon mom, you've gotta try for one hundred!" to which Millie replied, "No, I don't!" Vergie left Kim's house the next morning sobbing because she knew she had seen her mother for the last time. It was hard for her to drive away.

A few days after her 99th birthday, Mildred's health began a noticeable decline. She became more agitated and her arthritic back pain increased in intensity. She began to pick at her food and became much more lethargic. The last time Kim weighed her, she weighed just 77 pounds. She no longer had the strength to go to the bathroom down the hall or shower by herself, so Kim put a commode in her room and began bathing her in bed. Yet when Bobbie, John, Tom, Marlys, Nayda, Mary Ellen, Gwen and J.B. visited, she brightened up. Kim and Paula finally took Bobbie aside one day and said it was time for Bobbie to exercise her medical power of attorney to allow Kim to give Mildred a small dose of antidepressant to ease her agitation and to administer an analgesic stronger than Tylenol to lessen her arthritic pain. Mildred had steadfastly refused these medications, reminding them of her mantra, " I want to be who I am!", but neither Kim nor Paula felt they could ease her suffering without some additional medication. Furthermore, Kim was having difficulty turning Mildred in her bed to bathe her and put new dressings on her bed sores without hurting her. The pain in her little body was mounting as it began to shut down. Soon she was no longer able to get out of bed to use the commode. The sisters and Tom talked it over and reluctantly agreed to add the medications, but only a half-dose of each because of Mildred's weight.

Five days before Mildred's death, she had a very restless day, but became peaceful by morning. "She's letting go," Kim said to Bobbie.

Sunday evening, Mildred called "I love you, too," in the sweetest little girl's voice back to Mary Ellen who had said, "I love you, Millie," as she and Tom left for the evening. Bobbie was struck by the possibility that Millie was in another place in her mind and was experiencing a happy moment when she'd been a child, perhaps saying good night to her mother. The next day Mildred's words could not be understood and she rested quietly in her bed. Her lungs gradually filled, but she remained peaceful, her breathing shallow. Paula removed her oxygen on Wednesday.

At 10:12 a.m. on Thursday, February 15th, 2007, Mildred slipped peacefully away. Tom and Mary Ellen were by her side. Gwen and J.B. arrived within minutes. Bobbie had left to have a biopsy of a lump in her breast and missed Mildred's passing by about fifteen minutes. Before she left, she whispered in her mother's ear, "Mom, I have to go to a doctor's appointment. I will be gone for about an hour. Tom and Mary Ellen will be here any minute. If you need to make your journey while I'm gone, it's OK. I just want you to know all your children and grandchildren are fine and we love you dearly."

In true Millie fashion, she did it her way.

Millie on her 99th birthday surrounded by family and friends.

Elegy

MILLIE HAD LEFT DETAILED INSTRUCTIONS about her funeral. It was to be held at Holy Trinity Episcopal Church in Sunnyside. It was to be a full mass with hymns she herself had chosen. Her body was to be present, "so I can hear the hymns." The organist was to be one of her former students. There was to be no eulogizing except a brief homily by the priest. Her seven grandsons were to be her pallbearers. Except for Mildred's chosen organist, who declined because she had dearly loved Mildred and didn't think she could get through the service, these details were put in place.

In a twist of irony, Mother Deborah, the priest in Sunnyside, had met Mildred at St. Mark's in Mesa, Arizona, when Mildred attended church there in the 1980s. The Rev Brian Prior, (Rector of Episcopal Church of the Resurrection in Spokane Valley and later the Right Reverend Prior, Bishop of Minnesota), co-officiated. John Sahr served as subdeacon and Paige Calcagni, Millie's great granddaughter who had been baptized in Ellen Milby's baby's christening dress in 1989, was the acolyte. The church was full and the service followed Millie's wishes. During his homily, Reverend Prior exhorted the congregation to sing with greater gusto because had Millie been able, she would have directed them to do so. John D. Sahr, Millie's grandson, played cello selections for background music at the reception following the service. Three family members could not attend: Betsy and Michael Dollard who were snowbound in Albany, New York,, and Jen Williams, Karl's wife, did not arrive from Texas until late that evening, also because of weather delays. A dinner for family and friends was held at the Williams' in Richland later that evening.

Several weeks later a small family group gathered again in Sunnyside to place Mildred's ashes next to Lloyd's in their niche in the courtyard columbarium at Holy Trinity. It was a lovely spring day. Flowering trees and shrubs were in the peak of their spring bloom throughout the valley and their fragrances were abundant. Tom presented each of his four sisters, his wife Mary Ellen, and Gwen necklaces with some of Mildred's ashes and her picture on the inside. Engraved on the locket cover was a rose, Mildred's favorite flower, and on the back was inscribed, "Millie".

Such a tiny woman to be such a force in so many lives! Such a woman whose footsteps were sure, whose integrity was intact, whose love of her family was unshakable, and who would never yield ground despite the odds!

Millie's mantra throughout her life was simply that she wanted "to be who I am."

And she was.

Notes

THIS IS A WORK OF creative nonfiction. It's "creative" only in the sense that I recreated some conversations my mother had as a child from her descriptions of the events and her reactions to them. The rest of her story is the result of interacting closely with her for the last thirty years of her life during which I kept asking for more information or clarification when we'd talk about an event in her life. She gave more details when I pressed her again as the years went by, but she never varied the storyline. All the quotes come from actual conversations I wrote down frantically, some of which I recorded and some I found in her own writing. My little dictation recorder was rarely at my fingertips when I needed it, so I wrote on the backs of envelopes, sticky notes, doctor's office visit notes, several spiral notebooks, my journals, recipe cards, margins of books, anything that was handy at the time. I often wrote about certain events many times, and eventually when I collected everything into multiple boxes and compared them, I found they each told the same story with few if any differences. I collected newspaper accounts, letters to and from family members, her journals, recital programs, and concert information. I checked the historical events, and wrote two graduates of Sunnyside Senior High School (Jim Reeves and Peter Mallery as well as John Mallery, Jim's older brother to ask for their recollections of the summer of 1955 when Jim Mallery died of polio. I ordered microfiche through the Spokane Valley library. Most of all, I observed my mother Millie in action, which was a trip and a half. I am still out of breath.

BIOGRAPHICAL MATERIAL AND NOTES
FROM OTHER SOURCES AND FAMILY LORE

To UNDERSTAND THE IMPACT ON society of the Great Influenza Pandemic of 1918 which my mother experienced first hand I refer to

FLU: The Story of the Great Influenza Pandemic of 1918 and the Search for the Virus That Caused It. Kolata, Gina,1999, Touchstone/ Simon & Schuster, Inc.

Also the following:

MIlton Eagle, April 13, 1917

Athena Press, April 13, 1917, p. 3

Ch 7: interurban street car. An electric railway operated ran from Walla Walla, WA, to Milton, OR beginning in 1906. In 1950 it was included as a subsidiary line-haul railroad of the Northern Pacific Railway Co., and in 1970 it was merged into the Burlington Northern Railroad Co. and then abandoned.

Robertson, Donald B. Encyclopedia of Western Railroad History, Vol
III OREGON
   WASHINGTON. Caxton Printers, Ltd. 1995   385.0979 R ISBN
0-8700-4366-8

Ch 8: Potter, Sam'l O. I., Materia Medica, Pharmacy, and Therapeutics,
"Influenza" pp 703 & 704, et al.P. Blakiston's Son & Co., Philadelphia,
1906

Ch 10. "Step Hen." Author's note. Of all the chapters in this bi-
ography, this has been the hardest for me to write. Life was very
difficult for my mother after her own mother's death, but In those
few months of 1922 my mother became so vulnerable to the negative
circumstances in her life that I am amazed that she survived as the
emotionally intact person I knew. I am in awe of her; I was then; I
am now even after her death. Over a period of about thirty years she
gradually entrusted me with the intimate details of what happened
to her in her childhood and allowed me to ask for additional and
very personal details which she described. I believe she wanted me
to risk telling the parts of her story that she could not share with her
contemporaries during her lifetime.

CH 12: Portland YWCA: Building Buildings: Early Efforts;
Hungerford-Levine, Nancy and Schechter, Patricia A. http://
womhist.alexanderstret.com/portywca/buildings/earlyefforts.
htm

Ch 13. "antimaccasars": Mildred's aunt Ellen, a fastidious housekeeper, called the cloths placed on the backs and arms of sofas and chairs
to prevent soiling "atamascars". The name originated in the mid
1800s when macassar oil was used to smooth hair, especially men's.
Antimacassars were frequently made at home by crocheting delicate
patterns then pinning the finished cloths to the backs and arms of

chairs to extend the life of fabrics. They were also used in theaters, trains, buses and airplanes into the sixties.

Ch 14: "Laurelwood Academy Expenses" in 1922-1923 are detailed in the Laurelwood Academy yearbook of 1922-1923: Tuition was $10.84 for each of the six periods (or sessions) rounded to a total of $65.00 for the year; Room rent was $9.00 per period for a total of $54.00 for the year. Board was a minimum of $12.00 per period, or $72.00 for the year. Students were required to buy two $8.00 meal tickets at the start of each period for a total of $96.00 for the year. Unused portions of the meal tickets were refunded. According to Laurelwood's description of the board plan, "...This will admit each student to a nicely arranged dining room where a reasonable amount of good, plain, wholesome food will be served..." Mildred probably got a refund on her meal tickets because she ate very little

Arthur paid the tuition which left an approximate $125 balance for Mildred to work off by working four to five hours a day in the laundry. Mildred had no other income for personal use that year.

Ch 14. Laundry. Mildred is shown in the laundry in the 1922-1923 yearbook of Laurelwood Academy posing as if she and another woman were folding a sheet. Other girls working for their board and room are also shown. Mildred is also shown with girl students on the steps of Buena Vista dorm, in the student body picture, and in the music department picture in the Laurelwood Academy yearbook of 1922-1923.

Ch 14. Mildred's Subjects: "Courses of Study" are listed for the entire school grades 9-14 in the Laurelwood Academy yearbook, 1922-1923. Mildred was in the Normal School strand.

Ch 14. Death of Martha Albertson Fisher from the research of Harold Milby:

"AGED ATHENA WOMAN DIES AT SON'S HOME

(East Oregonian Special)

ATHENA. May 8, -- Mrs. Martha Albertson Fisher died at the home of her son Dr. Scott Fisher Wednesday morning, [May 2, 1923] at the age of 84 years. She had been ill for some time and came to Athena two months ago to make her home with her son. She is survived by the following children: Dan and Jack Fisher of Clayton, Idaho; George Fisher of Brookings, Oregon; Levi Fisher of Bloomington, Texas; Dr. Scott Fisher of Athena; Mrs. Ida Jones of Baltimore, Maryland; Mrs. Lucas of Santa Cruz, California, and Mrs. Mattie Jones of Salem, Oregon.

Funeral services were held Thursday [May 3rd, 1923] afternoon in the Christian church with Rev. Russell conducting the service. The remains were taken to Milton for burial. "

Ch 14   The petite Martha Albertson Fisher had become a veritable terror in the years following her husband David's death in 1910. She remained for a few years in her Brownsville home, but the family decided she was not taking care of herself and should live with one of her children. Mary Ellen Fisher Lucas was the closest daughter, so Martha was packed up and moved there despite her protestations. In the years she lived with Mary Ellen, Martha sank deeper and deeper into senility and her care became very difficult. When Mary Ellen had an offer to go to California to live with one of her daughters, she knew there was no way Martha would be welcome there and besides Mary Ellen was exhausted from her constant need to be at her mother's beck and call. The next closest sister was Ida Fisher Jones who lived in College Place, Washington, just south of Walla Walla. Mary

Ellen quickly packed up her mother's things and put her on the train to College Place and called her sister to tell her she was done taking care of her and that their mother was on the way. Ida whose marriage was on the rocks did not want her mother to come and was furious to learn she was already on her way! As to be expected, Ida and Martha did not hit it off at all as Ida who had a temper of her own, had three children of her own to care for and senile little Martha's famous temper and stubbornness was at full throttle. After the detective that Ida had hired to find her errant husband located him in Baltimore, Ida decided she was going to pack up the children, Effie, Nina and Melvin, and confront her husband Tom to his face in the bakery where he was said to be working. And she did. Once again, Martha was shuttled off to another of her adult children, Scott's and his wife Florence's home in Athena, OR. Martha lived there only two short months before her death. At that time, none of the family, including Scott Fisher was solvent, so Martha's remains were quietly buried in Milton rather than the more costly choice of having them sent to Brownsville, Oregon, where her husband David was buried.

Ch 14. <u>Letter to My Daughter.</u> Maya Angelou, Random House, p. xii

Ch16. Athena: See National Geographic..and Dee Brown's book, <u>I Will Fight No More Forever</u>

Ch 16: This was the "non-treaty" Nez Perce band's last chance to avoid being forcefully moved onto the Umatilla Indian reservation whose environs were much reduced in size and quality from the lands they were accustomed to and which they believed were their rightful home. Once on the reservation, they knew they would be denied access to not only their traditional and bountiful hunting, fishing and berry gathering areas but also the sites where they had buried their ancestors for generations in the Wallowa Mountains. The exhausted and sick band of people, composed mostly of the aged and young had walked, hidden, and fought for nearly 1600 miles on their flight toward freedom in Canada. In previous skirmishes from which the Indians had always managed to slip away the U.S. soldiers had killed most of the Indians' horses and the majority of their more vigorous middle-aged and young men had been killed or captured in earlier battles. They were about forty miles south of the Canadian border in Montana Territory, less than a two days' journey when Joseph made the fatal decision to let them rest overnight. When they were surrounded by U.S. cavalry men, Joseph held his head high and looked general Nelson Appleton Miles in the eye and made his famous speech in which he said, "I will fight no more forever."

Wikipedia et al " Chief Joseph".

Ch 16: www.cityofathena.com

Ch 19. Histories of Washington State People: StoryLink.org

A Letter Written from a 1900 Railroad Trip from Spokane to Athena, OR.

Written by Annie Hall who travelled from Edwall, WA to Athena. Began on Northern

Pacific; changed to Union Pacific at Colfax. (hard cc in files)

King Street Station-Seattle Wiikipedia.com

Between 2nd & 4th Sts. Built in 1904 by GNRR & NPRR

1 block from Union Station

Union Station-Seattle served the Union Pacific RR & Milwaukee Road; corner of S.

Jackson St & 4th Ave, 1 block from King St. Station in current Pioneer Square are

PRESIDENTS IN MILDRED"S LIFE: (18)

26th	1901	Teddy Roosevelt	R
27th	1909	William Howard Taft	R
28th	1913	Woodrow Wilson	D
29th	1921	Warren Harding	R
30th	1923	Calvin Coolidge	R
31st	1929	Herbert Hoover	R
32nd	1933	Franklin Delano Roosevelt	D
33rd	1945	Harry S. Truman	D
34th	1953	Dwight D. Eisenhower	R
35th	1961	John F. Kennedy	D
36th	1963	Lyndon B. Johnson	D
37th	1969	Richard M. Nixon	R
38th	1974	Gerald Ford	R
39th	1977	Jimmy Carter	D
40th	1981	Ronald Reagan	R
41st	1989	George H. W. Bush	R
42nd	1993	William J. Clinton	D
43rd	2001	George W. Bush	R.

Ch 17: Seattle/Broadway High School. The Broadway Whims, vol XXIII, No 4, Oct 7, 1924 (student newspaper) and interview with Mildred.

Ch 17. "...too much bloom..." story told to her daughter during a bus ride from Walla Walla to Sunnyside in the late 1950s during which mother and daughter conversed in French the entire way.

Ch 17. Louise. Mildred had never liked her middle name 'Lorraine,' so when she enrolled at Broadway High School she recorded her middle name as 'Louise.' Her HS diploma reads "Mildred Louise Milby."

Ch 17. Mildred's Broadway High School graduation announcement

Ch 18: Broadway High School, located at E. Pine St and Broadway Avenue on Seattle's Capitol Hill was opened in 1902. It was closed in 1946 due to the loss of one quarter of its students to the internment of Japanese-descendant families during WWII. The remainder of the students were transferred to Lincoln HS. The building was later used as Edison Technical School and is now a branch of Seattle Central Community College.

Ch 19: "The Road Less Traveled" appeared in the 1916 publication of a collection of Robert Frost's Poems" Henry Hold And Company. It originally was entitled "Stopping by the Woods on a Snowy Evening."

Ch 19: The Dishman Railroad Station is still standing (June 2015) as Mildred's story is being written. It is in great disrepair and is used as a fruit stand in the summer. I drove Mildred from her retirement apartment to see it in 2005 and she was amazed that she recognized it, even with the orange and white fruit stand awning attached on its north side. She remarked how 'nice' the station master had been to her on the day she arrived to attend college at Spokane University.

Ch 20: "Veritas est Lux"; Spokane University's motto: a loose translation of the Latin meaning "Truth is light"

"Spokane University"; Wikipedia Spokane University was situated on twenty-three wooded acres about ten miles east of metropolitan Spokane near the communities of Opportunity and Dishman in the Spokane Valley. It was founded by the Christian Church in 1912 and began operating in 1913. Suffering irreparable financial losses (students not being able to afford the tuition and living expenses) during the Great Depression, it ceased operation in 1933. Two years later it was reorganized as Spokane Junior College which two years later was transferred into a more accessible site in the city of Spokane.

One of the main buildings is now being used as a wing of a convales-
cent center, and the property near the corner of Ninth and Herald
Streets became the home of the old University High School beginning in 1960 and is now University Elementary School. The present
University High School, completed in 2004, is located on Pines at
32nd Avenue.

Spokane University: Moseley, J. Edward, "The School Among the
Pines" - 13 Years Later"; "The Conifer" News of Alumni and Ex-
Students of Spokane University (1913-1933); p. 1; Vol 1, No.1; Nov.
1, 1946.

1929 Summer School at the University of Washington $50.00 gift
from Ellen and Fred is noted in Mildred's account book.

21: Interlude
 Maizie Margaret Thayer
 Marshall Cranston Milby born Oct. 10, 1929 in Walla Walla.
 Delwyn Lloyd Milby born November 11, 1930, Walla Walla

Ewan:
Ch 22: "Palouse" is a name of undetermined origin, probably a combination of an indian word designating the area of rolling hills and
prairies and one French-Canadian trappers used to describe it as
"land of short and thick grass." Wikipedia, "Palouse". Palouse is also
the origin of the name of the "Appaloosa" horse breed. Wikipedia:
Kirk, Ruth and Carmela Alexander, *Exploring Washington's Past: A
Road Guide to History.,p. 198*

"The Ewan Story", Washington State Library: Institute of Museum
and Library Services:
Washington Rural Heritage, WCLSJ289_pp 1,2.

Eaton Grange: ibid "The Ewan Story"

We Got Here From There: About Schools in the Vicinity of St. John, Washington 1883--1990,
"Early History of Rock Lake", Junior Women's Club of St. John, Washington, 2nd printing
1990, Ewan teaching staff: J.S. Albright, Glen Miller, Vern Siegel, E.L. Steinke, Mrs.
Minnie Pierson, and Mildred Milby

Splawn, A. J. Ka-mi-akin, *last hero of the Yakimas.*

Note: Kamiakin was the son of a Palouse indian and grandson of a Yakama Indian chief. Growing up with the Yakamas, he was chosen one of their leaders and refused to agree to yield any of his people's lands to settlers. The Yakamas had roamed hundreds of thousands of acres from the upper Yakima Valley, south and west around Mount Adams to the banks of the Columbia River where Kamiakin had forged alliances with fourteen other tribes. As a result of many disagreements and broken promises and treaties between representatives of Territorial Governor Isaac Stevens and various indian tribes, Kamiakin gathered his allies to resist, but was finally defeated in 1858 by troops and volunteers of Washington Territory in a series of battles known as *The Yakima Indian Wars of 1855.* He retreated to Canada and Montana, then in 1860 he returned to the area near the Palouse River near present-day Starbuck where he had been born. In 1864 he moved to Rock Lake where settlers tried to run him out. Tired, impoverished, refusing any charitable assistance from Indian agents, he died sometime in 1877 without having capitulated any of his principles. His remains are buried at Nespelem, in Okanogan Co. Ironically, the name Kamiakin roughly translated means, "He (who) won't go."

1931,1932, 1933 Annuals of Ewan High School.

Note: As of May 2011 little remains of Ewan other than the grain elevators, the church, the community hall, and a few houses scattered here and there. An ice storm in the winter of 1996-1997 blew the water tower over.

From Mildred's account book:
Account of 1930-1931

Salary	*$1350*
Paid off Debts of	*-$405.93*
	=$944.07
Board & Room @ $35	*-$315.00*
	=$629.07

Expenses:

retirement fund	*$12.*
insurance	*$22.*
Christmas	*$50.*
fees, etc	*$16*
	-$100.00
	=$529.07
Plus music lesson income	*$142.17*
	=$671.24
Less clothes	
& entertainment	*-$227.24*
Saved up until May	*=$444.00*

CH 24: SUNNYSIDE YEARS: 1933-1966

Sunnyside: sources for historical facts consulted:

Historylink.org

Exploring Washington's Past: a Road Guide to History, revised edition, Seattle, University of Washington Press, 1995, p.145.

Roberta M. Sahr

Sheller, Roscoe, *Courage and Water: A Story of Yakima Valley's Sunnyside.*

City.sunnyside. gov

Steadley, Cecilia Rebecca. Cecilia's father Anton Frank Steadley was an illegal immigrant from Germany and whose last name was really Steudle. Officials could not figure out how to spell Anton's surname because when he was discovered hiding aboard ship, he could not speak a word of English. Thus, the spelling of his naturalized name.

SImpson, Claude & Catherine. North of the Narrows,: Men and Women of the Upper Priest Lake
Country, Idaho, University of Idaho Press, 1981.

CH. 24: dining room: Later, when Cecilia lived in the house she set up her quilting loom there.

Chapter 26: Prisoners of War: German POWs worked on my Uncle John Golob's farm hoeing beets @ 1944. In the last year of WWII Germany began to falter and run out of men to fight in the army. Boys in their early teens were conscripted for army duty (some volunteered). Without much training or support they tried to defend the battle lines as the Allies approached their cities. Many fought bravely for their country and died. Many were captured to their great relief.

Thirty-five years later I learned that many Japanese-Americans families in the upper Yakima Valley were forced from their homes, farms, and businesses in the spring of 1942 as a consequence of Executive Order 9066 issued in January by FDR after the bombing of Pearl Harbor. They were sent to "War Relocation Camps" such as Heart Mountain in Wyoming for the duration of the war. Many found their possessions, homes, and businesses had been taken over by others when they returned to their homes. This event had been omitted from our history books during my early education Only a few miles down the valley, if people in Sunnyside knew about the relocation camps and the wretched living conditions forced upon Japanese-Americans, they did not discuss it openly. Not only did the bombing of Pearl Harbor raise the level of patriotism in the U.S., it also fueled suspicion and hysteria.

Re: Germans in the community. During WWII many of these families, including the Sahr family who lived on 120 acres east of town limited their social activities. They mainly interacted only with their German friends and those who attended Messiah Lutheran Church, and minimal other activities such as shopping for groceries and farm related interactions in town.

Staying at the Golob farm: The farm was located (still is) about three miles north of town on Sheller Road, formerly known as the "Half Pavement" Road. The bedrooms were in the unheated upstairs, and it took a lot of courage to run up there and climb into a cold, cold bed in the winter. To help us out, Aunt Pearl warmed some porcelain setting eggs near the stove and when they were ready we would carry them in a dish towel and put them between the sheets at the bottom of the beds. Our older cousins Don and DIck were used to this routine. I don't remember them getting any warm eggs! These eggs were used to trick hens into laying more eggs to hatch. To them they must have felt like the real thing because they really worked!

"Baby Boomers" officially the big surge of children born in the U.S. followed the end of the war. However, there was a noticeable increase of babies being born as service men returned to their homes before the end of the war. Tommy was in this category.

CH 26: CCC Camp. Civilian Conservation Corps. Many camps were built throughout the nation as a part of President Roosevelt's New

Deal program which was put into place after the Depression to put men to work. The camps were shut down about 1940.

CH 27:WWII: ration tickets; VE Day; VJ Day

* Germany/Hitler: "sturm und drang." Wikipedia: a German term in music and literature translated as "storm and urging" which characterized purposefully imbuing audiences with extremes of emotion. Hitler gave rousing speeches which awakened German patriotism without regard for the human rights of non-aryans, non-Christians, certain "despised" faiths, and homosexuals.

Chapter 30: Polio: Letter from John Mallery 11/13/2010

Polio - 1955: dates and facts from various articles in Wikipedia "Polio Pioneers" - Wikipedia;

Oshinsky, David M. Oxford University Press 2005. Pp 1-7.

*"Polio Toll Rises in New England", Yakima Daly Herald August 13, 1955; "Massachusetts Polio
Toll Rises" ; "Thomas Mann Dies in Zurich"

Polio vaccine not yet approved by Y.V.Medical Society. Valley children won't be vaccinated until shots are approved. YVH August 2, 1955, p 6.

""Don't Neglect Children's Shots During Polio Wait" by Dorothy Whipple, M.D., AP Writer. Yakima
Herald Republic, August 1955.

*polio insurance policy Yakima Morning Herald, August 13, 1955, p. 6

Ch 17. Mildred's cousin Charlotte: reappeared suddenly in Mildred's life in the summer of 1984. The Sahr and Schlien families were camped at Reeder Creek Camp Ground on the west side of Priest Lake, Idaho, when Charlotte rolled up in her pickup/camper. She had contacted Mildred out of the blue the previous May just as the Schliens were packing up to head north from their winter home near Mesa, AZ, for the summer. As it turned out Charlotte was living in a little adobe house out in the desert about an hour from Apache Wells where Mildred and Chett lived during the winter. Charlotte was planning a road trip to Canada that summer, so Mildred suggested that she join them at Priest Lake, never dreaming Charlotte would do it. But up she rolled with two dogs and two cats. The Sahr family was absolutely charmed by her. She was a crusty dame, about seventy-two years old and wore a flat-brimmed leather hat with a feather stuck in the silver concho she had pinned to the hat band on the crown. Her grey-streaked hair was usually partially gathered at the back of her neck and one long braid hung down her back. She wore loose shirts, long flowing skirts, and men's leather boots. She was outspoken and sometimes curt, but in her own way, absolutely charming. She made a huge point of saying how much she admired Mildred and said frankly that she had been a brat while Mildred was living with her and her parents. Charlotte was divorced and had a son Charles Preble who was an Episcopal priest living in Reno, Nevada, with his wife Jana and their two young daughters. She wanted Mildred and Chett to accompany her to Canada for her last big trip, because she had recently had a diagnosis that her cancer was now beyond medical help and she had decided to "...go out the natural way..." after she returned to the desert. But Mildred demurred saying a trip to Canada was "not in the picture..." (Mildred's favorite way of saying,"no") for them, and after a few days Charlotte and her menagerie huffed down the road by themselves. As it turned out, she never made it to Canada. One of her dogs became very ill and she had to find a vet, then her own health began to fail. In the fall when Mildred and Chett returned to Apache Wells, Mildred contacted Charlotte whose health had stabilized for a while, and drove out to her home. They had several enjoyable visits before Charlotte died May 9, 1979. Mildred lost touch with Rev. Charles Preble.

Coda:
It is interesting to note that none of Mildred's children remember ever seeing a photo of Marion Milby. When Marion passed away Arthur's children were not notified until after her brief funeral. As per Marion's wishes her body was *not* interred in the Milby plot in Milton-Freewater, but was sent by train somewhere in New Hampshire, possibly Coos County, where she was buried in her family's plot. Arthur did not accompany the casket. Mildred never talked about Marion with her father and refused to dignify his comments when he reflected on his life saying he "...had had two good wives".

"In the end, all you have left is your story."
"Australia," the movie

Made in the USA
San Bernardino, CA
23 February 2016